BEFORE THE AFTER

FERNANDO PRUNA

&

CYRIAQUE GRIFFON

A TRUE STORY

Author: Fernando Pruna

With: Cyriaque Griffon

Cover and Back Cover Design:

Claudio Castillo and Andres Pruna

Prologue: Vicente Morin Aguado

Assistant Translator: Yusimí Rodríguez López

Editor: Fernando Pruna

****

COPYRIGHT

Registration Number: Pending

Effective Date of Registration: Pending

Year of Completion: 2021

Date of 1st Publication:
February 2021

Nation of 1st Publication:
United States

International Standard Number- ISBN: 9798731994668

Table of Contents

With all my love,

I dedicate this book to

Carolina, Carla, and Cristina,

My three daughters,

In case they ever feel the curiosity to know and the desire to understand some of the things that occurred before their arrival.

In case they have questions that they can no longer ask their progenitor personally.

PROLOGUE

Once upon a time, there was a lizard that stole the happiness of the Cuban people.

Until now, the Castro regime has achieved the propagation of its version of a long chain of events—62 years is a long time—called Revolution. Along the way, more than a few scholars have sought what I have called "the counter-story," or a focus that differs from the official narrative of one of the highlights of the period between the second and third millennium of the Christian era.
I came late to this alternative telling of the nation's past, but I came lest the effort be abandoned, when in November of 2018, Professor Carlos Alberto Montaner's valuable recommendation opened the door for me to the International Book Fair of Miami. Thus, I truly came face to face with a reality that becomes ever clearer, until being called by its only possible name: HISTORY.

After Montaner, the person responsible for such a radical change is Fernando Pruna, and his decisive cause is explained upon reading the monumental *Habana 505*. Now Pruna has written a book himself—the first of a trilogy – *Before the After* —available in Spanish and for the first time in English, which is my reason for writing this introduction.

Yes, because despite finishing my degrees in history and philosophy between 1977 and 1980, one evening at dusk, beneath the large tents on the campus of the immense Miami Dade College, Fernando raised in me again the primal doubt of every scholar: I only know that I know nothing.

I was not a novice, either, having read *Journey to the Heart of Cuba*, though its author was "a terrorist disguised as a journalist, counter-revolutionary and CIA agent of Cuban origin..." (cited from Cubadebate, official media of the Communist Party of Cuba).

As I said before, I had already progressed somewhat as far as the new way of facing Cuban history, when I shared an unforgettable dinner with Fernando at the Versailles Restaurant, where the now self-evident friendship and collaboration began.

In passing, as in Communist venues the norm is to justify oneself, the blame could fall on that emblematic restaurant, and its inviting rooms would answer for all that was to come.

How can a seven-hundred-page book, written by someone who is not an expert on the subject, change an old Marxism professor's understanding of history?

The answer is as simple as a banana still being a banana when it is peeled and eaten, and for me it came as a punch in the face, Buzz Aldrin-style—Aldrin being Neil Armstrong's tenacious partner on the first real adventure of humanity on another celestial body.

At age 85, after being condemned to death by execution at age 23, captured in Pinar del Rio, and having the historic honor of being the first counter guerilla to face Fidel Castro: Fernando's long pilgrimage—17 years—through Cuban jails: the "all-inclusive" La Cabaña, Isla de Pinos and Villa Marista, qualifies him to unveil the truth for us.

I warn the reader, after such antecedents, not to expect a dramatic reading, because Pruna Bertot starts off by telling us, for some two hundred pages, about the joys of life. No one even imagined that there would be a lizard capable of stealing happiness from the people—much less the tragedy that would come.

Read, and you will find out that I am not being untruthful in telling you that a small lizard (Hemidactylus) did exist, christened Fidel.

Far from fables or symbolism, the story is the crowning touch on this exceptional trilogy, the starting development of which is to tell us of a happy world that vanished from one day to another, without warning.

The so-called Cuban Revolution absolutely denies Marxism, especially the determinist pretension of Karl Marx, who could not evade the predictive endeavors of science in Victorian times, wanting to emulate with Darwin the enormous task of social engineering.

At least the Englishman who provoked José Marti's irate reply to an ignorant person when he told him: "That man has a mountain on his forehead!" was more rational in his evolutionary ideas that are the foundation of modern biology.

Allow me to explain myself:

Before facing the crude university of several prisons, where he wasted no time incorporating French and Italian into his vocabulary, Fernando received instruction at the highest academic level in Maine and Massachusetts as a teen, and in New York as a university student at Columbia.

At age 23, he won a seat in his birth country's House of Representatives in the 1958 elections, which were very controversial due to fraud. A congressman is a congressman, although he might blush now in his later years.

The part of his story now available in this new version is a chronicle as Havanan as those of Cabrera Infante, with the attraction of not being literature, as this irreverent adventure-lover has focused on telling us his experience without embellishing it with anything other than life itself, and I assure you that to him, life was indeed beautiful.

Fernando loved—literally many women—with everything he had, since he had money, physique, and opportunity. He met the most beautiful female celebrities of his time, between Havana and New York.

Denise Darcel, the protagonist in the immortal *Veracruz* with Sarita Montiel, occupied a table—together with her sister Helene—at the Havana Yacht Club, an exclusive place which the dictator Batista never conquered, as it has been said, given his peasant origin: part Indian and mulatto.

Santos Traficante agreed to entrust Fernando with a table at the Sans Souci, while in El Monseñor, Bola de Nieve thanked him for his tips with his sincere smile of dignity.

Never satisfied with his gallantries, he danced with the sublime Ginger Rogers and roamed Havana with Nidia Rios, the Cuban top model at the time, whose image was a creation of the same Korda who would convert Che Guevara's slight figure into an icon.

El Tropicana and El Nacional were never strangers to him, in the era of Sinatra and Ava Gardner, until the bearded men from Sierra Maestra arrived.

To paraphrase the famous author of *The Old Man and the Sea* (coincidentally, a friend of Fernando's family), six months before entering a burning chapel—he was enclosed in a log hut, waiting for the fateful firing squad, in the outskirts of the city of Pinar del Rio—the "before the after" of our friend could easily have been titled "Havana Was a Party."

And then, a lizard they would call Fidel climbed high up in a coconut tree.

There is special merit in revealing to us the Havana that was lit up night after night, where Pilón coffee cost three cents, and the U.S. dollar reached the exchange rate of 98 cents to one Cuban peso.

Democracy was in trouble, because an artful peasant—of peculiar natural intelligence, although illiterate—barged into the presidential palace for the second time, supported by the military and police.

Imagine how, in 1940, when for the first time he aspired to the presidency via election, after governing behind the scenes as commander of the army, Fulgencio Zaldivar had to add his first surname, Batista, through a well-paid notary transaction, due to only his mother having been counted in his poor birthplace in Banes, eastern Cuba.

Fernando Pruna's book adds notable merit to his experiences, revealing Fulgencio Batista Zaldivar, and his era, from the fascinating yet clear perspective of knowing him well, as his father was the general-president's financial lawyer and his mother a personal friend.

Cuba's history, written by the Communists, has severed part of reality, with the objective of magnifying Fidel Castro's saga. It is impossible to understand the Castro regime without knowing the opponent's personality and the era in which these acts occurred.

So, use caution, reader, as you will find undeniable testimonies, beyond all reasonable doubt—capable of making your eyes widen. At the end, it is possible you will reach a conclusion like mine: this is not a counter-history; it is the HISTORY of exactly how the acts took place.

The new "socialist" state created in 1959, besides being patterned after Marx's famous *Manifesto*—published a century earlier in the Europe that still didn't know Tesla's inventions— was born of a farse in every sense of the word when it comes to historical facts, and seeks to immortalize itself, amplifying unlimited falsehoods.

For the uninitiated in self-esteem, the Havanan chronicle of Fernando Pruna Bertot induces one to sin by way of envy. I've heard the phrase "a healthy envy," and, well, it could apply to this case. What is certain is that philosophical musings fumble to explain how the country could disappear by the hand of a few dissidents in such a short time.

If any explanations exist, we must begin to find them by reading books like this one.

Ex profeso, I won't tell you anything about the text; I won't even quote my friend, the author. I only suggest that you ask yourself many questions, for example: Why did the rebel soldiers, with Fidel Castro in the lead, rush to occupy—without paying, of course—the luxurious rooms in the capital city's best hotels?

And don't stop investigating—there was a lizard christened Fidel. The testimony is found in this book. It's a story of love for a beautiful woman, where we will find ourselves with a celebrated American actor and a highly intelligent little girl.

This anecdote is almost relevant enough to explain the singularity of the Cuban Revolution, and along the way it brings us to Fernando's next books: the pages of which will recount his long struggle against a political process that left an anthropological mark difficult to erase in millions of human beings.

After asking myself so many questions, I interrogated the author; and, as his answer does not appear in the book, I will copy it here in its entirety, as a postscript:

"Now that you are 85 years old, I just want to know the raw truth: have you come to hate the Castro family?"

"Vicente, I'll tell you the truth: to tell you that I hate the Castros, as in a personal sentiment of hate toward them—I don't think I feel that.

What I feel is that the Castros have done irreparable damage to our country: damage so great that perhaps the evil won't be cured for many years. And of course, I'd love to banish them from the globe; rather, I would like for them to have never existed.

I feel a need for policies, but not hatred. I don't like them, of course, but "hate" is a word that has never been part of my personality. I don't think I feel hate for anything or anyone."

Vicente Morín Aguado, Miami, 15 of January 2021.

Figure 1 Fernando and Andy Pruna at Bellavista farm circa 1945

CHAPTER ONE

THE YEARS SPENT IN MY FREE CUBA.

"This is the most beautiful land that human eyes have ever seen."
Christopher Columbus
October 29, 1492, when he landed at Bariay,
Oriente Province, Cuba

Bellavista Farm, Nazareno, San Jose de las Lajas, Havana, Cuba, 1945

"Come, Fernando, get on the saddle!"

On that beautiful sunny day, the boy skillfully got on the horse; then, his little brother mounted behind him. Both posed proudly, ready for the photograph.

Vacations were always blessed events of the calendar, sanctuaries in which sandcastles were made on the beach before diving into the turquoise waters of the Caribbean and going to have fun in the middle of the lovely patterns that combed the multicolored fish. They also played war, continuously inventing fierce battles between Indians and cowboys. They crawled. They hid in caves. Friends became play enemies, who they ambushed in the woods, surprising them with plastic guns. They imitated the sounds of shots with their mouths. The enemies put their weapons down and surrendered. Neutralized, they were taken, prisoners, and cross-examined. They had a fabulous time negotiating their release. They threatened to kill them. Playacting. And then, suddenly, the game was over. It was great fun to play war, to play delusive death. Later, they became friends again. The enemy were released before rushing to the house, where a colossal snack awaited, destined to satisfy the hungry stomachs of the warriors waiting. The children's laughter resounded. The delicious scent of the grilled meat prepared by the cook tickled their noses. Living in Cuba was beautiful.

My name is Fernando Pruna Bertot. I was born in Havana on November 19, 1935. My father, Dr. Fernando Pruna Blanco, was

Figure 2 *Fernando Pruna, photo token by Dr. Pruna from inside his car – Miramar, Cuba, circa 1941*

a lawyer[1]. His clients were mostly members of the more affluent Cuban society who entrusted him with the defense of their most special financial interests.

My mother, on the other hand, was deeply engaged in social welfare, trying to help the poor and needy. She was a militant and did everything in her power to promote literacy and moral guidance. She was a devout Catholic and a fervent believer in the Church's teachings.

We lived in a comfortable house, my parents, Andy, my younger brother, Velia, the governess who had taken care of my brother and I since we were born, and me. When we were not in our country home, we lived in a lovely spacious apartment that occupied the entire 17th floor of an imposing building[2] overlooking the Malecon Drive in Havana with a magnificent view of the sea and the city.

My father often enjoyed political discussions with Ernest Hemingway at the Floridita Bar. We had a friend who was a neighbor of Hemingway's countryside home in San Francisco de Paula. Frank Steinhart was his name, and every time we went to visit him, he accompanied us to the writer's house later. My father was my best friend in the whole world, and I adored him.

As a child, I had my friends and my ways of life in Cuba. However, abruptly, I had to change everything to prepare for my future. My parents wanted me to go to the best schools to build a bright future and be as successful as my father. I needed to speak English correctly to work with our American friends. I was eleven years old

---

[1] Fernando Pruna Blanco (Born: August 23, 1905, Havana, Cuba, died: November 3, 1993, Miami, Florida, USA), was the son of Manuel Pruna Latte and Maria del Carmen Blanco. He was the father of Fernando and Andres Pruna Bertot, and obtained his Doctorate Degree in Civil Law at the University of Havana, graduating on April 30, 1930.
[2] Someillan Building, Vedado, Havana, Cuba.

when my father informed me that I would soon leave home. I would leave the country as an adult. He explained that I would live in the United States, in the most prestigious school one could imagine. His words terrified me.

"Where is that school?" The boy asked, slightly restless, apprehensive, and curious at the same time, to find himself in vast, unknown lands that seemed so far off his universe."In the United States, up in the northeast," his father replied. "Make the best use of your summer vacation while you wait." In Cuba, he began his education in Havana, specifically on the corner of San Rafael and Manrique, two streets in the city's downtown. It was the address of the Catholic Pious School. His education began with certain irregularities since his parents eventually understood that he had started his studies much too early. He was so young when his mother sent him to school that when he finished kindergarten, his parents decided to pull him out of school for more than one year until he was older. In the meantime, his mother taught him how to read and write. He resumed his formal studies, but this time in the Vedado area of Havana, at the Columbus School, known as the former German School, which name changed during World War II for political reasons. There he remained until completing third grade, and from there he went to Ruston Academy, relatively nearby, where he finished the fourth grade, since his parents had by then decided to send him to the United States to continue his studies.

While attending the Catholic Pious School[3], I must have been four or five years old, and I had my first brush with what could have been the end of my life. I was still in Kindergarten, and our classes ended around lunchtime. We were then taken to a massive lobby at the entrance of the building to wait until being picked up, usually

---

[3] Escuelas Pías de la Habana.

by a member of the family or a responsible person working at our home. The lobby was crowded and noisy, with so many people coming to pick up their kids. Usually, I would be picked up by Velia, who was like a second mother to me. But on this occasion, an older black lady came towards me and told me that she had been sent by my mother to pick me up. Being a very naïve kid, I did not doubt that this was simply another lady working at my house, so I told the priest in charge, Father Luis, who was probably overwhelmed with such a crowd, that my mother had sent someone to pick me up. He said: "OK, son, I will see you tomorrow."

I walked out of the school with this lady I had never seen before and started chatting with her while we walked together down Manrique street towards my home, which was only a few blocks away. In the corner, a short distance away from the school, there was a store that sold candy, and I looked at the display and asked the lady if I could get some chocolate squares, which I loved. She said okay and proceeded to buy a few pieces which she pleasantly handed to me. I was delighted because Velia would have never bought me any chocolate before lunch. I was a talker, and now that I had received chocolate, I continued to chat with her continually. I was surprised when a couple of blocks later, she asked me for more precise directions as to where I lived. She also asked more questions, mostly about my family, which I answered as best as I could. I did not think anything of it.

Of course, I was not aware that I was in imminent danger. At that time in Cuba, there were rumors that very young boys were kidnapped from time to time to fulfill religious sacrifices related to radical African religions and sects. Probably, more than a reality, this was used as a way to scare children into being more obedient. However, kidnappings for a ransom did occur, and this was a real concern. As I look back to this incident, there is no doubt in my mind that, in fact, I had been kidnapped by the sweet older lady, though I will never know what her real motive was. What I will never understand is why she changed her mind about completing or going forward with the kidnapping. I was undoubtedly under her power, and she could have easily done it. But she did not. I think that my constant conversation with her somehow changed her mind. I have no idea why she desisted. I continued to guide her to my home, and soon we arrived at the bodega at the corner of where I lived. My home, which was then a large apartment on Campanario street, was only half a block away.

I pointed to her where I lived and, she simply said: "Go, I have something else to do, and I will see you later." I happily ran to our building and up the three flights of stairs and banged on the door. When my mother opened the door and saw me, she went crazy. Velia had gone to pick me up and had come home without me. The priest told her that I had left with a new maid. My mother almost had a heart attack. When I explained who had brought me home, she could not believe it.

Honestly, I have never forgotten this incident. You sort of wonder what went on in the lady's mind that she decided to deliver me home. What did I say to her that made her change her mind? And finally, what motivated her to pick me up at school in the first place; she did not know who I was. After the incident, I never saw her again. I think this was another reason why my mother pulled me out of school for another year or so.

Those years of study in Cuba were pleasant, not only because he went back every day and enjoyed the warmth of his home and Velia's tasty cooking. He also learned to play baseball and, besides, during all those years, he took riding lessons with a renowned Spanish expert in equestrian jumps whose last name was Solís. The students respectfully called him, Professor Solis. First, he rode in a stable located in Miramar and later in the Palatino Club, which had excellent facilities for horseback riding. In this sport, he got to master the show jump, which is an equestrian discipline consisting of a synchronized event in which judges evaluate the capacity of the horse and the horseman to jump over a series of obstacles in a given sequence. He trained to compete and be part of Cuba's equestrian team when the time came to leave Cuba. Fernando loved horses, and he rode his own in the "Desamparado" Farm, owned by his grandmother, Clotilde Ortiz, located in Jibacoa, as well as in the "Bellavista" Farm, owned by his parents, near the town of Nazareno. Both farms were in the Province of Havana. One of the horses, his favorite, was a beautiful Palomino named "Relampago," a gift from his Confirmation Godfather, Francisco Flores de Apodaca Unanue, owner of the "Central Carolina" sugar mill in Jovellanos, Matanzas, and a very close friend of Dr. Pruna.

Figure 3   Family at Bellavista farm with Relampago.

When Dr. Pruna decided to send Fernando to a school in the United States, he consulted his close American friends, Barron Otis, and Werner Bruchlos. Most helpful was Mr. Bruchlos, who was married to Ellen Otis, because they had sent their oldest son, Barron, to Eaglebrook School. As a result, Doctor Pruna decided to send young Fernando to Eaglebrook, the ultra-exclusive pre-prep school located on a mountainside of the Pocumtuck Mountain Range in Deerfield, Massachusetts. His goal: to provide his son with the best possible education. He wanted to expose him to the American way of life, as much as culture, sports, arts, and English. All this in an exceptional natural environment, where he would not only learn to ski well (since the school had its ski station) but would also have excellent teachers and make long-lasting friendships.

I spent my first Christmas in the United States at the home of Mr. and Mrs. Bruchlos. They owned a sizable two-floor apartment[4] in New York City. I helped to decorate their gigantic Christmas tree, which was two stories high. I had just turned 12 in November. On Christmas Day, it started to snow. It was the first time that I had seen snow falling from the sky, and boy did it snow. It is now known as the Great Blizzard of 1947 because it was a record-breaking snowfall that began on Christmas and did not stop until December 26. The measurement of the snow reached 26.4 inches in Central Park in Manhattan. I was delighted.

On Christmas Day, I received as many presents as their sons, Barron and Hugh. The two brothers became my good friends. I spent a fabulous three-week vacation at their home, and it was one of the most beautiful Christmas celebrations that I can recall.

Sadly, both Barron and Hugh Bruchlos had unexpected premature fatal endings.

Barron had a brilliant mind and a photographic memory. He could read a page from a book and then recite it back without looking at the paper. Unfortunately, Barron lost his way through gambling

---

[4] Address of apartment: 257 West 86 Street, New York City.

and drugs. He owned a food shop in Greenwich Village in New York and ran an illicit gambling card game in the back of the shop. On December 6, 1960, he was found dead in the backroom, smothered to death. Although his father made every effort to find his killer, the crime went unpunished. He was 28 years old when murdered.

Hugh, who was approximately my age, was killed in a car accident on September 14, 1963. On a snowy night, his girlfriend at the wheel, both driving home from school, the car skidded off the road. The passenger door swung open, and he was thrown out of the vehicle and catapulted to the trunk of a tree. He died instantly.

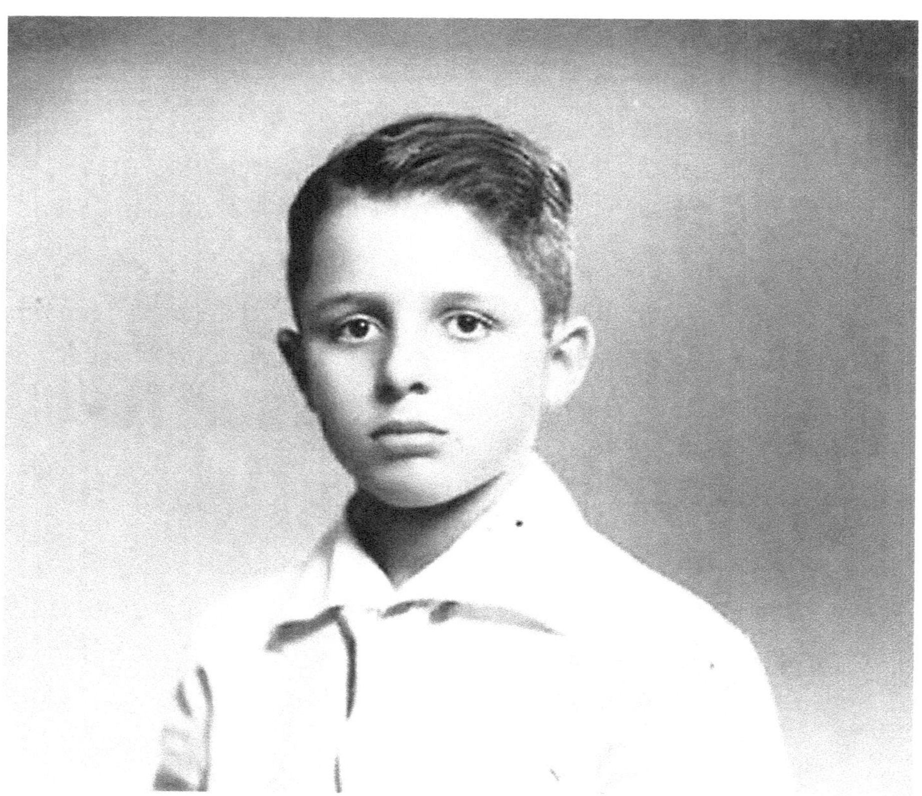

Figure 4 May 21 1945-First Communion – Fernando 9 years old.

Figure 5 Dr. Pruna delivers Fernando to Eaglebrook School. Deerfield, MA, circa Fall of 1947

It has always intrigued and puzzled me how in a few years, the Bruchlos family disappeared from this world. Fate has a fantastic way of deleting the existence of people, no matter who they are.

At Eaglebrook, Fernando gave himself to two of his passions: music and sports. He loved jazz, and he created a small band of musicians that entertained the gatherings organized by the school.

His friend, Peter Duchin[5], played the piano and accompanied him with the trumpet. Though it was that year that he had seen snow for the first time, he became an excellent skier and competed successfully in multiple ski events, winning prizes and awards.

He also made the baseball and soccer teams. During the years he studied at Eaglebrook, from the fifth to the ninth grade, graduating in 1952, he also learned to speak and write English correctly. He wrote for the school newspaper, "The Hearth." Besides, importantly, he made great friends who would remain so for a lifetime[6]. Fernando attended Eaglebrook School for five years until graduation.

An unexpected journey

The first days of June 1948, the day in which Eaglebrook School ended its classes, which marked the beginning of summer vacation, I was pleasantly surprised by the arrival of my mother and father as well as my brother, Andres, who I always called Andy. I was 12 years old, and Andy was 7. My father decided to take a long drive in the United States. He shipped his car, a 1948 De Soto 4 door sedan, on the ferry from Havana to Key West. My mother, brother, and father also traveled on the boat and arriving in Key West, got into the car, and drove to Deerfield, Massachusetts, arriving on time for my last day of school. They found me with a broken elbow, the result of a recent accident that I had playing baseball. I had a massive cast on my arm and a sling around my neck where the arm rested. My father informed me that for my summer vacation, he had planned

---

[5] Peter Duchin became a famous pianist and orchestra director as was his father, the internationally renowned pianist Eddy Duchin. Peter and Fernando are still friends today.

[6] Among his lifetime friends were Michael "Mike" Robert Etachy, Gardner "Pat" Cowles III, Perry Lewis, Eduard Lansing "Lanny" Ray, Andy Burden, Bill Echols, Jerry Crevier, Neil Divine, Peter Cooper, John Naramore and many others.

to show all of us the United States of America. And that is what he did. If I recall correctly, that is what his father had done with him when he was a high school student at the Horace Mann School in the Bronx, New York.

Driving back to New York City, where we spent a few days and visited Coney Island, we initiated what seemed to me an interminable journey. The plan was to cross the country diagonally from New York to San Diego, California. Then from San Diego, we went North to Los Angeles, where we spent a week or so to rest a bit from the road. From Los Angeles, we drove to Vancouver Island in Canada. My father wanted to continue driving to Alaska, but they advised him not to because the road was not in good condition. Besides, we might not get back to my school in time; classes started in mid-August. The last part of the trip was from Seattle, Washington, to New York City, where I took a train at Grand Central Station to get back to Deerfield with a group of Eaglebrook students. My father, my mother, and Andy drove back to Key West and from there back to Cuba on the ferry.

The trip lasted almost three months, from June to mid-August 1948. My father did all the driving, which, according to my mother's accounting, tallied twenty-seven thousand miles. We drove only on Interstate Roads; we still did not have the luxury of turnpikes or expressways, interstate highways were a thing of the future. We visited every famous national park that we found on our way. We crossed the Arizona desert, saw the Grand Canyon, Petrified Forest, visited Hoover Dam, and, in California, we went to Yosemite and Sequoia National Park. Of course, Yellowstone, Mount Saint Helens, Grand Coulee Dam, Crater Lake, and so many other places that escape my mind. Amazingly, some memories stand out and are still in my mind. They took off my cast in Los Angeles, and I could not straighten my arm for several months. Dr. Loew, at Eaglebrook, told me not to worry, that it would straighten out on its own. During the trip, I remember that gasoline sold as low as 11 cents a gallon, and Coke was only a nickel. It was difficult for

my brother and for me to be inside a car for so many months, but today I would not trade the experience for anything. It was the most educational trip that I have ever taken in my life. It also made me understand and realize the greatness of this grand country, the United States of America.
The most exciting memory is that the car had a Cuban License Plate, and this fact created a great deal of curiosity everywhere we went. People were amicable but dumbfounded when they looked at the tag on the car. "Where do you people come from? Cuba? What do you mean?" It brought us a good number of new acquaintances. Coming from Cuba in 1948 was, to most people in the US, like saying that we came from God knows where.

An unexpected comment came from a usually not too expressive person. It was Thurston Chase, Eaglebrook's headmaster: "Dr. Pruna, congratulations, you have given your sons the best possible educational journey. They will never forget it."
He was right.

After graduating from Eeaglebrook School, Fernando attended Hebron Academy[7], a Prep School in Hebron, Maine. With thousands of acres of land, its mountains, its lakes, its forests, it was the ideal scenario to explore as well as to ski. Fernando didn't take long to stand out in sports. At Hebron Academy, one needed to excel in every sport discipline practiced there if one wanted to participate in the New England inter-school competitions. Consequently, Fernando competed successfully in ski tournaments with the approval, support, and admiration of his classmates.

"Wow! A Cuban skier and there is no snow in Cuba; it is so amazing," his American classmates chorused.

---

[7] Hebron Academy was founded in 1804 and is considered one of the oldest and most prestigious preparatory schools in the United States.

I was not always a heroic skier winning competitions. In a ski meet with Lewiston High School, on their ski hill, we ran a slalom competition. Lewiston High had limited resources, so instead of using bamboo poles as the gates and markers for the slalom competition, they used heavy green tree poles that they had just cut for the occasion. Of course, each pole had a little flag waving on top.

The ski slope was quite icy from a drizzle the day before, which made for exceedingly difficult skiing maneuvers. When my run time came, I was overly confident, and sure enough, I lost control, and instead of going through the last two gates, I straddled the poles between my legs, taking all of them down. Four flagged poles passed under me at a fantastic speed, and I was sure that I was castrated. The pain was unbearable, and I screamed out as I fell in a crouched position. It was a very embarrassing moment for me because there were a lot of people watching the race, including most of the boys and girls from Lewiston High School. All that I can remember is that I looked up and around only to see most of the boys laughing at the incident. However, the girls turned the other way, literally turned around, in timid respect, not to look at me in my desolate state. Despite the pain and the predicament, I was impressed. Those girls had a lot of class.

Figure 6 Skiing at Hebron Academy. Fernando (at right).

Figure 7 "The Sans Souci"at a dance: Hebron Academy circa 1955

Fernando showed, from the beginning, initiative, and drive, and he liked to try everything. He got involved in several school associated activities. When gifted for real events, there is nothing more pleasant than to stand out in other disciplines. His passion for writing won him the position of Literary Editor of the school newspaper, "The Hebronian" for two consecutive years. He was President of the Glee Club and the Record Club and was part of the School Band, in which he played the first trumpet. He also created a jazz band and played at school dances. He named the school band "The Sans Soucis."

While at Hebron, he made everlasting friends, especially with the Headmaster of the School, Mr. Claude L. Allen, a well-known educator, and an outstanding human being who always showed concern for Fernando's life and destiny.

It Is unusual for a student to have such a lasting and significant relation with a school headmaster. But I can sincerely say that

Mr. Claude L. Allen was an amazing human being with a deep sense of empathy. He was tough and stern, but his heart was made of gold. He followed my life and tribulations with a keen interest in my welfare. Many years later I finally was able to visit Hebron Academy again. Claude Allen invited me and paid for my expenses. When I visited, he was no longer the headmaster of the school and I was informed that he was in the hospital having suffered a heart attack. I went to the hospital a few miles away from the school and spent a good part of the afternoon visiting him. We had a wonderful conversation. He wanted to know everything about my Cuban affairs. I did my best to explain. A few weeks later he passed. The news was deeply felt by me. I still keep in touch with his family, particularly his lovely daughter, Connie.

It was also during those years that Fernando discovered another of his passions and fascinations: beautiful ladies.

Top on his list was the incredibly unique and most attractive Sandra Branson, a Maine native and a student at a nearby private school for girls only. Fernando never forgot her.

Sandra Branson was a charming and most attractive girl from Portland, Maine. She was the daughter of a well-known and respected surgeon. I met her at one of our school dances with the Wayneflete School in Portland, which at the time was mostly a girl's school. Hebron Academy arranged a couple of dances a year with them. We would visit them once, and then they would visit us once. And that was it. We did not see girls that often at Hebron.

It turned out that this girl, Sandra, was not only attractive but also very courageous, a free spirit. From the first moment, I liked her very much.

On a weekend that I was hanging out with my closest friend, Mike Estachy, practicing our long jump and throwing a few shot puts, a car pulled up next to the playing field, and I saw a girl waving at us.

It turned out to be Sandra with a friend, whose name I do not recall. She simply said, "I came to visit you. Is that OK?"

Of course, Mike and I were delighted with the surprise visit, and after some small talk, the girls invited us for a ride. Although we were breaking the school rules, we accepted, and a few minutes later, we were exploring the countryside with these two lovely girls. Mike and I knew that we were totally out of bounds, but this was a ride we could not turn down.

Purposely avoiding details, I can surmise that we became close. I started to call her Sandy. The weekend visits continued at an accelerated rate, and it was beautiful and unforgettable.

That year, Sandy left Wayneflete and started to attend another girl's private school in Vassalboro, Maine. The Oak Grove school was an exclusive girl's finishing school with a strict headmistress, famously known as Mrs. Owens. The new school, of course, ended the weekend visits.

Hebron Academy also had a couple of dances per year with Oak Grove, and Sandy and I wrote to each other and socialized at these dances.

The day that I graduated from Hebron Academy in June 1955, Sandy Branson, who was already on vacation, arranged a visit to Hebron. She drove to the school from Portland, and we spent the day together. We said a very romantic goodbye, and I wondered if I would ever see her again. She went back to Portland, and I went back to Cuba.

A year later I got a call in Havana, and it was Sandy, she was on vacation in Cuba with her mother and father. We met, we went to the beach together, we went sailing at the Havana Yacht Club, and it was a beautiful get together, although she got a sunburn from a long day of sailing under the hot Cuban sun. Her father got furious at me for the sunburn. I felt terrible.

Then we parted, and we never saw each other again. My life took radical twists and turns.
For some inexplicable reason, I have never forgotten this exceptional lady. Over the years, she remained both in my mind and in my heart. No doubt, there was mysterious magic chemistry in our relationship that outlived time and distance[8].

As I look back at my years as a student at Eaglebrook School and later at Hebron Academy, I must confess that they were some of the most beautiful years of my life. I am so grateful to my mother and father for having allowed me to study at such excellent educational institutions. I am so thankful to the brilliant teachers that worked so hard to provide me with an education. I feel so fortunate and so blessed to have cultivated such beautiful friendships that have lasted a lifetime[9].

It would be unforgivable on my part, not to mention Mr. L Edward Willard, Jr., an extraordinary English teacher to whom I am most grateful for working so hard and trying so graciously to improve my writing skills in English. I distinctly remember his making us write a few paragraphs on any subject on a daily basis while he sat dangling, his feet in the air, on the chalk tray of the blackboard, an amazing feat in itself which he could perform only because he was very slim.

---

[8] Back in the States, many decades later, Fernando was able to communicate with Sandra Branson. She still lives in Maine and has a lovely family. Sandra had been told that Fernando had been killed in Cuba and for many years believed him dead. They still communicate from time to time and remain friends.

[9] I particularly want to mention the name of some of my closest friends at Hebron Academy. First and foremost my best friend, Michael "Mike" Robert Estachy, who was like a brother. But I also wish to mention other dear friends like James "Jim" Goodman, William "Bill" Dockser, Richard "Dick" Parker, Barry Schwartz, Ralph Russell, Neil Divine, and others who have been my friends all my life.

Figure 8 The President and the General - Fulgencio Batista

2

OUR "DOUBLE PRESIDENT" FULGENCIO BATISTA ZALDIVAR.

"Salud, Salud, Salud."
The three words with which Fulgencio Batista ended his speeches.
(Health, Health, Health)
A bit of Cuba's political history

I know very well the history of our "double president" Fulgencio Batista[10]. It is logical, since my father, Dr. Pruna, a lawyer, moved in the high spheres of the government and had represented, for several years, various interests of the President himself and of other prominent political figures of the time.

Rubén Fulgencio Batista y Zaldívar[11] was, above all, a singularly intelligent self-made man who eventually reached the grade of General and President of Cuba. Born at the beginnings of the 20th century, he was of very modest peasant origins. At the age of twenty, he decided to embrace a military career. At the beginning of the 1930s, when he was just a sergeant, Batista found himself, for the first time, in the middle of a national political imbroglio: he was the main instigator of a rebellion that would later be called "The Sergeants' Revolt." Members of the army protested their adverse working conditions, and especially their abusive low wages.

---

[10] Fulgencio Batista: From Revolutionary to Strongman by Frank Argote-Freyre.
[11] Fulgencio Batista y Zaldívar, (born January 16, 1901, Banes, Cuba—died August 6, 1973, Marbella, Spain).

That is how Batista got to power for the first time, by conspiring and helping to overthrow the government of the dictator Gerardo Machado y Morales, who ruled Cuba with an iron fist for numerous years. Carlos Manuel de Cespedes y Quesada, who had replaced President Machado, was also soon forced by Batista to resign. It was the time of the so-called musical chairs game: as soon as someone posted their butt on the chair, someone else came and made him fall to sit on the throne; those were times when "friends" stabbed you in the back to replace you in the seat of power.

In his first coup d'etat, September 4, 1933[12], Batista introduced the influence of the army in the real political power of a government, and he would become a loyal ally of the United States. Cuba was then governed by what was called The Pentarchy of 1933[13]. Five men ruled the country. Although Batista was not one of them, he put himself at the head of a Military Junta that, even without the presidency,

---

[12] The coup deposed Carlos Manuel de Céspedes y Quesada as President, installing a new government led by a five-man coalition, known as the Pentarchy of 1933. After only five days, the Pentarchy gave way to the presidency of Ramón Grau, whose term is known as the One Hundred Days Government. The leader of the revolt, Sergeant Fulgencio Batista, became the head of the armed forces and began a long period of influence on Cuban politics.

[13] The Pentarchy's inability to rule the country became evident at once. The group lacked not only the support of the various political parties and groups, but also of the United States. The Roosevelt administration, surprised and confused by events in the island, refused to recognize the five-man government and rushed naval vessels to Cuban waters. When one member of the Pentarchy promoted Sergeant Batista to the rank of colonel without the required approval of the other four, another member resigned, and the regime collapsed. In a meeting with Batista and the army on September 10, 1933, the Directorio, with Batista's consent, appointed Dr. Ramón Grau San Martín as provisional president. Pentarchy of 1933, formally known as the Executive Commission of the Provisional Government of Cuba, was a coalition that ruled Cuba from September 5 to September 10, 1933 after Gerardo Machado was deposed on August 12, 1933.

pulled the strings of power in the country, short leashing various presidents. With the approval of Uncle Sam, who saw in this an ideal situation in which to develop and extend the financial interests of the United States in Cuba. From 1933 to 1939, he remained the head of the army and promoted from Sargent to Colonel.

In 1940 Batista ran for President in a free and honest national election, obtaining the victory in the ballot boxes. After governing for four years, in 1944, he ran again but lost to the candidate he had defeated four years before, his long-time adversary, Ramón Grau San Martín.

After his defeat, Batista decided to leave Cuba and lived some years in exile in the United States. He was elected senator in "absentia" in the 1948 Cuban elections and returned to his country after this victory.

On March 10, 1952, a few months before the next scheduled presidential elections, he made use of his military connections in the armed forces of Cuba and with their backing struck, reinstalling himself as President of Cuba, kicking out the constitutional president and carrying out a coup d'état. Carlos Prío Socarrás, who was the President, escaped hastily, and Batista soon began to prepare new elections that would take place two years after the coup.

Cuba's presidential elections of 1954 were carried out on November 1 that year. Fulgencio Batista was elected president of the Republic for the period 1955-1959. His opponent, former president Ramón Grau San Martín, was suspicious that Batista would commit fraud, so he resigned his candidacy two days before the elections. Batista was then elected president without opposition. So, he became president for the second time. He had won the 1954 elections.

For this reason, I call him our "double president." He came, he left, and returned, as if he were two different persons, but it was two mandates, separated by the interval of some years.

Many Cubans have never forgiven Batista for the March 1952 Coup. They accuse him, and perhaps rightly so, of breaching the 1940 Cuban Constitution and therefore interrupting the consequential flow of a stable democracy. However, it is also true that Carlos Prio's presidency was profoundly corrupt and chaotic and witnessed the rapid deterioration of the rule of law.

Many things have been said about Batista's performance in politics. Still, it is a fact that while greatly enriching himself, he also governed the country most effectively, expanding the educational system, sponsoring a massive program of public works, and fostering the growth of a robust capitalist economy. Indeed, there was corruption, but he also got things done, and he put a stop to the chaos of gangsterism of the Carlos Prio presidency. However, in his last few years of power, his administration became more brutal and corrupt, and his insistence on retaining control at all cost was finally his downfall.

Personally, Batista had a tremendous individual magnetism that was very appealing to the military. His looks didn't make it easy to know where to place him in the human species. I believe his parents were of mixed race of black and white with a native Indian vein and perhaps more than a drop of Chinese blood. To sum up, a physical appearance that was quite impressive and virile. Sleek black hair and an attractive smile.

Sometimes, the General joined Hollywood stars, who went to the Island for vacation. However, many racist Cubans who were proud of their white Spanish origins didn't like him because he was a mulatto. Others despised him because he was involved in the shady business of the American Mafia in Cuba.

When Batista saw my mother in social events, he called her "The Anticommunist." True, my mother had a reputation as a radical anti-communist, possibly because of her religious formation or a reflection of her perception of World War II and what she believed were Russian atrocities.

So then the President became an actor with the role he liked to play the most: a gladiator that would do anything to fight against the communist plague and his new enemy who tried to destabilize his government. That rebel, a little-known young lawyer of shady and questionable background who had not yet grown his revolutionary beard.

"Condemn me; it doesn't matter; history will absolve me."Fidel Castro, from his book: "History will Absolve me ." "They may find me guilty, but the eternal court of history will absolve me."Adolf Hitler,1924, during his trial for his failed coup in Rathaus, Germany.

"Condemn me; it doesn't matter; history will absolve me."Fidel Castro, from his book: "History will Absolve me[14]."

"They may find me guilty, but the eternal court of history will absolve me." Adolf Hitler,1924, during his trial for his failed coup in Rathaus, Germany.

---

[14] La Historia me Absolvera.

CHAPTER THREE

THE JULY 26 MOVEMENT

Origins. The 26th of July Movement's name originated from the failed attack on the Moncada Barracks, an army facility in the city of Santiago de Cuba, on 26 July 1953[15].

The Moncada Attack.

Fernando and his father rarely got involved in the political turbulence that agitated the country from one end to the other. Fernando had other concerns. After all, the agitators that had become the government's alarm were nothing more than small underground groups. The President knew what he had to do to give them checkmate.

Nevertheless, Batista had it out for some rebellious members of the youth wing of the Orthodox Party, and, mainly, for a young 26-year-old lawyer encouraged by a subversive flame. He was among the first to oppose the new regime. The lawyer felt justified and had the right to take legal action against Batista for breaking the law by carrying out a coup d'etat against the elections scheduled to have taken place on June 1, 1952. He had pressed charges against him at the Havana Exception Trial Court[16]. This young man's name was Alejandro Fidel Castro Ruz.

---

[15] The Moncada Attack was the origin of the July 26 Movement, but the name of this organization only became official, (it was founded), when Fidel left the Presidio Modelo on May 15, 1955.
[16] Fidel Castro based his allegation on a formal accusation whose legal basis was legitimate, backed by a constitutional article (1940 Cuban Constitution).

Young Castro had tried to present his candidacy to Parliament through the Orthodox Party. In his posters for the primaries election campaign, he posed with a thin mustache and a thoughtful and proud expression, his eyes, calculatingly questioning, focused on his hopes for the future; his head appeared between two slogans: "Dignity versus money" and "Freedom or Death." His voice was deliberately ardent and passionate. Batista's coup – which the General vindicated as an outburst of light – cast a shadow over the hopes of the first opposition party. Batista's political adversaries embodied the fulfillment of the people's dreams of social justice and denounced what they described as gangrenous corruption at all levels of government.

Nevertheless, Fidel failed in his political initiative losing the primaries. Frustrated by his limited achievements through traditional channels in the political arena, Castro chose to achieve his goal through armed struggle, carried out in secret, with some partisans of the Orthodox Party and other young people recruited by him. Fundamentally, Castro was a terrorist motivated by a socialist philosophy. During his student years at the University of Havana, he demonstrated total disrespect for the rule of law, and the police accused him of being associated with political gangsterism. As a student as well as an adult, Fidel clearly understood that he had no chance to obtain political power through a free electoral system. Restless, in his deep ambition, he chose terrorism as his tool for political power. His nature was that of an outlaw.

Dozens of men, students, workers, and some farmers organized extremist groups. A significant number of insurgents were determined to take by force the Moncada Military Garrison in Santiago de Cuba. They chose July 26 as the date for the attack to take advantage of the confusion and joyful atmosphere of the Carnival Festival that was at its peak on this date. Castro planned to assault the fortress, neutralize Batista's soldiers, take the arms stored there and call for a general insurrection on the radio to destabilize the Province of Oriente. The Moncada Military Garrison had ample storage of guns and ammunition that they hoped to use to provoke a general uprising. The initiative resulted in a complete disaster. The surprise element was rapidly removed from the equation. The alarm immediately raised, and Castro's men were quickly disarmed and arrested. The attack lasted only twenty minutes. The city of Santiago's military compound, the country's second-largest military fortress, and an attractive symbol for the revolutionary aspirations, unshaken. Batista's reaction was rapid and aggressive: persecution, arrests, cross-examination. Fidel Castro and his brother, Raúl Castro[17], as well as most of the attackers, didn't even reach the interior of the Moncada Military compound during the attack. Given the vertiginous and apparent failure, the brothers prudently fled, and Fidel, with a few of his followers, was able to take refuge in the premises of a nearby farm by the name of Siboney[18].

Neither Fidel nor Raúl ever fired their guns. Fidel Castro abandoned the battlefield leaving behind wounded rebels and others who were exposed and eventually captured. Historically documented, the soldiers tortured none, and the insurgents committed no assassinations. However, the soldiers of the Moncada Garrison were angry, considering that they had been the victims of a vicious assault in which 22 soldiers lost their lives. Many of them were relatives of the surviving ones. Enraged, they executed, mercilessly, in the hours following the attack, without a trial, a significant number of the revolutionaries arrested on the outskirts of the Garrison as well as in areas close to Santiago de

---

[17] Raul Castro was arrested a day later walking on a railroad track.

[18] The Moncada Attack: Birth of the Cuban Revolution by by Antonio Rafael de la Cova. The Siboney Farm had been rented before the attack by Fidel and used as a gathering place to coordinate the attack. Now it would serve as a refuge.

Figure 9 Fidel Castro after his arrest being questioned by Colonel Rio Chaviano. Circa August 1953.

Cuba. Still, only 8 of the attackers were killed in action while 56 were assassinated in the following days after the attack.

Because of the massacre, social and civic figures asked Batista to intercede for the rebels and stop the killing perpetrated by the raging soldiers who had suffered the attack. Batista responded by energetically ordering the military chief of the Moncada Garrison, Colonel Alberto del Río Chaviano, to respect the lives of the rebels arrested. From that moment, Chaviano stopped the executions.

The Bishop of Santiago de Cuba, Monsignor Pérez Serantes, sent a note to the commanding officer of the Moncada Military Garrison and held several meetings with him. He asked the Colonel for permission to go and find the fugitives, mainly Fidel Castro, and also requested assurance for the safety of those that surrendered. Responding to Batista's order, Colonel del Río

Chaviano agreed. So, Monsignor Pérez Serantes was able to directly and personally save the lives of Fidel Castro and a few other insurgents who had hidden with him. Fidel surrendered in the presence of Monsignor on August 1, 1953. Later, the attackers who had survived and who had been arrested went to trial.

A few hours before his voluntary surrender at the farm, Las Delicias, Fidel Castro, anguished and deeply frustrated by his catastrophic failure and potential consequences, grabbed his 45 caliber pistol and pointed it, in a fit of despair, to his head, intending to kill himself. Closest to him, Mario Chanes, quickly jumped and grabbed the gun from his hand to prevent suicide. Jaime Costa and Juan Almeida, also present, helped in disarming Fidel. If it had not been for these three close members of his group's rapid action, Fidel Castro would have shot himself[19].

All this happened in the Eastern Province of Oriente, far from Havana, which remained at peace and mostly indifferent to the events that occurred in Santiago de Cuba.

Anniversaries

September 4 and March 10 symbolized dates for celebration at the Columbia Military Camp, in Havana. Politicians, military officers, diverse representatives, and influential figures from all over the Island received an invitation to take part in these celebrations.

---

[19] Mario Chanes de Armas, Jaime Costa Chávez (The Catalan) and Juan Almeida Bosques also participated in the Landing of Granma some years later and all three obtained the highest possible military rank in the Rebel Army: commander. However, both Chanes and Costa were imprisoned by Fidel after they turned against him when he took the communist route. Only Almeida followed him to the end and became General and led the Cuban Armed Forces and had a top ranking position in the Communist Party. On the contrary, Jaime Costa Chávez was sentenced to 30 years in prison in case 412 / 64H. Mario Chanes de Armas was sentenced to 30 years in prison in case 556 / 61H.

"Double president" Batista organized a massive reception at the Military Headquarters every year to commemorate his two presidential periods. Fernando knew the place well because he had accompanied his parents to official acts and celebrations there. Batista paraded before the diners sitting at the long elegantly set tables. A gallant gentleman elegantly dressed, sometimes in a proud military uniform and wearing the angular visor cap that he removed at times to show the shine of his sleek hair, and sometimes in his impeccably starched white linen suits.

He went to the Pruna's table to say hello to Mrs. Pruna, whom he much appreciated. His face showed the origins of a continent, depending on the angle from which you were looking at him. On that specific day, noticeable were his oriental eyes under his arched bushy eyebrows that he could furrow with the charm of a great movie actor.

"Good evening, Mrs. Pruna. How are you this evening?"

"Very well, thank you. So how are you, Mr. President?"

"Well, too, thank you. I hope that you are enjoying yourself. I am very happy that you could come and join us."

He launched one of his usual gallantries with a mocking eye.

"Also, may I ask how the excellent anti-communist is?"

So they both laughed. Batista didn't always pride himself on the political skills that took him to the presidential seat for the first time in 1940, because he owed having defeated his longtime political rival, Grau San Martín, to the support of a coalition of political parties that included The Communists!

"I presume that you are still chasing them?" Mrs. Pruna asked.

"Of course. We are. Just like our American friends. Is that not so? Yes, just like our allies. We chase them; we catch them, and then we know what to do with them. The ones who have caused us so much trouble have been arrested, they will soon go to trial. It will be a fair trial. I can assure you of that. Nothing to fear, all is well." Affirmed the President.

Richard Nixon, vice president of the United States then, supported Batista. He had recently visited Batista in Havana. Nixon had been the vanguard of the anti-communist movement in the United States, he, as well as Senator Joseph McCarthy, had been eager to clean the world of communists.

There was no doubt that Fidel Castro, Batista's sworn enemy since the assault on the Moncada Headquarters, would be punished for his acts. Nevertheless, he could consider himself supremely lucky for not having been executed right away. The soldiers, raging for believing that there was no justification for the aggression in which fellow soldiers and close family members had died, had decided to take justice into their own hands. They executed a significant number of the rebels at the very moment of their arrest with the consent of the military chief of the Moncada Garrison, Colonel del Río Chaviano.

When the Moncada attack began, Colonel del Rio Chaviano was absent from the Moncada Garrison. He was taking part in a private bacchanal or sex orgy organized by some close friends in Santiago to celebrate the Carnival. Abruptly notified of the attack in the middle of his party, he rapidly put on his pants and at full speed headed for the Garrison. When he arrived, the attack had already concluded. Confused, frustrated, and probably embarrassed, he lashed out furiously against the insurgents.

Fidel, fleeing hastily, managed to get to the Siboney Farm, where, with a group of nineteen men, he decided to go into the surrounding woods to evade arrest. Though they didn't go far and wandered half lost in a five-kilometer perimeter, they were able to remain undetected for a while and gain time. With the passing of days, the rage of the soldiers gradually mitigated. Besides, Batista had ordered to respect the lives of the ones arrested. When Fidel and his group finally turned themselves in under the direct and personal protection of the Bishop of Santiago de Cuba, Monsignor Pérez Serantes, the executions had already stopped. However, there is no doubt that Fidel was incredibly lucky those days, and, unfortunately for the Cuban people, he would indefinitely remain a fortunate man throughout his life.

This time, like many others in his vertiginous political life, Castro got away with it.

"However, those rebels who attacked the headquarters, are they communists?"

"In any case, they are terrorists, just as dangerous as communists."

Batista smiled again. With his American allies, he had nothing to fear.

Plagiarism

When Fidel went to trial, he ended his defense in a closing statement with the following words:

"I am not asking for my freedom. One counts on the support of the Cuban people, although you condemn us. Today's silence is not important. History will tell all."

Later, when Fidel published his political pamphlet under the title, "History Will Absolve Me," he changed the last words he had said during the trial. He chose other more dramatic adjectives: ***"Condemn me, it doesn't matter. History will absolve me."*** These words remind us of those, very similar, pronounced by Adolf Hitler in his defense when a German Court tried him after his failed coup in Rathaus, Germany. ***"They may find me guilty, but the eternal court of history will absolve me."***

Fidel had always sympathized with the Nazi leader. Plagiarizing him was a way to show his admiration for Adolf Hitler and Nazism.

Fidel Castro ended his defense in those terms, on October 16, 1953, during the trial against the assaulters of the Moncada Headquarters. He also used his defense statement to expose and criticize the regime of his enemy. The free press gave ample coverage to the event. There was freedom of the media at the time in Cuba. The defendants sentenced to 15 years in prison in the Isle of Pines, a world created by a previous dictator, Gerardo Machado, in the twenties, the "Model Prison."

The process against the attackers, including Fidel Castro himself, was a fair civil trial with all the guarantees of a due process and deprived of any judicial bias. The legal process applied the Civil Penal Code in force in Cuba, with zeal and absolute attachment to justice[20]. Fidel, as well as some of the defendants, acknowledged that, and expressed it publicly after the trial in several appearances and printed publications in a grateful and respectful tone. Doubtlessly they had been treated justly and generously, and they knew it.

Other people questioned if Fidel and other attackers should deserve execution. According to General Roberto Fernández Miranda[21], Batista's brother in law, the crime was, according to Cuba's Penal Code in force then, primarily a military crime, since it had occurred in an Army Unit. Nothing kept them from being judged by a military court. Therefore, should be executed at the same place where so many men had fallen because of their

---

[20] At the beginning of the trial hearing, Case 37 consisted of 15 Pieces - number 16 was being worked on - of 200 pages each. 122 accused were to be tried and 26 lawyers would act in their defense. – Bohemia Magazine.
[21] Mis Relaciones Con El General Batista by General Roberto Fernandez Miranda.

actions. General Fernández considered that a mistaken civil spirit had prevailed in Batista's judgment, but he kept himself from censuring his brother in law for the wrong decision he had made. He knew that Batista had made a grave mistake, which indeed, as time would tell, he had.

Several Cuban jurists and renowned politicians of the moment shared General Fernández's criterium. The truth is that, historically, this "civism" of Batista resulted in one of his most dangerous, among so many other mistakes. Fidel, having learned the lesson well, has never shown any civil gesture of this or any different nature to his enemies. During his Communist government, Fidel executed or sent to prison, for long years, as many opponents as he considered convenient to kill or imprison, without an accurate and fair legal process and without caring at all whether or not they were guilty or innocent. In all of his political career, Fidel proved unmistakably, his ruthlessness and his total absence of empathy or fairness.

If a similar act had occurred during the communist revolution in Cuba in which a critical military barrack was attacked and multiple soldiers murdered, the perpetrators would have been interrogated for months at the central G2 Headquarters (Villa Marista) until confessions were obtained and signed by the accused. After that, they would be judged by a top-level Revolutionary Military Court, totally controlled by him, that would sentence most, but probably all the participants, to death by firing squad. There would never be due process, and the sentence would be firm without possible appeal. Within hours after the trial concluded, the punishment would have been implemented. Based on historical knowledge of the communist judiciary system, all of the accused would have been found guilty and duly executed in front of a firing squad. During their long years of power, Fidel Castro and his brother, Raul Castro, made it very clear that the death sentence applied by a firing squad was the revolutionary response to anyone that crossed their path, without exception. Death by firing squad is the most crucial embodiment of terror that the Cuban Communist Revolution wields.

The **1940 Constitution** of **Cuba** banned **capital punishment** for peacetime offenses, but the **penalty was** officially reinstated by law as well as in practice following the **Cuban** Revolution in 1959. The death penalty was never judicially applied to anyone during all the years that Fulgencio Batista governed Cuba.

The assault on the Moncada Headquarters turned out to be historically determining for Fidel Castro and his combatants. It meant the birth of the "July 26 Movement", a name Fidel Castro proudly vindicated with the feeling that the Cuban Revolutionary movement had begun to root. Despite the complete failure of the assault on the Moncada Garrison from a military point of view, Fidel was able to turn that setback into a far-reaching political victory. He achieved the objective of becoming a figure known at national and international levels. In a blink of an eye, the almost anonymous and mediocre young lawyer with a gangster like background became an essential figure in Cuban national politics. Fidel didn't care about the bloodshed caused by him or the human sacrifices made by others for his achievement of such a goal. For Fidel, the end always justified the means, regardless of any moral or ethical considerations.

Fidel's political victory was propitiated, to a great extent, by the cruel, illegal and unjustified executions carried out by the furious soldiers assaulted at the Moncada Headquarters. These unleashed executions, unrelated to the assault as such, had a negative repercussion on the Cuban people, who from then on considered Batista a murderer. Batista didn't personally order the executions performed under the command and approval of Colonel del Río Chaviano[22]. Still, Batista has been historically blamed for those acts because he was the President of Cuba when these events took place and, therefore, was responsible for the executions. Batista made, unwillingly and unconsciously, one of the most significant contributions to the Revolution by converting the bizarre and failed military assault on the Moncada Headquarters into a clear political victory for Fidel Castro.

Batista ran again for President in 1954, even though the polls published were far from favoring him since he placed in the third position, behind his political adversaries. However, his political opponents renounced only days before the election, leaving Batista to run unopposed. It is also a fact that Batista had the support of the United States. Washington was willing to recognize any trusted government that would make sure to tighten the pegs to prevent the communist advance.

The ghost of communism was everywhere, even in Hollywood circles. Senator McCarthy's paranoia made the blacklist grow. Film director Elia Kazan quickly became the target. The FBI fought to demonstrate the communist infiltration in the film industry. Gary Cooper was called to testify, and John Garfield was accused of being a sympathizer. A Los Angeles Studio denied even Dolores del Río a role. The Committee of Un-American Activities was sure to be making good publicity in this Witch hunt. The great party of McCarthyism was at its peak.

Resistance to the government came from underground movements inside the cities. However, Batista remained calm. He could overthrow any government in a matter of a few hours.

---

[22] Batista's Information Minister, Ernesto de la Fe, declared that Colonel del Río Chaviano should have been brought before a court-martial for failing to comply with the rules of war and executing the prisoners. That was what allowed Fidel Castro to turn a military defeat into a political victory. — Antonio Rafael de la Cova, *The Moncada Attack*.

Batista was sure he could suffocate any uprising attempts. Eventually, he began to gag the media and establish government censorship on publications.

During this time, Fernando, still very young, remained a thousand miles away from these struggles and debates. He focused on other offensive strategies. While McCarthy carried out his witch hunt, Batista courted Lansky, one of the greatest Mafiosi of all time, and Vice President Nixon flew to Havana to support President Batista as well, young Fernando's policy was aimed at other grounds he found equally or even more fascinating: beautiful ladies. During school vacation, between conquest and conquest, he worked as a ski instructor at a fancy winter sports station in New York State, Belleayre Mountain Ski Resort, which allowed him to make some extra money in addition to the allowance provided by Doctor Pruna from Havana. "Next semester, if everything goes well, I will go to College. In the meantime, I would like to make some extra money. I have an offer to work for the Grolier Society in New York City," he told his father.

He had seen an advertisement requesting marketers. However, after graduating from Hebron Academy, he felt he needed a sunny vacation in Cuba first.

After entering Columbia University, Fernando went to the Grolier Company's offices in New York. In the interview, everything went very well.

His studies provided him with a good base, but that was not enough. He made up for that with – business and enterprise management skills for which he was just a natural.

Doctor Pruna was proud of his son. He was confident that he would succeed. While being a student at Columbia University, Fernando began to work for the Grolier Society, an enterprise created at the ends of the 19th century, named after its founder, French Jean Grolier, a symbolic figure among readers of good books. The enterprise distributed encyclopedia collections, and Grolier was one of the most prestigious names in this field. The young man soon became familiar with Grolier's selling methods. He learned it well. The door-to-door immediately became part of his routine. He worked from afternoons to nights because the best time for sales was when everybody was home, the whole family together. Fernando showed the beautiful encyclopedic volumes with an eloquent display of his skills as a salesman. He became the best of the team and moved up the ladder in a short time promoted to sales manager and regional sales director. The young man effectively earned good commissions through sales in his assigned sector of the Bronx to Staten Island as well as Queens and some areas of Long Island.

His rapid promotion allowed him to make between one thousand and one thousand five hundred dollars a week, a fortune at that time.

His financial success soon showed. He dressed almost exclusively from Brooks Brothers, on the corner of Madison Avenue and 44 Street, remarkably close to the Harvard and Yale Clubs, as well as the New York Yacht Club. An elegant wardrobe. Luminous. Chic.

Fernando was a stylish, radiant attractive young man. He soon purchased a splendid new Oldsmobile in a select concessionaire in Park Avenue. It was an impressive black convertible with white leather interiors. Since he settled at the University, some companies showed interest in his marketing abilities, and soon he was engaged in part-time jobs in the financial sector.

"Now, my son, do not forget that you must continue your studies. Columbia University offers you the best teachings in business and enterprise management."

Doctor Pruna couldn't stop repeating that, worried about his restless and testosterone-charged son.

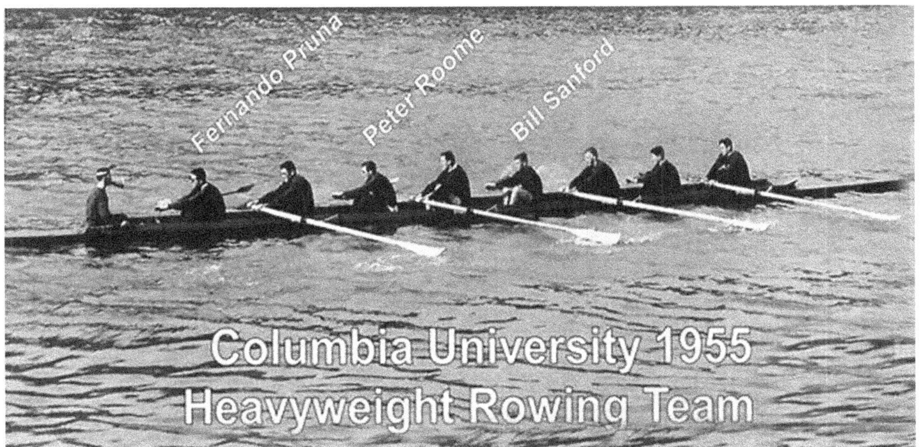

Fernando Pruna
Peter Roome
Bill Sanford
Columbia University 1955
Heavyweight Rowing Team

CHAPTER FOUR

THE GENERAL AND HIS GODFATHER FRIENDS

"Lansky was maybe an outlaw in the United States, but not in Cuba. He had been welcomed as the ideal man to bring order to business. Batista's purpose was to turn Havana into the Monte Carlo of the Caribbean, with the help of Mayer Lansky".
Robert Lacey, "Le parrin des parrins, Meyer Lansky ou la vie des gansters."

The Significance of an Early Release from Prison.

After carrying out a coup in 1952 and having to prepare his presidential campaign for the 1954 elections, Fulgencio Batista had placed his longtime business partner, Andrés Morales del Castillo, in the presidential seat for some months. After this transitional period, his chief political adversary, Ramón Grau San Martín, launched accusations of flagrant fraud and resigned his candidacy a few days before the elections. First, however, he called the people to boycott them. Nevertheless, Batista was elected head of State, without opposition. The General was satisfied to be "legitimately" in charge again.

For his part, Fidel Castro, whom Batista had sentenced to 15 years in prison, only served 22 months of his sentence and was released on May 15, 1955. Some said Batista had released him so that he could later kill him. Still, the truth is that, during their relatively short stay at the Modelo Prison in the Isle of Pines, Fidel and his comrades lived comfortably at the Prison Hospital with all kinds of benefits. An Amnesty Law was approved, which favored him as well as his comrades in arms, and President Batista signed it. The Amnesty was, in fact, total forgiveness for the crimes committed in the assault of the Moncada Garrison. Amnesty was not conditional freedom; it was complete freedom, and they could leave the country if they so wished.

Despite the excellent treatment that Fidel and his companions received during the 22 months that they spent in the Isle of Pines Prison, they remained bitter. Shortly after the triumph of the Revolution, on May 1, 1959, he condemned to death officer Juan Capote Fiallo, who was the Director of the Modelo Prison during Fidel's imprisonment. Capote had not committed any crime, but Fidel never forgave him for a letter he mailed, while imprisoned, to Naty Revuelta (his mistress) mistakenly delivered instead to Mirta Díaz-Balart (his wife). The misdirected letter caused Mirta so much resentment that she began the divorce proceedings. Fidel intimately felt that, therefore, Capote had indirectly brought about his divorce, even though Capote had nothing to do with the letter's destination. However, Fidel, always vengeful, had Capote accused of false crimes and personally ordered, after the triumph of the revolution, the execution of Officer Capote. Ernesto "Che" Guevara carried out the order in La Cabaña Fortress.

Rafael Díaz-Balart, a Congressman then, stands tall among the ones who firmly opposed the Amnesty. He was the brother of Mirta, Fidel's wife, and therefore his brother in law, who knew him better than anyone else. His speech opposing the Amnesty that would free Fidel Castro is one of the most eloquent and meaningful speeches ever pronounced by a Cuban Statesman. His clear vision of who Fidel Castro was and what he represented was a precise and accurate prediction of the destruction, hatred, and death that his brother in law would bring to Cuba if he ever came to power. His warning about the risk constituted by granting amnesty to Fidel Castro had eloquent clairvoyance because everything he predicted came true.

Shortly after his release, Castro departed to Mexico. Amazingly, Batista sent him ten thousand dollars to finance his departure[23]. Perhaps he was guided by the old Spanish saying: "To enemy that flees offer a silver bridge."

From afar, Fidel would set in motion an entire plan to organize his return, with the help of the Soviet Union and international communism.

In Business with the American Mafia

In Cuba, Fulgencio Batista recalled his American goldmine: the kings of organized crime. The godfather of godfathers. A gangster who, for his part, was delighted to have an extraordinary playground in beautiful tropical Cuba, thanks to the General. They were old friends who had been collaborating for the prosperity of both, for some twenty years.

Meyer Lansky, whose real name was Meyer Suchowljansky, had been born in Tsarist Russia at the beginnings of the 20th Century. In Havana, he operated with complete impunity, having left his business in US territory a little aside because of his legal problems in that country. In Cuba, he was making his way everywhere, but, above all, in the international gambling casino of the Nacional Hotel. When Batista latched on to Lansky, his fortune grew. In New York, under the Prohibition, a very young Lansky had felt attracted by the capos of that environment who came from the

---

[23] "Perfiles del Poder" by Pedro Corzo. Also mentioned in "La Lucha Guerrillera en Cuba" Volume One, by Colonel Ramón M. Barquín (May 12, 1914 – March 3, 2008).

Figure 10 Fulgencio Batista, Meyer Lansky and friend. Havana, Cuba

Italian and Irish mafias: Charles Salvatore Luciano, nicknamed "Lucky," from the Sicilian mafia, and another one, Benjamin "Bugsy" Siegel, an archetype of the elegant Mafiosi with a Hollywood worth physical appearance, that made, according to legend, women faint. In association with his childhood friends, business flourished with the rhythm of dice and the noise of roulette wheels. Casinos, hippodromes, night-clubs. His business prospered thanks to the tacit approval of the local politicians who filled their own pockets. A series of nightclubs and casinos in Las Vegas and New Orleans, during the thirties and the forties, should be added to the list.

Batista had already resorted to the Mafia at the end of the thirties. When he climbed to power for the first time and later, during his presidential period up to 1944, so began his influence in the economic gears of gambling and other related activities in his country. Other notable figures of the same category of Lansky appeared in the Cuban scene, staying for many years, such as Lucky Luciano. The Italian-American had been released from prison in the United States under the condition of never stepping on US territory again. However, the tempting propositions increased with Batista's blessing. The capo of Sicilian Mafia then left Europe and returned, secretly, to Cuba. At the end of the thirties, Batista had already handed over the control of the casinos and hippodromes, making sure, on the other hand, that he would receive a substantial share of the profits. Making history, the most famous names in the criminal underworld gathered in Havana; one of the most critical Mafiosi summits openly held in the halls of the Nacional Hotel: Frank Costello, Vito Genovese, and Santo Trafficante Jr., among others. A crime syndicate reunion crowned by a show starring Frank Sinatra.

After the 1952 coup, relations with the United States were at a peak level, and Batista approached Lansky once again to reorganize the gambling business in Cuba. Lansky was cordially invited to bring order to the casinos because there had been some nasty scandals involving the gambling business in Cuba. Lansky was the casino cleanup man, the one you would call to restore trust in the damaged image of certain saloons which had been shadowed by accusations of fraud. For example, the scandal of the razzle-dazzle. With eight dice on the table, the gambler only had a one in a thousand chance of winning. However, the croupier had to use all of his seduction skills to convince the player that the odds were in his favor. When the Sans-Souci practiced this kind of game, other nightclubs did the same thing. Most of the time, this provided more profit than all the other games put together, thousands of dollars per night. Tourists began to complain, investigators stepped in, but the pressure of the casinos made them give up.

This matter got to Batista's ears. The cheating upset the government, which ordered the closing of all the casinos on

New Year's Eve for a few hours. Since returning to power, Batista resorted to his underworld associates to help him polish the glass vitrines of his gambling facade. So worked the system, sometimes paradoxically, thanks to the significant figures of corruption, who kept a close watch on their saloons, to keep them from any cheating accusations.

Meyer Lansky turned Havana into a rotating plate of drug smuggling, while Santos Trafficante Jr. gave Batista a big bite of the casino's profit. Trafficante was the second of the great godfathers of the Island; Nicknamed the "green-eyed killer." His activities revolving around the profitable "racket" of "*la bolita*" – underground lottery – in Tampa, Florida, had been threatened. His father, Trafficante Senior, had died two or three years before. The son took over entirely: he was at the head of the biggest nightclub of the Island, the Sans-Souci Cabaret. With the endorsement of the gambling union, he managed surreptitiously other saloons. Many other Mafiosi also had interests in gambling at the casinos. Whether at the Nacional, the Capri, or most of the places dedicated to pleasure in Havana. The FBI closely watched them as well as Albert "Mad Hatter" Anastasia, one of the biggest shots, or Lefty Clark, who controlled the Tropicana casino. Narcotics, prostitution, gambling. The doors of the Sans-Souci, Sevilla-Biltmore, Comodoro, or the Montmartre Club were open to make big profits. When it was not their trustworthy men, it was the gangsters themselves who carried bags with hundreds of thousands of dollars from gambling, at night. Girls stood in the windows, showing off the smoke spirals they expelled through their nostrils, before emptying part of their bags in the pockets of the National Police. Organized crime continued their operations with some US contacts in the mafia world with Batista's approval.

With few exceptions, the American Mafia ran the gambling business in Cuba, but they kept to themselves and did not cause any disturbance of the peace. You could walk the streets of

Havana day or night and feel perfectly safe. Common delinquents were kept at bay by a very well-organized police department. Social disturbance only showed its face when the revolutionary underground movement started to anger the government with terrorist activities.

Fernando's young brother, Andy, was aware of the student's protest against a corrupt dictator, but, despite the rebellious nature that is so natural in the teens, politics was still part of an alien world, reserved for the older guys.

Andy preferred to have fun, like any young man his age. Besides, Dr. Pruna had nothing to reproach himself; if Batista had an interest in any new corruption scheme, he wouldn't go to Dr. Pruna with it. However, honest, intelligent professionals were useful to Batista: they provided his government with a sort of legitimacy. Andy understood that very well.

From Social Benefactor to Chicken Farmer

Regarding Mrs. Pruna, she had intense activity in her local social life. She was also engaged in the religious policies of the Catholic Church, and she also taught Catechesis. She observed that teachers received their wages. Sometimes, she went to the most remote places, on horseback, to help the ones living far from Catholic churches and schools. She had managed to obtain some subvention from the government on behalf of the very needy. She advocated for literacy teaching without defects. "Children must learn to read": that was her creed.

For her initiative, Mrs. Pruna had decided to start a seemingly promising project in the family-owned farm, Bellavista. She had decided to start a chicken farm. The United States was exporting eggs to Cuba. She felt that the Island would be able to produce eggs for the people, and it would no longer be necessary to import them from the United States. This kind of business could also be very profitable as long as you didn't disturb the interests of the government. Mrs. Pruna invested heavily and had several large rudimentary tropical structures built with palm tree frond roofs.

Soon, thousands of chicks arrived and were comfortably housed in Bellavista. The males would become, broilers and the females, layers. Her business initiative started to do very well. She brought to the market thousands of eggs every week.

Optimism, however, didn't last. The American producers, viewing a threat for their export market, started their protests. The Cuban eggs were cheaper and fresher. Batista was informed. He likely received a big check in his account for lowering the duty prices of the eggs imported from the United States. The prices came down so much that soon, Mrs. Pruna's business stopped being profitable. Once more, the Americans flooded Cuba with their eggs to destroy the market. Mrs. Pruna realized that the government her husband advised was so unethical that the General himself had torpedoed the made-in-Cuba egg market.

"It seems that Batista's primary interest was money. Just for the sake of having it!"

Andy had understood this too.

Figure 11 Solange, under the Cuban sun.

CHAPTER FIVE

5

SOLANGE, AN ANGEL

"J'attendrai, le jour et la nuit,
J'attendrai toujours,
Ton retour…"
Lyrics from French song, "J'attendrai"

Havana, Summer of 1955

"Mama mía!"

Fernando left New York and flew to Cuba once again for his vacation. Tonight, he was sitting at an outdoor table next to one of the entrances of the El Carmelo Restaurant, having a soda with his dear friend, Charles Lee. The restaurant was in the lovely Vedado section of Havana on Calzada Avenue, a favorite of the elegant society who would flock there to enjoy a snack or a drink after having attended a musical concert or a theatre. Both young men barely 20 years old and as bemused as anyone at that age whose game consisted of merely staring at the beautiful ladies that walked in and out of the restaurant. They followed them with their eyes until they vanished in the crowd or the distance when they turned the corner. The place was full — wealthy American tourists. Exotic dancers. Actresses. Mermaids of the international upper class. Mafia associates. Politicians. In their wake, the ladies left a trail of subtle perfume that seemed inaccessible, and yet, curiously, it would appear that it was within reach of the hand and that one could grasp the scent and become impregnated with it.

However, Charles and Fernando had no money, as was the case most of the time, and watching the girls passing by was free.

"Mama mía!" Charlie repeated. "Look at that!"

An angel had just walked in. She had a magnificent face — a gracious body.

She walked as if she were dancing.

"A grand prize!" Charlie affirmed without taking his eyes off her.

"She reminds me of that actress. What's her name? In any case, she is the kind of woman that I love and that, to be sure, I will have someday."

"You poor thing, wait to see some other chicks. You've got to have what it takes to seduce something like that."

"Shit! I am penniless. Soon, I will leave my studies, and I will start to work to make some money so that I can give in to the good life and gorgeous women."

Both laughed. Sitting in the restaurant terrace, they searched their pockets and found a fifty-cent piece they used to share one Coca-Cola served in two glasses. No tip for the waiter. A man followed the dancer. Her friend of the moment,, perhaps, Fernando's imagination began to wander. Her Lover?

She used her grace to sideslip between two tables inside the restaurant as if she were executing a new ballet step.

Her husband?

This new funny angle revealed other attractive curves and ended up seducing Fernando. He didn't realize the young girl had slightly run into a client sitting at one of the tables.

"How subtle!" Charlie exclaimed.

What do you mean?"

"I have never seen anything like it!"

"Please explain?"

"Haven't you seen into whom your beauty ran when she passed between the two tables?"

"Shit! How amazing. It's Lucky!"

"The same!"

The one who kept close relations with Batista's government. The king of the Italian American Mafia, with the most suitable nickname, the one who dealt with the goods that provided the Mafia with many dollars. The United States had expelled him and sent him back to his homeland, Sicily, but the man had returned for business in Cuba. The beautiful dancer had graciously disturbed the reputed king of the underworld: Lucky Luciano.

"How lucky is Lucky! I only wish to be bothered by a butt like that one." Fernando had let the luminous beauty vanish. His fantasy of the moment. The curtains dropped.

"I've been fortunate. Even if the angel had come to our table, I wouldn't have been able to offer her a drink, in fact, not even a coke."

La Arboleda Bar at the Hotel Nacional

With a Coca-Cola split into two glasses and penniless, what could be more natural than going a few days later impeccably dressed to the saloons of the Nacional, a center of the upper-class pleasures? However, the two young men were used to these contrasts. Charlie was the son of Conrad Lee, the President of Gillette in Cuba, and Fernando's father was a remarkably successful attorney. The Hotel Nacional de Cuba is a historic Spanish eclectic style hotel in Havana, which opened in December 1930. Located on the seafront of the Vedado district, it stands on the rocky promontory of the Taganana Hill, offering a commanding view of the Malecon Drive. A favorite of famous people. The incredibly sublime Ava Gardner visited it always. Frank Sinatra stayed there regularly. Ernest Hemingway was part of the hotel decoration. Among Hollywood stars and politicians, the Italian American Mafia often attended the premises. Santos Trafficante, Meyer Lansky, and Lucky Luciano held their meetings there in absolute peace.

You can go to La Arboleda Piano-Bar at the Nacional Hotel for whole nights and feel the hours vanish with the rhythm of a piano keyboard. This night Frank Dominguez[24], the well-known composer, played. How many stories, passions, dramas could be told by this rocky hill in Punta Brava, on the opposite side of San Lazaro Harbor! However, that night, the beautiful unknown lady that had appeared at the National Hotel eclipsed any mystery and vanished any other beauty from Fernando's mind.

At the hotel saloon, Frank caressed the keys of his piano with very languid fingers. An intoxicating voice rose. He couldn't understand the lyrics, but the words spoke to him.

"J'attendrai, le jour et la nuit,
J'attendrai toujours
Ton retour..."

The Singer hypnotized him: it was "his" mysterious, sensual, seductive lady. The alluring beauty seen at the Carmelo Restaurant a few days before.

---

[24] Frank Domínguez (born Francisco Manuel Ramón Dionisio Domínguez y Radeón on 9 October 1927 in Matanzas, Cuba – died 29 October 2014 in Mexico) was a Cuban composer and pianist of the *filin* (feelings) movement.[1] Born in Matanzas, he began to play piano at 8. His most famous song, "Tu me acostumbraste", was written in 1957

Solange's husband liked to show off his young and beautiful wife. He got a strange erotic kick out of it. When she entered a room, all eyes turned on her. If she was on stage, success was guaranteed, and he felt gratified watching the audience captured by the beauty of his lovely wife. The clients of La Arboleda also appeared seduced, and Fernando was no exception. Without hesitation, he was the first one to approach and congratulate the young lady when she finished her song.

"No doubt, you are French?"

"Exactly."

Solange Podell[25] had been born in Paris, educated in almost every art discipline: dance, singing, theater. She was part of the Russian Ballets in Paris. "I am not surprised," Fernando thought, "she has the grace of a gazelle.". She had been cast for television and collaborated in the show The Wheel of Fortune in New York. Later, she met her husband, David Podell, who was beginning his medical studies, and she moved to Canada with him when he continued his education in that country. Since she got married, she used her American last name, Podell, and had a daughter, Claudia. "I also have trained young actors. I have dedicated myself entirely to prepare a Shakespearean Theater Company in Canada. We received English companies. Classic theater players."

"So you don't act in the theater?"

"I only train actors, almost as young as I am. I like it very much. I trained at the Comedie Francaise in Paris."

Solange seemed to want to tell the young man her life story. She explained that when she was very young, she had appeared in her first film, in France, under the direction of Marc Allégret.

---

[25] Mademoiselle Trystram (French Edition) a biography of Solange Podell by Cyriaque Griffon.

Afterward, having appeared in some ten other films before starting her theater studies. She was still a teenager when Hollywood tempted her, but she preferred to better herself in the New York Actor's Studio.

"And you?"

"I am simply a student, I have just graduated from Hebron Academy in Hebron, Maine, and Columbia University has accepted me in New York City, where I will begin my studies this September."

"So, we will be occasional neighbors? I go to New York very often. I sometimes work for CBS."

"That sounds fantastic. Do you also work on television? I find you to be very charming, and you have a lovely and seductive voice."

"Thank you, I appreciate your words. Yes, I sometimes do television."

"Indeed, I am delighted that we've met."

"I feel the same way."

"If I may suggest, we could meet later tonight at the Monseigneur restaurant, it's less than one block away, and it is a charming place with a French atmosphere; if you will accept my invitation," he proposed. "If you like music with piano and violins, this is the place and the occasion to delight your ears. Also, who knows, you could perhaps entertain us by singing some of your lovely French melodies again."

"It will be a pleasure," Solange ended with a sweet smile.

David, who was now standing next to her, nodded accordingly.

"I think that after a drink we could all go together. We can walk there."

Figure 12 At the Monseigneur restaurant, Vedado, Havana.

Across from the Nacional Hotel, there was a great restaurant owned by a businessman named Efrén J. Pertierra. He was a Cuban rumored to be associated with Lucky Luciano in the gambling business. Monseigneur." A meeting place for the crème de la crème of society," It was attended by the wealthy. Those people liked everything, French. Superb cuisine, music played by a string ensemble imported directly from France, beautiful people. Errol Flynn and Nat King Cole had dinner there from time to time. It was also the favorite place of the Cuban pianist and singer Ignacio Villa, better known as "Bola de Nieve," who sang in French while playing the piano. Tonight, the ensemble directed by Jacques Loussier[26], a pianist that would years later reach international fame.

Fernando's total interest in the Monseigneur was, for now, the delectable figure discovered by chance some days before, when he was at the Carmelo Restaurant with Charlie Lee. No doubt, he fell under Solange's spell. The young woman sang again. Her voice slipped between the notes of the French pianist accompanied by violins and other string instruments—photos were taken to capture the moment forever. Fernando made good on his invitation by signing the bill on behalf of his father.

Solange sincerely loved her husband. Beyond her will, she felt disconcerted by this mysterious, bold, smiling, attentive, and, above all, terribly seductive, young man.

He was, maybe, the most attractive man she had ever seen. So that feeling that seems to push the soul beyond the stars was

---

[26] **Jacques Loussier** (26 October 1934 – 5 March 2019) was a French pianist and composer. He arranged jazz interpretations of many of the works of Johann Sebastian Bach, such as the *Goldberg Variations*. Loussier's style is described as third stream, a synthesis of jazz and classical music, with an emphasis on improvisation.

reciprocal: Fernando felt he was growing wings. Their links were so disconcerting that, from that moment on, the three friends wouldn't stop seeing each other during their brief vacation in Cuba.

Fernando couldn't stop thinking that he needed to see Solange again but in New York City.

Mexico, Late Summer, 1955

After leaving Cuba, while Solange and her husband enjoyed the last days of summer in Acapulco, two men spent their first night together in Mexico. They had just met. It was political love at first sight: Fidel Castro had met a young Argentinean doctor, trained in the Marxist-Leninist doctrine. This young man had spent some months in Guatemala, where he became enthusiastic by the reforms carried out in that country. He had met some exiled revolutionary Cubans who had taken part in the assault on the Moncada Garrison. Earlier, the Guatemalan President, Jacobo Arbenz, was overthrown by a coup sponsored by the CIA. The secret operation destined to put an end to a policy that US President Eisenhower judged as dangerously communist. In such a context, Fidel Castro's new friend could do nothing else but to allow being recruited by the Cuban revolutionary initiative. That night, both comrades spent long hours discussing the "imperialist enemy," while they planned their next steps: conquering the Cuban territory through armed struggle. This discrete meeting would be the key that opened the door of the Cuban Revolution. At sunrise, Ernesto "Che" Guevara would join the July 26 Movement.

New York, Fall of 1955

Solange had cautiously kept the phone number Fernando had given her before leaving Cuba. She had thought about him while in Mexico. Strangely, Solange could not keep him out of her mind. When she reached New York, the first chance she had, she called him.

Fernando. How are you?

Oh, what a great surprise. Solange, I am so pleased to hear your voice. How are you? How is the family?

Claudia is well, but my husband is not. He fell sick in Mexico. He cannot go anywhere. At least, for now. I should remain by his side and take care of him, but.

What?

I confess that I am so bored here. It's true. If at least I could go out for a breath of fresh air. Even my husband has suggested that you could accompany me, go out for a while and enjoy some distraction.

Before he arrived in the United States, a few months before, the audience had discovered Marcel Marceau, the man who didn't speak but who incredibly expressed himself, in the antipodes of musical comedies and classic Broadway performances. New Yorkers were conquered by this luminous and agile creature who traveled to fascinating, invisible worlds, walking against the wind, climbing an imaginary ladder emerging out of nothing, pulling strings from another dimension. He was a huge success.

Fernando saw the artist's face painted in white and crowned by a spring hat, in which a little red flower danced, ceaselessly, with the rhythm of Marceau's jumps. His eyebrows looked like a circumflex accent, and the lips painted in deep red. His eloquent silence spoke to your most profound inside. Solange knew him personally, so after visiting him in his dressing room to congratulate him, they decided to call it a night. In the taxi that drove them back, she was very close to him, and Fernando was burning with the desire to be the love mime performer. It would have been enough to say nothing and put his lips on Solange's ones. Only the eyes spoke. They returned peacefully, as good friends.

"If your husband has no objection, I can accompany you again tomorrow night, if you wish."

"He will surely have no inconvenience. He doesn't like me to keep myself from going out. I would also like it very much."

So, they went out. Fernando chose an excellent place. They had dinner and danced at the luxurious Persian Room of the Plaza Hotel on Fifth Avenue and Central Park South. Dancing very close to her, he sensed the delicacy of her perfume. He also felt the warmth of her body in his delicate senses. New York City at night in October can be electrifying. It was a cold delicious fall evening in the city, one of those that you know that you will never forget.

Maybe they had a little too much to drink. The champagne was perfect. In the taxi that drove them, once more, back, Solange was so close to the young man that the slightest movement of the car let him feel the touch of her silk dress. He leaned forward and kissed her. The young woman gently rejected him at first, and yet, he continued to kiss her over and over again. She wanted to resist but failed.

"No, please, it's not right."

"I couldn't help it. You are a delicious woman. Will you forgive me?"

"Yes, how can I not?"

"You are."

"What?" "An Angel. A Sun Angel. A delectable Angel. My angel."

"You say such funny things."

"Should I pick you up again tomorrow across from the CBS studios?"

"Of course. You better. I want you to pick me up. I'll be waiting for you."

However, it was necessary to dream a little in those last days of happiness. Solange and her husband had to return to Canada very soon. It was time to part.

"I've had such a charming time with you. I feel so very close to you."

"Yes, I feel the same."

"I want to come back immediately but "

"When?"

"Now, I have to wait until Christmas. I can't come back sooner, but I will be counting the days."

While he longed for Christmas to come, Fernando thought that he could recognize every public telephone cabin on Broadway from where he regularly called Solange. She always called him day or night to a telephone he had installed in his dormitory bedroom at the University.

"I miss you."

"I will be with you in New York for Christmas. Please be patient."

"Also, I have an idea. Perhaps, we can plan a trip to Havana?"

"Yes. I'll do whatever you want me to do."

He didn't tell her that he was all out of money; that he had spent almost every dollar his father had sent him for the trimester, or that those long-distance phone calls had bankrupted him. Fortunately, for the last weeks, he had been eating at the little Chinese Restaurant on Amsterdam Avenue, one block from the University. It wasn't expensive, and all the bread he could eat was free. Thanks to the complimentary bread muffins, he did not starve to death. However, he didn't care because he would soon see Solange again, and she would be alone, completely alone, for the first time. She had told him:

"I will be in New York in a few weeks to stay for some days before my husband arrives. I'll be alone. I hope you will have time to see me."

Solange arrived with her daughter Claudia and her babysitter. She had rented a suite at a comfortable hotel, right on Central Park South. The little girl and the babysitter occupied an adjacent room that was utterly independent form hers. Solange and Fernando saw each other every day and soon, also, every night.

When they went dancing at one of the most exclusive and intimate night-clubs in New York, the Embassy Club at the Ambassador Hotel, on Park Avenue and the corner of 51ˢᵗ Street, Chancy Gray's band wrapped them with a languid "Something's gotta give."

"When an irresistible force such as you
Meets an old immovable object like me.
You can bet as sure as you live.
Something's gotta give
Something's gotta give
Something's gotta give...".

They danced most of the evening up to the club's closing time. Dancing to the rhythm of Chauncey Gray and his band would remain anchored in Fernando's memory forever. Something's gotta give. "Algo debe ceder." Solange would never forget either. And yes, something did give.

While Fidel Castro collected funds in the East of the United States to organize his revolution and pronounced speeches, Solange's husband arrived in New York. The happy trio linked one night to the next in Manhattan's smoky evenings, from the Copacabana to the Stork Club. Solange's husband paid for everything, thanks to the generosity of his wealthy mother.

"Tonight, my friends, we are going to the Elmo!"

Only the regular ones called it the Elmo, short for El Morocco. In the elegant atmosphere of the nightclub, sitting on the famous striped benches imitating zebra's leather – a renowned decoration by Vernon MacFarlane – on which having photos taken was considered a must. The El Morocco's official photographer, Jerome Zerbe, had defined clients this way: "Here we admire the New York and International upper class, of which our guessing is they have houses full of treasures. They are the ones who master the art of dressing more elegantly. Women wear the most beautiful jewels. They are dream people, which you watch and expect to meet or which you would like to resemble".

The next day, they met at the Stork Club, which had the same façade it had back in the thirties, though, on Christmas Eve, 1931, Prohibition agents had closed the club for being a "speakeasy." In 1934, the Stork Club enlarged with the night club located at 3 East 53rd Street. Since then, this address was always frequented by New York's aristocracy. In this place, you could expect to meet Sinatra, Elizabeth Taylor or Marilyn Monroe, to have a drink with them, to ask them for an autograph or a picture. Maybe even a dance, perhaps something even better.

The Stork had recently been in the center of a controversy, particularly for their admission policy. The owner was reticent regarding clients of color. Some years before, the singer Lena Horne, arm in arm with George Jessel, had been reproved at the club's entrance by the owner, Sherman Billingsley. He asked her:

"Who made the reservation?"

To which Jessel, who didn't find it hard to reply, said:

"Abraham Lincoln!"

"Excuse me?"

"Abraham Lincoln himself made the reservation for us!"

Moreover, both characters stood, with unquestionable dignity, before an astonished and a little embarrassed Billingsley. One time, Josephine Baker accused the Stork of racism because, after ordering a steak, she had to wait for an hour for service. Grace Kelly, who had witnessed the scene, went to Baker, held her arm, and left the club with her friends, disgusted, after promising she would never go there again. She kept her word.

For Fernando, to tour the dancing floors of these legendary clubs with a lovely company meant some instants of intense joy. Pleasant moments after having started his studies at the university some months before and after having worked in the late afternoon and evenings.

"Run!"

"What?"

"Come. Take my hand and let's run! Let us run together".

"You're crazy!"

- "Yes, I'm crazy! Crazy about you! Let's be crazy together!"

Fernando and Solange left the club and began to run until they lost their breath, holding hands in the cold, wet December night. Their footsteps beat and resounded on the sidewalk, like in a musical comedy where they dance on the asphalt. As if they were children or like Gene Kelly and Debbie Reynolds. Chip Chap! They jumped from puddle to puddle. In this way, they would forget everything in the streets of the big city until the lights went out. When they turned around, the others were nothing but dots behind them. Fernando and Solange, who had barely turned the corner, leaned against the building wall and embraced their lips together. Without opening their eyes. Breathless. They exchanged furtive kisses that intensified to the beat of their heartbeats. It was a risk if we consider that David and Kirk, his friend who was with him, were about to turn the corner. Then the little musical comedy ended. The kisses remained secret—deeply hidden Kisses.

In the same instant, another group of friends started moving. Fidel Castro had traveled to New York too, accompanied by a select group of his associates. Only, he was neither a bearded man nor was he wearing the olive-green uniform; he wore a fine mustache and pronounced his speeches dressed in an elegant suit, his propaganda aimed at recruiting the exiled Cubans and raising funds. In New York, in New Jersey. In Philadelphia and Miami. He kept his mind on his final goal: Absolute power.

Figure 13 The Persian Room, The Plaza Hotel, New York City

CHAPTER SIX

DANGEROUS LIAISONS

"Nothing human is alien to me."
Mario Kuchilán – Cuban newspaperman[27].

On the road from New York City to Havana. December 1955

"Will we see you in Havana?"

Fernando nodded to the proposal.

"We will take the plane to Cuba, and you will join us by car to Key West and then a short flight to Havana if you want. I have a car in New York, a Studebaker. It works great. I will gladly lend it to you. It's a beautiful drive to Key West. When you get there, you can take the Ferry or a plane if you prefer."

David's proposal made the young man enthusiastic. It was a very generous offer.

"Velia, our nanny, could take care of Claudia, Fernando suggested. I recommend her to you."

If Velia took care of Claudia, it meant Solange would be more available. Velia had been a trustworthy employee of the Prunas for many years; since Fernando and Andy were born. "And she is insured," the young man added, hiding a smile.

---

[27] One famous quotation by Terence reads: "**Homo** sum, **humani nihil a me alienum puto**", or "I am human, and I think nothing human is alien to **me**." This appeared in his play Heauton Timorumenos.

"Consider that Velia has taken care of me since I was born. She came into our service when I was only forty days old. She is like a second mother to me. She is a beautiful person, the perfect one to take care of Claudia, your daughter. You can't find anyone better."

Fernando borrowed Solange's husband's Studebaker and, with a friend from Columbia University, he got on his way immediately to Florida, more precisely to Key West. Andy, Fernando's brother, who was studying at Eaglebrook and was on vacation, joined them too, as well as Kirk, a Canadian friend of Solange's husband. The latter was also studying medicine at Queens University in Kingston, Ontario, Canada.

Was David Podell aware that, by lending Fernando his car, he might also be bestowing him his wife?

Havana is twenty minutes away from Key West by plane. The distance is only 90 miles. Arriving in Cuba, Solange and her husband stayed at the Rosita Hornedo Hotel in Miramar, a chic district in Havana. It was splendidly modern with very high ratings. Recently built and, curiously, its windows were all parallel aligned. Their hotel room had a fabulous view of the Gulf of Mexico.

"Solange! Solange! Solooonge! Hola!"

Fernando screamed. The young lady went to the window.

"You are just crazy! Screaming like that. What are you doing here?" She smiled.

"I just got here. I've seen you've arrived and here I am. Are you coming?"

"Where?"

"I don't know. Anywhere! Maybe for a walk; for a ride. I want to see you and be with you alone, to talk for a while."

In the afternoon, the pair of lovebirds met secretly in a discreet nearby street, and from there, they drove straight to a secluded motel located on one of the most lively and elegant boulevards: Quinta Avenida, Miramar, in Havana.

They parked the car in a purposely hidden from view garage attached to the motel and walked into the motel room through the back door. Fernando picked up the phone to let the front desk know that they were taking it. There was no visual contact with the management. Discretion was the norm.

They sat on a sofa and started to chat in almost whispers. Both very close to each other. They embraced. They kissed softly at first. The crescendo of passion slowly crept in.

Solange's heart fluttered, and an overwhelming, unexplainable feeling muddled her mind and all of her. She felt lost, unable to control her emotions.

Solange's chest rose slightly with her sighing. It was a feeling of deep yearnings. There was also a feeling of despair. She felt too well, and this made her feel guilty. However, she got up abruptly, gathering all of her strength, doing her best to shake off her overflowing passion and desire, with a rush.

"I must go," she said to herself. "I must escape this moment." Somehow, she had to break out of the emotional lock. Maybe it was the place. She did not like it. However, also, it was her conscience; things came to her mind. She thought: My husband, my daughter.

She smoothed out the dress that she had not completely removed after kissing Fernando endlessly. She fixed her hair with her hands as well as possible before running out to the street, escaping like a vulgar thief, while Fernando was momentarily washing his hands. Under Fernando's astonished eyes, as he was coming out of the restroom, Solange ran out like a terrified deer.

The colorful Fifth Avenue in that district of Havana was terribly busy. The young, elegant lady dashing down the sidewalk didn't go unnoticed to a patrol car of the secret police. She ran along the street, surrounded by palm trees and beautiful houses. Fernando quickly ran after her until he caught up to her and held her in his arms.

"What has gotten into you? What happened? Have you gone crazy?"

"Oh, Fernando, I find all this to be sordid."

"What? What do you mean?"

"That place into which we have sneaked, I feel shame, Fernando."

"You did not find it convenient?"

"No, and I don't want to talk about it. I don't think you understand. We are the ones who have not acted conveniently."

"I don't know what to say. I fail to understand."

There was the embarrassment of thinking about her daughter Claudia, who was with her for vacation? The dreadful thought of cheating on her husband whom, she thought, deeply confused, she still loved despite everything. The confounding effect of being magnetized by the handsome young man she wanted and desired, and at the same time, her need to refuse with all of her strength? A paradoxical contradiction and a trivial synthesis of all love stories. She kept telling herself that Fernando was a perfect playboy, a seducer, and a womanizer. Still, she felt trapped in his spider web when his sweet smile translated the expression of his eyes, hidden behind large dark glasses.

The speaker horn voiced, loud and clear, the chief agent on the patrol car that had followed them. His voice sounded behind them:

"Stop! Do not move! We are the police."

The Officer ordered through a speaker horn from the open window of the patrol car. The young couple obeyed.

The Officer got out of the patrol car and walked up to them. Three agents inside the patrol car observed cautiously.

"Miss, is this man disturbing you?"

"No, not at all! It's just a game."

"A-game, but it seemed you wanted to run away from him at any cost. Has he hurt you?"

"No, no." Solange insisted, disgusted at herself for causing such an embarrassing incident.

"I can assure you it is just a mistake," Fernando said to the Officer.

"I did not ask you. Please show me your ID. Are you Cuban? Documents, please."

"My name is Pruna. Fernando Pruna. Yes, I am Cuban."

"I said, show me your ID." The agent reprehended him.

Fernando didn't protest. With so many revolutionaries everywhere, any unusual behavior was suspicious in Havana. Controls had become a routine. The police made arrests everywhere. They arrested some students from the University of Havana and some from Santiago who had protested against Batista's regime. The police cars patrolled the Havana streets day and night, and they had the authority to arrest anyone they found suspicious of being involved in revolutionary activities. Government repression was particularly hard against those who agitated at schools and colleges, waving the revolutionary flag. The repressive police force didn't hesitate to arrest the ones who caused more trouble. Sometimes, it happened so fast that one could find himself arrested and submitted to violent cross-examination without much time to understand anything.

The misunderstanding had given Fernando goosebumps. He was concerned.

"Officer, it is a private affair between a man and a woman. Let me inform you that my name is Fernando Pruna, and my father is a lawyer who belongs to President Fulgencio Batista's close circle."

The young man gave his papers to the police officer. He gave him his ID as well as a safe-conduct pass, signed by President Batista himself that his father had given him for his protection.

The face of the patrol chief softened immediately and showed a discrete and respectful smile. The tension of the moment instantly dissipated.

"I am gratified to see who you are, young man. Please go on with your matters," was the agent's terse reply. "However, you should know that we have orders to arrest anyone who looks suspicious. We are very sorry for the incident, and I beg you to be careful, the street can be hazardous in these times."

"I understand, Officer, thank you very much."

As soon as the agent left the place, Fernando grabbed Solange's shoulder.

"What happened? We kissed, we hugged, and a minute later, you dashed off like a crazy woman."

"Sorry, Fernando, I didn't like that place. It was sordid. Being there with you was good, but the site was not. I am desolate. I am not too fond of this game."

"I am so sorry. You know that I only want you to be happy. You deserve to be content."

"It's not that easy with my husband. I have the feeling that he is holding me back, always controlling me."

"He hinders my life, my career. Just recently, he let me go to an audition in Toronto. It was a superb character in a play by a great Russian playwright. It could have been perfect for my career."

Solange lost herself for an instant, remembering her audition in Canada for a part in The Story of The Soldier, by Igor Stravinsky. She had already auditioned for that play in New York when she had gone to see the king of mime, Marcel Marceau, with Fernando. At the last minute, her husband had said no to her acting in the play. Also, he had done the same in New York. She had a superb project with CBS for a television show and even a part in a movie with Orson Welles and Eartha Kitt. At the last moment, the same situation, he said no.

"My husband decided we should go to Acapulco for some days. So, I had to leave everything. The result was that the studios no longer want me to work for them. They put me in the "blacklist" of actresses. It's quite rare that the studios hire someone for a live performance, and then to let them down at the last minute, that is unheard of, inconceivable."

"If you feel this way, you should leave him, Solange! You deserve more. As for me,"

He didn't finish the phrase or said the three more difficult words. Solange had already cut him short.

"Despite everything, I think David and I love each other. I might be fooling myself, but I think so. So yes, I don't know. I feel lost and confused, and I am frightened, very much afraid. You scare me, Fernando. You have the capacity to terrify me. Don't ask me why."

She was fighting herself. Her feelings for Fernando petrified her.

"I have to go back. Please? It's hard for me to be away from you, but I must. At least, for now. I need to recover."

"Will I see you tonight?"

"I am supposed to go to Tropicana Cabaret with David. Do you know who's singing?"

Solange evoked the artist with emotion.

"It will be magnificent. You should listen to Edith Piaf someday if you haven't."

She remembered when she saw the singer some years before in France. After World War II, both acted in the same musical magazine at ABC, the renowned Paris Music-Hall. Even under the Nazi occupation, the cabaret had not ceased singing to happiness and now, in a city liberated and drunk with joy, Maurice Chevalier, celebrated his return. The next year, Solange, a young actress at the moment, had just joined a troupe, as a dancer, with the singer, and they had exchanged some words about the work and their respective careers.

On her way back, after leaving Fernando, she returned immediately to the Fifth Avenue area. Outside, everything was a party, the sun, the colors, the sounds, the delicious effluvial. She should have felt relieved. However, she was depressed. When David asked her where she had been in the afternoon, she kept evasive. She told him about a walk and some privileged instants in the sun. She had to make the best of it since the sky was inexorably beginning to darken.

***"She sings dressed in black, without jewels
Wearing flat shoes."
Bohemia - Cuban Magazine***

Tropicana

One of Havana's Inevitable places was the Tropicana Cabaret, baptized with the glittering name of "Paradise under the stars." The stage was enormous; the palm trees rose from the dancing floors to the sky, going through the bold modern architecture.

The singers swayed among the tables swaggering with their sequin dresses. It was the Monte Carlo of the Americas, as the publicity announced, and it was created in 1939 on a large property with overwhelming vegetation in the city outskirts.

During the period that followed the depression, the club, initially named "Eden," was transformed into the "Beau-Site," combining a first-class cabaret and casino. However, it was soon rebaptized "Tropicana" due to its tropical environment. The syllable "na" was added at the end of the word Tropic because it was the last syllable of Mina, the name of its first owner. By this time, it belonged to Martin Fox, one of the few Cuban owners of this sort of nightclub. The environment of Paris suburbs mixed with the Cuban warmth. The asphalt shone under the car lights. It was drizzling in Havana, but just a little: in the wet atmosphere of the tropics, the spotlights illuminated a small spot on stage. In the antipodes of the iron worlds, in a glittering sequined dress that made a "Fru Fru" sound and the feathers, to which the regular audience of the Tropicana understood, flying in the air, she appeared. The first notes of a perfect color gave way to the performance. The orchestration was brilliant.

"It is magnificent," Solange whispered, her ears devouring, *"La vie en rose."*

She cried with emotion before the small woman. On the outdoor stage, in the center of the Tropicana, the raindrops fell on "La Móme."

The young woman couldn't help thinking, "those are rain tears falling from the sky."

The "Grand of France" as the newspapers described her, traveled to Cuba twice before. She sang at the Sans-Souci, first, and then the Havana Montmartre, the next year.

"No, no!" she said to the light technician, who gave her a disconcerted look. "I want white lights. Very simple, nothing else".

"Are you sure?" The choreographer said to her. "People will hardly see your Dior designer dresses."

"I wear a black dress so that the audience can see precisely my gestures and the movements of my hands, not my dress," she replied.

She didn't care at all about people seeing her Dior designs; the audience should only focus on her voice and her gestures. When dealing with an artist of this stature, category, and cachet equal to a Nat King Cole or Bing Crosby, there was nothing to argue about; you had to let her do whatever she wanted to do. You felt you could forgive her anything once you listened to her voice, even with an empty stomach or a dry throat since she demanded that nothing to drink or eat be served while she was singing, not even a glass of water. With the lights illuminating the stage according to her wishes, the voice of "La Mome" brought joy to the hearts. It was exhilarating. The audience agreed to go dry while L'Hymne de L'amour spread over the tables, causing a big ovation. Solange didn't stop whispering, "It's beautiful." At the end of the performance, Solange and David went to say hello to her in her dressing room, but the icon was in such high demand that they soon left without being able to say a word to her. Back home, David asked Solange some questions again.

"Well then, where were you this afternoon? We had barely arrived, and you disappeared. I believe that you went to see Fernando, didn't you?"

"For the last time, I did not. What do you want to imply? I was walking by the beach, relaxing, enjoying the view of the sea."

"I think he is a little bit persistent, overpowering."

"What do you mean? I don't know what you are talking about."
"Come on, please, he revolves around you like a bee around honey. Also, you seem to enjoy it, to be attracted to him. The way you cross gazes with him, the way you look at him. If you think

I haven't noticed anything, you are wrong. Tonight, it seemed as if you were somewhere else."
"Well, I got carried away by emotion. Piaf was sublime."
"You two have a bond. I feel it. I can sense it. I know it."
"Shut up, will you? You are talking nonsense. You are delirious."
"I'm going."
"You're going what?"
"I'm going mad!"

"Mad? What are you saying!"

"You have understood me very well. Mad with jealousy."

"You don't know what you're saying. Nothing is going on between us. Fernando is just a friend."

Several plots and strategies were going on at the same time.

Elsewhere, another conversation pursued.

"He has held me back. The time I spent in prison. Lost time."
"It is necessary to recruit the best, to go back and free the people. Free them from the tyranny — the oppression. I will wield a weapon and kill him. He must die."
"He will see what I've got for him," Ernesto exaggerated.
"He hinders my career," Fidel continued talking.
"I will wield a weapon and kill him if I have to," Camilo repeated.

Fulgencio had already spared his life, but, in the name of the Revolution, Fidel had to make him pay for his crimes, as he deserved. There would be no forgiveness for Batista or his followers. Fidel had been forgiven, but he wasn't willing to forgive. Never.

Complicated Family diplomacy

"Good morning, Mrs. Pruna, I have taken the liberty of calling you."

"David, how are you? So lovely to hear from you."

"Precisely, I wanted to talk to you. I think Solange intends to leave me."

"What are you saying? Are you serious?"

"I think it's true. Solange is seeing your son. I think that she is seriously attracted to your son. "

"What? Impossible, Solange and Fernando are nothing but good friends. They appreciate each other."

"No, I'm not so sure about that. It is more than that. In fact, I believe that it is very much more."

"Listen, I will talk to my husband about this matter. He will have a conversation with our son if necessary. Honestly, David, I think you might be wrong. Your wife appears to be very much in love with you. Besides, you have a lovely daughter, and you are married. No, I cannot believe what you are saying."

Elsewhere.

"Dad, you already know, that young lady I have told you about, Solange, the beautiful French actress."
"I think I'm aware. David has spoken with your mother on the telephone. David called her yesterday. I am amazed but not surprised, knowing you."
"So what has he said?"
"In what quagmire have you descended?"
"Her husband is mad, furious, like insane. He might even want to kill me. Solange has mentioned this. She even said that he was looking for a gun. Can you believe this?"
"What are you talking about, Fernando? Can't you be a little more prudent? If this is the case, you must forget about her. You are playing with fire. Listen to me and do as I am ordering you to do. Don't get yourself in more trouble. I will talk to him. I will try

to soothe him. To calm him down. It seems that he is very much in love with his wife."

"Do you realize what you are asking me to do? It is not fair. I love her."

"Don't argue. You have no right to claim. I see only one thing that you can do to avoid more problems. Take the first plane to Key West and drive back to New York. It would be best if you left Havana as soon as possible."

"Do you think that the situation requires such drastic measures?"

"Go back to New York and resume your studies at the University. You should not see her again, at least for a long while. Though it would be better if you forgot entirely about her, there are other women in the world, you know. I suggest you evade married women in the future. For heaven sakes, what a mess. It would help if you got going."

"How long? I mean, for how long should I not see her."

"How should I know! Could you not ask me such an insane question? You are not aware of the complications that you have caused. It would help if you got back to the University. Don't see her again for at least a year; that should be enough time for things to calm down. Better to not see her again, but I know you. Let me handle this; I will invite both of them to the Havana Yacht Club for lunch. I wish you could act more sensibly and diplomatically with women. Particularly with married women! In the meantime, pack your bags. I am putting you on a plane — no ifs or buts. You are gone."

"Solange, we wish to invite you and David for lunch at the Havana Yacht Club. I think you would both enjoy it."

Solange hung up a little nervous, although Mrs. Pruna had assured her that Fernando wouldn't be there. The situation would be much more relaxed. The refined atmosphere of the Havana Yacht Club was the perfect setting for sensitive negotiations. Nonetheless, Mrs. Pruna and Solange kept their distance.

"Come, Solange, let me ask you for a dance. It should be more comfortable to converse. You see, I find all this a little disturbing, but I think my son is very attracted to you and that you perhaps feel the same way," Dr. Pruna began.

"I indeed like to be with him. To dance, to be in his company. To talk to him, But."

"Would you leave him for Fernando?"

"Whom?"

"Your husband. David."

"No, no, I love my husband. I love my daughter. No, and a thousand times no."

"I believe that you have to forget Fernando, he is young and honestly, if I must say so.... "

"But I have no intention to leave my husband..." Solange interrupted.

"He is a young man, only a student, and as such, he has no money and even less to assume the responsibility of a family. Take care of your little daughter. Also, besides, it wouldn't be very reasonable to leave David. It wouldn't be wise. He will soon be a doctor, won't he? Your husband is financially sound. He can provide for you and your daughter. You must weigh these factors objectively."

Solange, confused, befuddled, didn't even have time to answer. Dr. Pruna spoke first:

"I wonder if my son is right for you. He is a little, wild, let me put it this way: When he meets a beautiful female, he,"

Solange felt trapped in the net of a love triangle that was difficult to detangle, in which Fernando's shadow continually overlapped

David's figure. Solange looked askance at the table and noted that Mrs. Pruna, for her part, was trying to comfort David.

"You have such a lovely wife."

The Prunas did everything in their power to soothe David and discourage Solange. They accomplished their goal, and each territory remained safe. Weapons not drawn.

A cold war persisted, but the tension seemed to decrease. Solange sighed, relieved, waiting, maybe, for the next attack.

"Sometimes, I would like to have a few more months to see what my future will bear." She meditated, she needed more time to sort out her feelings and her desires. However, there was no more time. She must move on.

"In 1956, we will be heroes, or we will be martyrs."

Fidel Castro had just pronounced a spectacular speech in Miami. He was determined to invade the Cuban territory. They were getting ready in Mexico and believed that the General was eager to face the rebels, in the middle of the cold war between the United States and the Soviet Union. As for Fernando, he had not packed his luggage yet.

A hurricane was emerging on the horizon and threatened to shake these Cuban latitudes. It unleashes the forces of the elements. The barometer was falling, and the thermometer was rising. No doubt, the temperature was going up. You could feel the heat.

Figure 14 **DENISE DARCEL**

CHAPTER SEVEN

VIVACIOUS DENISE

"It's a tropical heatwave
That makes the temperature go up to 35 degrees."
Marilyn Monroe
Heat Wave, "There is no business like Show Business," 1954

The Monseigneur, El Vedado, Christmas of 1955

Tourists rushed to do their year's end shopping. The warehouses were full and the Galiano Street stores, illuminated. In the warm environment of the Restaurant Monseigneur, an orchestra played the sweet notes of a bolero. Solange and her husband started to dance. Fernando cut in and embraced his girl under the scrutinizing eyes of the husband.

"I wish you both a Merry Christmas," a young lady exclaimed. "May Santa Claus fill your fireplace and empty his bag of happiness!" She didn't realize that in Cuba, there were no fireplaces, but the joy was boundless.

She spoke with a delicious, lulling, and a solid French accent.

"Hey, this woman, she looks familiar, let me see!" A male voice exclaimed in a side table. "Isn't that? What's her name? The one that was starring in Vera Cruz, the Western film! That neckline is a killer, let me tell you!"

Men's eyes dived into the provocative cleavage. Women discovered that there was the subject matter for concern there and that the French bombshell had nothing to envy Jayne

Mansfield's hyperbolic breasts. That is why she had allowed herself, once, to address a photographer in these terms:

"Please, take these pretty flowers away. Can't you see they obstruct the view of my neckline! You don't want to hide such a view, do you?"

"Some years ago, France presented us with the magnificent gift of the Statue of Liberty to thank us for everything we had done for it. I don't know what we Americans this time have done to deserve this second gift, that comes directly from France. Here I give you,

So, began Dean Martin & Jerry Lewis Show, on that November 2 of 1951, on NBC.

"Mademoiselle Denise Darcel!"

Everything was sensual about Miss Darcel. Americans adored her, and the French lady knew it. She realized it immediately, just as soon as she landed on Uncle Sam's land, at the end of the forties. Like a diva wrapped in mysticism and wearing her mink coat, she got off a limousine to attend a premier. She was a sensation with her Dior designed dress. Journalists already said she had something that would make headlines. They had also noticed that she had an attractive female vice. That is, she wouldn't stop talking! Denise was a chatterbox, and she kept making gestures. She repeated her so sexy zze or zziss endlessly, and Americans found this charming exotic touch fascinating. She was also very unusual, and she liked to joke, which was, in a way, her trademark. A creative cocktail of humor and extravagance for a beautiful woman, dripping with sex appeal, who spoke her mind with a devastatingly sharp tongue. This post-war bombshell had everything to delight men. Above all, David, and, of course, Fernando.

Solange went to say hello to Denise.

"Bonjour! I see that we are both French and that we are in the same business."

"Are you a singer too?" The last one asked.

"Something like that. Also, I have made movies — even television. However, I particularly love theater."

From the beginning, Denise was amiable, talkative, and cheerful.

"Like me, then. May I introduce my sister, Hélène? She has one of the most beautiful voices one can listen to, and yet, she is so modest. She never praises herself. So, I do it for her!"

Denise burst out laughing. Hélène, a lovely-dark-eyed brunette, smiled and only said a discrete hello. It was evident that Hélène, despite her beauty, was very modest, and quiet, compared to her sister's overwhelming personality. Denise explained that her sister sang in hotels and night-clubs.

"I joined Denise in New York some years ago. Denise was beginning to make herself a name in cinemas on the other side of the Atlantic, at that moment. America frightened me a little, in the beginning. It is so big, and it's so far from my country! However, at the same time, it was all so exciting."

The contracts came one after the other. Then, Jack Benny, the renowned television showman, discovered her when she performed at a night-club in New York.

Jack Benny invited me to the Jack Benny's Show, in the broadcasting of December 31 of 1951.

"But please introduce your friends!"

Denise interrupted bluntly, addressing Solange.

"David, my husband. Fernando, our Cuban friend."

"So lovely to meet you, how are you doing? How are you? See me at the Sans-Souci cabaret tomorrow. I am singing there now. Tomorrow is going to be a huge night!"

Lefty Clark was opening his new two million dollar casino night club. He had recovered the Sans Souci to relaunch it under the stars. Lefty's real name was William Bishoff, known in the media as Lefty Clark, Clark the left handed. He came from Miami, and he handled the great Florida seaside resorts. He was a symbolic figure in these environments. Denise had been hired to be the star of the show, she had a good resume for being hired: large, beautiful breasts. She was going to be a walking, singing and dancing bomb. In Cuba, Denise made the Cuban essence burn. If she had been a cigar, men would have inhaled her and smoked her until they got burned. If Denise had been a glass of rum, they would have drunk her to the last drop, becoming intoxicated with her body. If she had to be a dance, she would have been a mambo, one of those that trap you, and you can't break loose.

Meanwhile, in the Monseigneur, when Fernando was not near her, David was not very far from her. Solange was not fooled by the fake smiles, nor her looks. Denise was so beautiful, so lively, so vibrant, so free, so sexy, that she was a threat to all women around her. You could see it in her eyes and sense it in her voice, in her palpable sensuality. Between movie and movie, she illuminated the nightclubs, the cabarets, and the elegant saloons of the grandest hotels of America, from Las Vegas to Los Angeles and from New York to Montreal, making her tours as a star attraction and captivating the audiences with her vibrant spirit and personality. In her favorite staging – wearing sheath dresses or other bolder and more attractive outfits – often completed with opera gloves, which she was so fond of, the audience always applauded like crazy. Denise was a French revolution in Cuban territory! As soon as a man started to walk away from her, another one took over and tried his luck. With Miss Darcel, it was something like casino gambling. Everyone expected to succeed, but most failed.

"I have worked my entire life. I mean that I started very early, from the age of twelve. We were five sisters at home! My father was a baker, and he struggled to feed all his daughters. During the war, the Nazis came to our home one day and shot my father dead. Just like that, they murdered him. At the end of the war, I found a job as a scented-rayon vendor at some big warehouses in Paris. Unexpectedly, one day, someone saw me and wanted to take pictures of me.

Can you imagine? He wanted to take pictures of me! I could not believe it. The photograph turned out to be my passport to America. They had discovered me. Like magic, soon I became: 'The Most Beautiful Girl of Paris' and 'The Most Photographed Girl in France.'

When I was a child, I used to dream of being an actress or a singer. So, I didn't play hard to get and took a ship to New York. So that is how my dream came true. Moreover, to top it off, in America, I couldn't ask for more! In France? No, I'm not so well known there. Ah, sure I'm a thousand times better known in Montreal than in Paris. Also, besides, I like Canadians, and they love me. So we even speak the same language. Well, it's a different thing, but, at least, I can express my style. It does me good."

A journalist approached.

"Denise, Denise. A few words, please!"

He wanted to capture the most critical moments of her life.

"What do you think of Americans?"

"Of Americans? Well, they think more about business than they think about love.

Isn't that true?"

After reflecting for one second, holding her chin between the forefinger and the thumb and frowning, with a studied pose, she added: "That is unless love is business. Heart business! Yes, it is an unstoppable market with its parts to conquer. I will say that Americans are very similar to French wine. They can go to your head!"

"Do you like champagne, Miss Darcel?"

"Of course, I like champagne. What kind of question is that!"

Denise burst into a sparkling laughter like bubbles, and after one or two silent sips, she exclaimed:

"Except for when thrown at my face!"

She had not forgotten that her ex-husband — well, one of her ex-husbands, had thrown a glass of champagne at her face during an argument.

"What do women dream about today?"

"About what? Men, of course! About the perfect man, about his spirit! It is just a beautiful image. However, the framework must be fair too. Please don't make me talk about men, I would be talking about them for hours, and then you would write whatever you want to. Once, I was very offended by despicable publicity about me. If money grew on trees, I would be willing to marry a gorilla! No, this is not true."

This woman had a disturbing sex appeal. Of course, it didn't disgust Fernando since he was not insensitive to her looks and winks. There is no business-like show business. Consequently, the mercury was going up in this gentleman's thermometer.

8

LIFE THROUGH ROSE-COLORED GLASSES

*"In Havana, there is not such a thing as boredom
It is the Paris of the Americas
The very sublime pearl of the Antilles
The sexiest city in the world."
Jay Mallin Sr, Havana Night Life, 1956.*

The Sans-Souci Cabaret, Havana, 1956

At the entrance of the Sans-Souci, on a corner, a blonde whispered in the ear of her lucky knight. She was selling him her charms, without a doubt, and was groaning sweet words between whispers. She pulled her hair back like an actress who had just seen a photographer approach.

"It's the kingdom of the three "R's" mon Chéri."

She even pronounced the word Cheri with a French accent, prolonging the r in the South American style, marking it stronger to provide it with a sensuality she considered to be Latin.

"The three "Rs"?"

"Rrrrr," she purred, like a tigress, to make a catlike Eartha Kit turn pale with envy, who was, nevertheless, the queen of purring.

She walked around him.

"Rum"

She executed a dancing step.

"Rumba"

Then, another dancing step.

"Yankee Coke and dollars?" She dared, walking to him with exaggerated swaying.

"Now, let's see. Rum, Rumba, and"

She burst into resounding laughter.

"Roulette!"

The name fitted the place perfectly. Leave your worries at the entrance. It was a paradise for the eyes, ears, and throats. During the seconds of silence between two musical numbers, one could hear the clinking of glasses overflowing with champagne. Nobody was bored. Ever.

However, a budding revolution had been agitating the island for a while and was sensed everywhere. It was in every corner of the city. It quickly recruited anyone who let themselves be seduced and cast under its spell. It could convince and befuddle. Also, proximately there were crowds of partisans. Men. Women. No distinction. In perfectly synchronized lines. A revolution that became so popular that those who didn't join it appeared suspicious. It counted on powerful, leather rutilant that fired and made thousands of people keep pace. This revolution struck you without warning, on every corner. It caught you by surprise, it imprisoned you for endless hours, at the same time, particularly during late-night hours. If it gave you a break, it was to hound you better and to hammer you with its rhythm. This Revolution was the Mambo. Havana became a bonfire of music, a roar of dollars, a tremor of bodies. With the rhythm of congas, clients danced frenetically on the dancing floors and became as disinhibited as the magazine dancers.

Some ten kilometers away from Havana, the Sans-Souci was built after World War I and frequented by wealthy Americans. It never closed its doors entirely. Not even during the 1929 stock market crash, when it became gradually less usual to see many tourists, and it started to welcome gangsters. Every day one could hear the mantra of the slot machines and the voice of the croupiers who always managed to renew the usual "Place your bets!".

When you entered there, you had the feeling of entering a homestead. It was magic just two steps away from the American Key West Airport. Weekend packages, inexpensive plane tickets, happy hour restaurants, nights in night-clubs, and nights at hotels for some hours of madness. Inside, dancers swayed their hips, and the bands played live music throughout. Two hours after landing, tourists could already give in to the roulette passion or craps to blackjack or baccarat. The game choices were many. Others came in full package-boats.

At the peak of the Sans-Souci pyramid, a place of honor was occupied by the number two of Mafiosi, after Meyer Lansky, Santos Trafficante Jr.

Figure 15 At the Sans Souci Cabaret. Fernando, Solange, David, Denise and Kirk.

When a client visiting some of its night-clubs recognized the owner, they would discretely elbow their roulette neighbor. With his glasses and his serious intellectual look, it was easier to take him for a university professor rather than for a Mafiosi.

The Sans-Souci was the kingdom of the underworld. They weren't stingy at all about investments, refurbishing it cost almost one million dollars. A million dollars then has a value of ten million dollars today[28]. Lefty Clark knew how to make the show permanent. Once, he tried to seduce the middle-weight champion, Rocky Marciano, with a 350,000-dollar contract – a trifle – to fight the Cuban champ, "Niño" Valdés. The show glittered at the Sans-Souci. You could play in an environment of easy dollars. At the same time, you could admire shows that would leave you astounded. All night long, the profligacy of colors, feathers, and devilish melodies that made a cluster of beautiful women shake. With their attractive dresses, some centimeters of fabric between the navel and the upper thigh, with the loud sound of the drums and surrounded by black or coffee-milk-colored young men.

Being at the Sans-Souci was like being immersed in a movie set, where a filmmaker revived a Cuban night cradled by a tropical breeze and the echoes of fascinating congas. The Cadillacs and the Buicks were parked not very far from the entrance. The night made beautiful women glow, jewels twinkle, and life worth living.

Sans-Souci. A name that acquired meaning depending on the amount of alcohol consumed or the sum of money won or lost at the roulette. If you were lucky in the game, you could even win a brand-new Cadillac.

One lost patience in front of the slot machines but saw life through rose-colored glasses and worry-free.

____

[28] 2019 Value of US Dollar.

That night, Denise was singing at the Sans-Souci for the opening of Lefty Clark's remodeled casino, among a constellation of musicians and dancers. She was singing her fetish song, the one that had won her recognition on her arrival in the United States: *La vie en rose*. Her languid version of *Ombres sur Paris*, her first film, had made many lose their heads. That small part as a cabaret singer opened the doors of the most prestigious night-clubs and movie theaters to her, even after having vegetated while she waited for a new role. The second film, "Battleground," came afterward, and the action took place in France during World War II. Denise appeared only for six minutes, but her sex-appeal spilled through the screen. Showing generously sculptured breasts under a tight black T-shirt, she cut a big loaf of bread with a huge knife. To do so, she needed to hold the bun against her breasts. In movie theaters, the scene caused a commotion with howls and whistles among the male audience. Later, some wild-eyed man walked towards Denise and said:

"You are the young lady who cuts the bread in Battleground!".

"Please, give a big hand to Denise Darcel!"

Denise lasciviously went down the stairs of the Sans-Souci, tightly wrapped in a white sheath dress. When she sang the first notes, Fernando became hypnotized. He put the voice aside and focused on her body. The sexual bomb had just exploded in his eyes, and he took in all the flashes. The war of the senses declared.

"*Quand il me prend Dans ses bras... Il me parle tout bas...*"

Denise didn't only embody beauty; she was generosity made flesh. When she danced and sang, her eyes devoured you while her lips embraced you.

"*Je vois la vie en rose.*"

Her limitations as a singer forgiven for her entirely charming accent and her famous "the" that became zze. A Parisian environment settled in the saloon. French performers were always more successful than the rest of the local or international artists. Maurice Chevalier had made the audience roar when he sang his "Ma Pomme," and Edith Piaf dragged the crowd with her "L'homme." So was la vie in rose, worry-free

Fernando looked at the small world around him. There was Solange. Married. Her husband was also there. Would Denise be married too? She seemed to be as free as the air, free as full flesh. There was also the exotic Hélène, so sweet and quiet that she intrigued him; so discrete that she almost went unnoticed, but very attractive. He felt trapped in befuddling female hanky-panky – though, "right now, my hanky-panky is you," he told himself while looking at Denise. Laughter burst, green bills were wasted, champagne glasses clinked. Denise and Fernando felt like dancing. She was dancing the swing with the rhythm of drums and metals of the orchestra, with a devilish mambo. Their feet beat on the floor, with one of Rosemary Clooney's last hits, that was all the rage.

"¡Hey, mambo! ¡Mambo Italiano!
¡Hey, mambo! Mambo Italiano
Go, go, go; you mixed up Siciliano."

"What an ambiance! I love it!" Denise exclaimed and sipped champagne before bursting into laughter, swaying her hips and provocatively showing off the promise of her milky white breasts.

How could one not enjoy such an ambiance? Havana was full of warm and exotic musical trends that were successive, intermixed, or enjambed; they were like snakes sneaking under the dresses of the dancers up to their skin pores and dragging them to perform those devilish dance steps. Encounters and affairs were also successive, intermixed, or enjambed. Mambo and Chachachá imprisoned you with their scent in deliciously magic trances that only stopped to allow the velvet like fingers of a pianist to explore the keys of the piano or the warmth of a jazz band invade the audience.

David seemed to have forgotten his rivalry with Fernando because of Solange. He revolved around Denise. Solange watched how this curious triangle moved before her eyes, curious of how far it would all go. A fit of certain jealousy climbing up her stomach.

"It's a little bit hot here. Shall we move somewhere? Perhaps get out of here!"

Fernando followed the actress.

"Would you show me some words?"

"*Quand il me prend dans ses bras...*"

Denise approached him closer and closer and kept singing.

"*Il me parle tout bas.*"

"I see la vida color de rosa," ended Fernando.

"Bring your lips close to mine, Darling" she whispered.

Denise and Fernando disappeared into the hot Cuban night not to be seen again until the next day. They left without saying goodnight to their astonished friends. In silence they looked at each other in disbelief.

Sometime before the disappearing act, at the ringside table, Fernando had proposed.

"Friends, I would like that we meet tomorrow to swim for a while and later have lunch at the Havana Yacht Club! That is if the hangovers will permit it."

Fernando was the one who made the invitation. The Habana Yacht Club was the upper class's favorite place: a delightful swimming pool, private beach, sailboats, yachts, fabulous cuisine, champagne bar. Nothing could beat the elegance of this icon, founded in 1886. Membership was closed. However, one of the only ways to be a member of the club was to marry the daughter of an active club member. They were, of course, stigmatized as "Fly Members"!

Alternatively, you had to be the son of a club member. It was the most elitist private club in Cuba. Dr. Pruna had been an early member of the club but, while abroad, had ended his membership. Years later, when he wanted his two sons to become members, he was asked to pay for all the years of absence, as if he had never interrupted his membership. Being a member of the Habana Yacht Club was not something you could improvise, not even with a vast amount of dollars. Even Fulgencio Batista,

Figure 16 Founded in 1886 The Habana Yacht Club - The most exclusive private club in Cuba before the Communist Revolution.

when he was President of Cuba, requested membership and was rejected, even after offering the President of the Club a significant sum of money to expand the grounds of the club. Also, he had no chance of ever becoming a member because he was not white, and the Havana Yacht Club was very strict with the issue of racial segregation. As for Fernando and his brother Andy, they automatically became members, precisely because their father had belonged to the club and had updated his membership. The Juniors perpetuated the family tradition of high society.

Solange, Denise, Hélène, and David. The presence of the other two young ladies cast a shadow on Solange, who indeed was more than a bit jealous. Fernando's disappearance with Denise had not gone unnoticed. For the occasion, the three of them were wearing very provocative but fashionable swimming suits, and they paraded around the swimming pool showing their chiseled bodies defiantly. Such a wind of freedom and joy to live emerged from Denise that she approached Fernando and aggressively tongue kissed him several times, their bodies in an embrace before the daunted group of friends. Having spent the night with Fernando, she treated the young man without apparent inhibition and total familiarity. She bit his lips sensually, and a drop of blood decorated Fernando's mouth, which she wiped off with another kiss. However, this wave of sensuality didn't go unnoticed by the administration. The director of the Havana Yacht Club wanted some explanation. He walked to Fernando and took him aside.

"I want to talk to you, Señor Pruna."

"Yes, of course, about what?"

"I'm going to have to suspend your membership and will forbid you to enter the Yacht Club. At least, for the time being."

"Why?"

"Don't pretend you don't understand. It seems that you do not respect anything. How have you dared to bring to our club all those half-naked loose foreign girls? There are children here, you know. We have rules and regulations, and we follow a moral code of conduct."

"You are making a mistake, Director. That is not quite the case. They are very talented and famous ladies. They are beautiful and belong to decent families. They are far from being the kind of girls that you are implying. To settle this matter, allow me to explain. Don't you see one of them is the world-renowned French movie star? Denise Darcel?"

"Who? Wait. Calm down, young man. You don't have to shout."

"I don't want to calm down. Who do you think I am? You invited the Spanish actress Sara Montiel with all the honors to our Club, for playing in the film "Vera Cruz" in which she had just acted. Furthermore, you had yourself photographed with her, and the photos published in our club magazine."

"Yes, indeed, that's true. However, what are you trying to tell me? So, what?"

"So, what? Don't you see that Sara Montiel is the actress who played with Denise Darcel in that very same film? Yes, in the same movie! Moreover, the most crucial role of the film performed by the French actress Denise Darcel, the same girl you are looking at right now. Denise Darcel is the Star in Vera Cruz!"

"Really? It could be."

"What do you mean, "it could be"? It's quite eloquent! If you want me to, I would be pleased to introduce her to you. You might enjoy meeting a fine lady."

In Vera Cruz, with Gary Cooper and Burt Lancaster co-starring, Fernando could have added, Denise kissed languidly that virtuous Burt Lancaster, effortlessly enviable for the whiteness of his shining teeth and his perfect smile. Maybe because of that, Denise put her lips on Lancaster with such apparent pleasure. ¡As for Gary Cooper, he was very tall; he was over six feet tall. Since Denise was not so tall, it was better that she kissed Lancaster, thus leaving Cooper for Montiel.

"So, what's your point?" The Habana Yacht Club's director continued, returning to reality.

"It's the same category of women and should be treated in the same way, so they can attend the Habana Yacht Club as the guest of a member without being considered 'easy' women. Quite the contrary. Famous, talented ladies."

"I confess that I am embarrassed, and I stand corrected. Your clarification is valid. Well, then, I apologize. It's just that there was certain ambiguity. How was I to know who the ladies were."

He continued, "I made a mistake, he mumbled. I beg your forgiveness; the incident immediately forgotten. Moreover, I would like you to introduce them to me."

"I will be pleased to," Fernando replied, hiding a smirk.

Meanwhile, the director ordered some bottles of champagne to welcome Denise Darcel, as well as Hélène Darcel and Solange Podell. He had become so enthusiastic that he didn't want to leave the group, and he kept talking to the girls and asked for photos for the Club's Magazine. The Director had a delightful time and Fernando was quite pleased.

Prejudice was an endemic trait of Cuba's high society. Marxists exploited the concept of class struggle. Indeed, social strife breeds unrest and, eventually, potential revolutions.

Later that night Denise approached Fernando when they were all alonge.

Figure 17 GARY COOPER, SARA MONTIEL, DENISE DARCEL, BURT LANCASTER – FILM: VERA CRUZ

"Fernando?"

"Yes, Denise?"

"Please don't feel bad for what I am about to ask of you. You are a handsome man, and I adore you, but I would like you to spend some time with my sister. I feel bad for her. She is so gentle and adorable. You know she is here with me. She helps me all the time. Please take her for a tour, show her a little bit of Havana. She has not seen anything. I am just too busy with my tours. She has been my assistant during all this time in Havana. It will be good for her. She needs some distraction, and I think that you could be the perfect tour guide. Could you do this for me? You and I can still meet every night after the show."

Denise curled up next to the young man like a purring kitten.

"All right, I promise. I will show your sister around old Havana, the historical monuments and fortresses, and she will enjoy it. I am sure."

Fernando discovered a sweet and quiet Hélène in the antipodes of her volcanic sister. She was of a very alluring exotic beauty that exuded calmness and serenity. Fernando was impressed.

"In France, did you use to sing in nightclubs?"

"Yes, I made my debut in Paris. Afterward, when Denise came to try her luck in the United States, I arrived a little bit later, some years ago already. I was fortunate."

"Was it Jack Benny who discovered you?"

"Yes, as I told you, he heard me sing in a nightclub in New York. Then, he invited me to be on his television show. It was crucial for me since the famous Jack Benny Show was one of the most seen in America."

Then she added, "It was a great moment: to have a program named The Hélène Francoise Show."

"Hélène Francoise?"

Her stage name was Hélène Francoise. Later, she used the fame of her sister and changed it for Hélène Darcel.

"Two weeks later, I was on his radio show, for the réveillon de San Silvestre[29]. They named the show 'Rendezvous Avec Une Francaise pour la Saint Sylvestre'."

Then, vertiginously, she succeeded in the saloons, the hotels, and the night-clubs. The Old New Orleans welcomed her in

---

[29] New Year's show.

Washington DC. She went for several months to sing in Mexico, and Montreal could listen to her sing as well. In New York, she sang at the Sherry-Netherland.

"I would like very much to listen to you. Denise says you sing divinely."

"If you want to, I will soon sing in New York City. Please come."

The vacation was coming to an end. Multiple and lovely gallant dates with Denise also were coming to an end. With her, it was an exertion of the senses. Exhilarating sex.

Would there be more? The actress was in high demand.

Denise's contract at the Sans Souci was coming to an end. She walked with Fernando hand in hand in front of the Riviera Hotel, on the enticing Malecon Drive sidewalk, right in front of the Ocean. The waves were hitting against the rocks and the sea wall and you could taste the salt in the air. She stopped for a moment to embrace the young man. Then, she handed him a note and looking seriously into his eyes, said:

"Listen, Fernando, when you get to New York, please give us a call. Take this; it is the number where you can find us, Hélène and me. It is my private home number. I mean it, Fernando, please call us; we will be waiting for you."

**Helene Darcel

9

MARVELOUS HÉLÈNE

Hélène never married
Some women, very few, only love once.
Hélène was one of those women".
Denise Darcel in conversation with Cyriaque Griffon.

New York, January 1956

It was time to return to the University. Denise was not in New York yet, as he expected. She was performing on a stage in Las Vegas. When Fernando called, it was Hélène who answered. By the time Denise returned, the press had echoed an emerging relationship. The actress cared so much for her sister that she could only be happy for her. She took care of her like an older sister when Hélène was the elder of the two.

"Hélène Darcel, Denise Darcel's little sister, and Fernando Pruna, from the Cuban sugar families, are dating. He is a student at Columbia University".

In his credited column, syndicated at a national level with upper-class gossips, Igor Cassin, whose pen name was Cholly Knickerbocker, published something on the nightlife of the Darcel sisters and the Cuban Fernando Pruna, every week.

Between the wedding of the comedian Efrem Zimbalist and the new affairs of Grace Kelly, a Hollywood star who began to flit around princely Monaco's cliffs, Fernando continually saw his name in some leaflet of the pink chronicles of the Palm Beach Post. The reference to the romance was concise, the age of his conquest was a little altered, and the older sister turned into, the younger one. The professional and family environment modified, and at times his last name was misspelled, but it didn't matter everything smiled at him. This sudden notoriety made him gravitate in the celebrity circles of show business, arm in arm with two lovely creatures. Life was like a musical comedy. Fernando's and Hélène's romance took off with *My Funny Valentine*, sung by Chet Baker.

Denise didn't seem jealous, quite the opposite. She adored her sister. She was satisfied with telling them about her last adventures.

"I took part in a show in front of all those pilots."

The show, filmed at Nellis Air Force Base close to Las Vegas, to entertain some thousands of combat pilots, was seen nationwide. Suddenly, with her patter and her slapsticks, zze French bomb had plagiarized even the zze from Zsa Zsa Gabor, both invited to the Milton Berle Show in front of a multitude of American soldiers. Denise liked American men, handsome soldiers, like the ones she encountered in Paris at the end of World War II. So the soldiers paid her a proper tribute.

"Hello, my darlings! I am delighted to see you. Oh, it's fantastic to see all these good-looking young men! I am so happy to be here! I like American pilots very much."

Denise had said all this in French, just in one breath. The devoted Berle audience gathered there had surely understood nothing at all, but Denise's sensual smile and humor were enough to make up for her language gaps.

"Two beautiful girls coming from two very different countries in Europe and nevertheless, they share the same coastline."

Milton Berle had said this as he stared roguishly at both girls' provocative necklines.

The spark lit, and Zsa Zsa Gabor, who wouldn't bite her tongue either, played the role of the pale, timid, shy one, next to her bold, brash, French colleague.

If Denise made at least some five or six thousand dollars a week from her contracts as a singer, Hélène didn't make that much, maybe two thousand dollars. However, Hélène's voice dazzled Fernando, who had never heard such a beautiful timbre in a voice or such sensitivity when singing. Hélène was pure "feeling." The movement of her body, hands, and arms, while she sang, was magically graceful and highlighted her exquisite elegance. The musical notes embraced her voice sagaciously and captivated the young man. "In this land, my only joy, my only happiness, is my man."

Hélène sang at various chic clubs in New York City: The Starlight Roof at the Waldorf Astoria, Chez Vito, the Casanova Club, and always at the Viennese Lantern, a fashionable club with a marvelous string ensemble to which it was a delight to listen. New Yorkers flocked to see her there after seeing a play on Broadway or enjoying a concert at Carnegie Hall. Listening to Hélène sing in French, Spanish or Italian, surrounded by violin players, was a feast to the eyes and the ears. She evoked European sophistication and dazzling elegance. Besides, her exotic beauty and her lovely figure were deeply seductive.

Then one day, totally unexpected, Denise faced Fernando and said:

"You can stay at our home for as long as you wish, Fernando, she said earnestly. I am inviting you to come and live with us permanently. Please come to live with us. Do you understand? What do you think, Hélène?"

Her sister nodded with a shy girl's smile. Soon, Fernando accepted the invitation and moved into their beautiful and comfortable Brownstone building apartment on 63rd Street, between Fifth Avenue and Madison Avenue. One of the most exclusive neighborhoods of the city.

Sometimes, when Fernando went for walks in the area, he would be pleased to encounter the famous Swedish actress Greta Garbo. She looked almost unrecognizable with her big dark glasses and her severe dresses. She appeared to be older than her age, her beautiful face with no makeup and withered by years of solitude. She was retired, by choice and disappointments, not only from films but from life itself. Whenever Fernando ran, casually, into her, impacted by her presence and could not help but to muse on how fleeting is passion, beauty, and fame.

The Gabor's were also his neighbors. They lived next door, a family of exiled artists from Hungary, which included the eccentric actress, very prolific in marriages, Zsa Zsa. Also, her sisters Eva and Magda and the mamma of the family, Mrs. Jolie Gabor. All the daughters were beautiful and the mother charming. Jolie loved to hear Hélène sing. When Hélène sang at the Viennese Lantern, "Mamma" Gabor was often there, sitting next to Fernando. She liked to talk to the Cuban young man. They appreciated each other, and while Hélène prepared herself for her performance, they enjoyed one or two Martinis, while they talked a little bit about everything.

"She sings divinely, this little French girl,' she said.

"Yes. I agree. Helene has a fantastic voice!" Fernando confirmed.

"Tell me, Fernando. Have you ever been married?"

"No."

"Keep her forever! Don't let her go. I can see that she is crazy about you."

Mamma Gabor could have also told him. "My daughter spends her time collecting husbands!"

It is a small world. Fernando had met Zsa Zsa, on some occasions, in Bayshore, Long Island, at Marie and Barron Otis's home. He was only a young boy then, still attending Eaglebrook School. Zsa Zsa had married – among others – the actor George Sanders. The actor was, at the same time, a close friend of Barron Otis, with whom Dr. Pruna kept a long-lasting friendship; from the time he was a student in New York, when they were both classmates at the Horace Mann Preparatory Academy, from where they graduated.

"I was Miss Hungary! Zsa Zsa would vindicate with her funny accent whenever she found the occasion."

**"Have you seen the well-to-do?
Up and down Park Avenue?"**

His life seemed plagiarized from the golden lyrics of 'Puttin' on the Ritz,' the song Fred Astaire sang. When the three of them walked up and down the streets of New York, Hélène, Denise, and Fernando, they were a chic trio, a striking and captivating one. A young and elegant Cuban nobleman with his perfectly made-to-measure oxford gray suit, his white shirt and tie, a voluptuous and vibrating Hollywood actress, wrapped in her white mink fur stole, and a sweet and good-looking singer, the epitome of charm. El Morocco, the Harwin, the Copacabana, the 21 Club, the Stork Club. Fernando, Hélène, and Denise couldn't be absent from these fashionable nightclubs, where exhibiting oneself or having fun with the All-New York Upper Class were of good taste. At El Morocco, Fernando posed proudly for a photographer. Sitting between an actress with a pronounced neckline, with her shoulders slightly covered by a fur bonnet, and the discrete singer with whom he was in love, the champagne bucket full of ice in the center of the table, next to a smoking Cuban cigar. Fernando danced with his girls, alternating, first one and then the other, though Denise unfailingly courted when they toured the clubs. If the godmother of the All-Hollywood and the mundane chronicles, Hedda Hopper, were informed, she would highlight in one of her columns that she had seen Denise Darcel arm in arm with a new gentleman at the Harwin. The other queen of gossips, her snaky rival Louella Parsons, would enjoy writing that Miss Darcel danced with her latest conquest at El Morocco.

A different type of press informed that students were protesting in Havana, and they were opposing Batista's regime. They demanded free elections.

Some weeks later, the Cuban president was the honored guest of the city of Daytona Beach, in Florida. He got off the plane with his wife and children. A parade organized to honor him. Tourists and local citizens waved Cuban flags when he passed. Batista liked seeing this place he had known during his exile again. Police kept under watch some exiled agitators, surely the same who had peacefully protested some days before, on March 10, on the anniversary of Batista's coup d'état. They claimed he had repressed the students' demonstrations that had taken place in Havana.

At the end of a semester at Columbia University, Fernando announced his new projects to his father.

Figure 18 A night at El Morocco with Helene and Denise Darcel

"Father, you know, it happens that all my extra-college activities do not fit well into the demands of the college courses."

"Do you mean your different jobs?"

"In other terms, yes. I don't get to tackle all of them."

"Well, then?"

"So, then, I need to choose. I am thinking about leaving college and finding other jobs to increase my income."

"Do you want to leave your studies?"

"I want to keep on working. However, I'm not going to leave my studies. I will register for the Columbia University night courses."

"I'm not sure that you are doing the right thing, probably not, but it's your call. You have the necessary ambition to succeed, but your education is critical. Education refines the tools you need to succeed. The foundation on which you will structure your life depends on your knowledge. The most important thing is that you do not spread yourself too thin, with too many activities at the same time."

On the other end of the line, Dr. Pruna remained silent for an instant and then whispered:

"Better said, chase several hares at the same time."

Was he talking about his love stories or his professional activities, Fernando wondered?

Dr. Pruna referred, from time to time, to the David and Solange episode at the Havana Yacht Club some months before. However, this French singer, though a little bit older, was so delightfully refined – and, above all, not married – that Doctor Pruna could do nothing other than to tolerate this relationship.

However, Dr. Pruna had other concerns dancing in his head. Within Batista's close circle, some said that Castro succumbed.

Others sustained that he was alive and that his July 26 Movement was growing, and that Castro was using effective political propaganda abroad: radio and news bulletins. The rebels always pursued their goals and worked in their logistics abroad. Students manifested at Universities and raised the tone of discontent. On the other hand, the General assured that he had the situation under control. He was confident that his head of the armed forces, General Francisco Tabernilla, was totally capable of overpowering the rebels and unquestionably loyal to him.

However, Cuban students felt otherwise.

"We want elections to take place right away. We demand immediate elections. Moreover, Batista insists on not wanting to organize new elections to vote for a new president."

"You better shut up!"

"We want to bring about change and kick Batista out of the presidency."

"He only sees his interest, that of his circle, of his buddies and his Mafia acolytes. There is nothing left for the rest of the people. They can rot in their misery!"

"Castro is touring the United States at this moment. He is in touch with our countrymen in exile. He is raising funds that will be useful to organize the logistics of our Revolution, to fortify the resistance, to train men for guerrilla warfare, and to purchase weapons. Batista doesn't know what is in store for him."

"Of course! Castro will be back. He will be back, and the Revolution will succeed."

Batista intensified repression and censorship. A gunshot or an arrest were awaiting those who got in his way. The General had executed 15 rebels that took part in the armed assault of the

Goicuría Military Headquarters in Matanzas on April 29, 1956. At the time, Fidel Castro was organizing an invasion from Mexico. He was training with long marches on rugged terrains, improving his guerrilla tactics, and preparing to execute his plans with the protection and cooperation of Mexican communists and international communism as well as the influential ex-president of Mexico, Lazaro Cardenas. During his stay in Mexico, he met with the Soviet Union's Ambassador on various occasions. The communists did not hide that they had his back. Radio Moscow openly expressed in its daily programs the sympathy they felt for the rebel. Interesting was the fact that even in Mexico, Fidel expressed his socialist inclinations publicly, and yet, in Cuba, the majority of the people did not pay heed to his political manifestations. Instead, they wanted to see him as the potential savior of Cuba. This political blindness only grew as time went by. The result was catastrophic for the Cuban people.

"Have you seen them
Walk up and down the streets
With an elegant military uniform
Ready for war?"

Soldiers could have appropriated this song by Fred Astaire to make it their military anthem. A yacht had left Mexico some days before. It was the "Granma." It arrived in the Cuban coasts with an anti-Batista crew made up of eighty-three armed to the teeth men On December 2, 1956. Their chief, Fidel Castro, was accompanied by his brother Raúl Castro, Ernesto "Che" Guevara and Camilo Cienfuegos, among other vital rebels. They had almost reached their destination when the Granma was sighted near the Eastern coasts by a Cuban coast-guard plane that alerted the command. Disoriented and half lost, the Yacht ran aground, in mud, six hundred feet from the beach, two miles or less from the Niquero military post, suffering alarming equipment losses and chaos. Rebels jumped into the sea, carrying only the indispensable to try to reach the shore. Their shadows slid in the night, entering the swampy areas, and splashing about in the mangrove. Castro's objective was to attack the military positions of the eastern province and make his attack happen at the same time as another armed insurrection was simultaneously carried out by a revolutionary young man of high prestige named Frank País in Santiago de Cuba, the capital city of the province. Afterward, these two rebel units with concurrent actions would join to control the entire region. That was the plan, but just as had happened with the attack on the Moncada Headquarters, it was another colossal military failure. Nothing worked as planned. The historically lauded Granma landing evoked by communist propaganda was, in fact, a shameful military failure and an organizational disaster.

Castro had thought, hastily, that his arrival would cause a revolutionary seaquake, but it didn't happen that way. In Santiago, the action carried out by the other group, with their red and black bracelets showing the name July 26 Movement, also failed. They attacked the prison to release the political prisoners, but the strike kept the city paralyzed. Batista ordered a state of siege, and the troops recovered their positions in the besieged city. Concurrently, Castro took too long to disembark, and the attacks couldn't be carried out at the same time as planned. Batista knew they were coming, and he welcomed them properly. Shortly after having landed, Castro's rebels were arrested in Alegría de Pío, and many of them were killed; the others fled and some deserted. Others were executed in the days following. Some preferred to give up the fight and disappear. Fidel Castro, aware of his failure and conscientiously perturbed, tried to kill himself out of frustration for the defeat and failure, but some of his closest comrades disarmed him to avoid his death[30]. The invaders who prevented his suicide were Mario Chanes, Jaime Acosta and Juan Almeida. All three in time earned the rank of Commanders, the highest military level possible in the Revolution. It is interesting to note that both Mario Chanes and Jaime Acosta dissented after the triumph of the Revolution by opposing the communist transformation of the Revolution. They were arrested and convicted, accused of counterrevolutionary activities. Both served long years in prison[31]. Only Juan Almeida remained faithful to Fidel until his death many years later. Fidel rewarded his loyalty by placing him as head of the Army and eventually bestowing him with the rank of General.

Despite the military debacle and the significant losses in men, war equipment, and food suffered, Fidel was still miraculously lucky. His ex-wife, Mirta Díaz-Balart, and his mother, Lina Ruz, went to see Fulgencio Batista, who agreed to meet with them, and they obtained a short truce from him, so that Fidel and his partisans, could turn themselves in alive.

Ordered by Batista, there was a ceasefire from the soldiers aimed at a fast but peaceful surrendering that guaranteed the lives of

---

[30] It was not the first time that Fidel had tried to kill himself. He wanted to kill himself before, after the failure of the Moncada attack. In both cases, some of his followers prevented his suicide.

[31] Mario Chanes served thirty years in prison, never having fired a shot, and never having belonged to any opposition or counterrevolutionary organization, his most serious fault, having been in the Moncada Garrison assault, in prison with Fidel and taken part in the landing of the Granma, who had the courage to oppose the new power that was installed usurping democracy and establishing a Communist regime in Cuba. Furthermore, he prevented the suicide of Fidel Castro. A man of unquestionable integrity and proven personal courage, his participation in all the most important historical revolutionary events qualified him to be one of the top leaders of the revolution. Fidel destroyed him for not accepting communism in Cuba. Fidel was ruthless against anyone that opposed him, particularly if the person had been one of his close associates.

the ones who turned themselves in. Instead, Fidel, his brother, and some other survivors took advantage of the truce to escape, guided by a resident of the Sierra Maestra named Guillermo García Frías, sent by Celia Sánchez, who knew the zone well. Some days later, Fidel was able to reach the Sierra Maestra Mountains and regroup what remained of his troop. Only seventeen invaders finally reached the Sierra Maestra. These men were all that remained of the Granma's failed invasion.

The news spread to every corner of the planet: Fidel Castro was dead, according to the press. They also lied that Raúl Castro, Ernesto Guevara, and Camilo Cienfuegos had lost their lives.

In New York City, Fernando continued his life mostly unaware of the Cuban events.

"Why don't you come back to Cuba? Doctor Pruna suggested to his son. "Here you can get involved in numerous business ventures."

"I am not doing too bad here in New York, father. I have been quite successful at Grolier. I have no complaints with Crosby & Crosby; I work directly with Peter Crosby. Having said this, it is true that I often dream about Cuba. I cannot deny that I miss Cuba."

"Believe me. You already have a place in business. It is your thing, and you can get very far, particularly here, in Cuba. The possibilities are enormous. There is much foreign investment, and you can see Cuban investors in the construction sector everywhere, especially in Havana."

The interest in investments, aroused by the excellent results obtained in Canada by Crosby & Crosby, without considering his other activity in a publicity firm, tickled the young man's capitalist papillae. There were plenty of opportunities for American investments in Cuba. Was it maybe the time to take advantage of his experience and network in his homeland? The idea seduced him more and more. Deep in his heart, Fernando wanted to go back to Cuba; he adored his island.

"I must think about it. If there is a chance, I will fly there. I've been thinking about the possibility of building a hotel since I understand that tourism is growing in Cuba. Maybe something more modest, a motel could be more viable. I have thought about initiating a promotion. Let's see what we can do."

"All you need is to find the ideal person at the right time, but I trust your excellent star. It will take you far."

"How far?"

"I see you in politics, my son."

"In politics?"

"It is the best way to protect your interests, your business. You have ambition. Do you remember how much you have always liked challenges? Since you were incredibly young. The first responsibilities at school. That's what I have instilled into you; now you can use it and benefit from it. Cuba is a little gold cup."

Then his father added: "Besides, you can also do much good for your country. I know you love people."

"We'll see, father, we'll see."

"Cuba needs someone like you to defend our ideas, our principles, our freedoms, versus the revolutionary effervescence. I think it could work well. You have the necessary spirit and energy."

"I read that some disturbances are going on. Can you explain?"

"Havana University is closed because of the student's protests. That, without mentioning Castro, who has clandestinely returned to Cuba carrying out a military landing."

"Where was he?"

"It seems that he was in Mexico, preparing an invasion, in secret."

"Isn't he dead, Castro?"

"That's what we are supposed to believe; that is what the press has informed so far."

What about Batista? What does he say?"

"Batista has not clarified the issue."

"Precisely because of that. Do you think this is the best time to do business in Cuba? With all this social and political convulsion. Frankly, I don't think it's a good time for business ventures."

"Are you kidding? Even if Castro is not dead, Batista has him in the crosshairs. He doesn't have a chance. Batista has a standing army of over forty thousand men well armed by the United States government. No, I tell you, come back, you won't regret it. Opportunities for you are here."

Perhaps Dr. Pruna was partially motivated by the fact that he missed his son dearly. Fernando had been away for much too long studying in the United States.

"Do you think many people support Castro?"

" I don't think so. Frankly, I believe that the rebels are nothing but a bunch of losers, bandits, outlaws."

Dr. Pruna was mistaken. The executions performed by Batista's soldiers, not only because of the landing of the Granma but also in the Sierra Maestra Mountains to create panic among those who helped the rebels, gained the regime the hatred and discontent of the residents. Batista's remedy turned out to be counterproductive. Once more, the effect of the soldiers' uncontrolled and vengeful actions was opposite to their purpose. The injustice perpetrated by Batista's troops inspired an anti-Batista wave that swung the balance towards the rebels and helped their infrastructure. The peasants who had been born in Sierra Maestra and therefore knew the area well began to help the insurrectionists.

After the failed landing of the Granma, Fidel Castro managed to escape and hid in the mountains with his brother Raúl and Che Guevara. In the South of the Eastern Province, in Cuba's most rugged terrain, known as Sierra Maestra, he established his Headquarters there. Out of the 83 men who landed, only a mean score remained. The rest had died in combat, been murdered, or deserted. However, Castro's troops were gradually gaining the trust of the disaffected with Batista's regime.

Fidel made use of an almost infallible propaganda and recruiting strategy: he promised to re-establish the Constitution of 1940, a model of democracy, to conduct free and democratic elections, and to respect and enforce law and justice. He also offered many incentives to workers and, above all, to peasants. The agrarian reform was his warhorse. Execute a legitimate land redistribution for those who had neither money nor land, by expropriating the big foreign and national landowners, and, above all, the American ones, who had thousands and thousands of unproductive hectares. Among the peasants, many were squatters; it means they were peasants who lived and worked the land without having property title. Fidel offered to make them owners; his liberal projections went beyond social justice. He promised a free Press. The communists echoed his political statements. Radio Moscow openly expressed its sympathy for the July 26th Movement. International communism secretly backed him up. As time would tell, none of his promises would come to fruition. Fidel never fulfilled any of his obligations.

Before Fidel gained power, he promised the people of Cuba, free democratic elections within six months of acquiring power. The immediate restitution of the 1940 Constitution, an accurate model of democracy. Total freedom of the Press. And top on the list, an agrarian reform that would give poor farmers real title to land that they would receive as a gift from the government. These and many more enticing promises made up his political agenda.

When Fidel came into power, he kept none of these promises. No elections, no freedom of the press, no 1940 Constitution. The Agrarian Reform modified, and land in Cuba confiscated and owned by the government solely. The small parcels of property distributed to some farmers were given without title and only as usufruct, a legal right accorded to a person or party that confers the temporary right to use. Not ownership of the land.

His political manifesto was simply a strategy to gain political power. His real goal was to retain control indefinitely at any cost. He was able to do this by transforming a deceitful democratic revolution into a totalitarian communist regime. Fidel was never an idealist; he was an ambitious and ruthless pragmatist. His goal was perpetual and everlasting power. Communism was the answer to his aspirations.

Erroneously advised, Batista decided to implement terror: the vision of a man hanging from a streetlamp made many give up joining the Revolution, but also won him many enemies.

Despite this, Batista could not control these small resistance groups. He had to face many fronts at the same time. Besides, in the countryside, the unrest had reached the students' circles in Santiago de Cuba under the direction of Frank País, the unquestionable leader of the underground opposition in the East. Havana University closed after the increasing students' demonstrations. Besides the July 26 Movement, another political movement that fiercely got involved in the armed struggle against power: The Students' Revolutionary Directorate (DEU), led by a student named José Antonio Echevarría, known as "Manzanita" (little apple), for his robust built. A political murder had just occurred in one of Havana's favorite nightspots. On October 2nd, 1956, an armed group of the Student Directory, had broken into the Montmartre Cabaret, one of Cuba's most glamorous nightclubs, and opened fire against the Chief of the

FIRST DOLLAR to go into "iron lung" container at March of Dimes Dance given by Bay Shore-Brightwaters Branch of National Infantile Paralysis Foundation at South Bay Golf Club Saturday night earns a kiss for Fernardito Pruna from chapter chairman, Mrs. C. Barron Otis, left, and treasurer, Mrs. Kenneth Percival.

Military Intelligence Service, (S.I.M.), Colonel Antonio Blanco Rico. The attempt was vindicated by the DEU, whose original plan was to eliminate the Minister of Interior, but he wasn't at the place. Therefore, they aimed at the second-best target.

In Manhattan Island, Fernando kept away from the students' revolt in Havana, from all the daily reality and the acts perpetrated in Cuba. His work for Denise's former husband, Peter Crosby (which he obtained thanks to Denise Darcel's intervention), produced substantial benefits. Fernando spent most of the time flying between New York and Toronto, handling Crosby's business in Canada.

Fernando still stayed with the Otis family at Bay Shore, Long Island, for most vacations, like when he was a child. It was his home in the United States. It was where he went to stay on every vacation when he could not manage to go to Cuba. Barron and Marie Otis were his parents in America, and he loved them dearly. For him, they were just Aunt Marie and Uncle Barron. Besides staying in Bay Shore, he currently went often to Southampton, this chic bathouse, where New York's upper class liked to get together on weekends or during summer. In that charming district, bordered by Great South Bay, it was common to see cabin cruisers dancing quietly to the rhythm of the waves collapsing against the dock. Charles Barron Otis[32] was a New York symbol of success and

---

[32] **Charles Otis** (1872 – 1944) was a prominent financial publisher in New York and New England who served as president of The Wall Street Journal and its parent, *Dow Jones & Company*, and publisher of his family-owned newspapers, *American Banker* and The Daily *Bond Buyer*. Otis, who resided in New York, died at his summer home in Yarmouth Port on September 30, 1944. He was succeeded as president of *American Banker* by his son, Charles Barron Otis, a Harvard Graduate (1928)who was later named chairman and publisher. Charles Barron Otis, named for his father's mentor, Clarence W. Barron, remained in the post for 30 years until his death in 1974, when his great-nephew, Derick Otis Steinmann, facilitated their sale to International Thomson during his tenure as publisher.

a legitimate American aristocrat, descendant of the Mayflower's crew. This financial press magnate owned several newspapers, including the American Banker and the Bond Buyer. Fernando sometimes invited his conquests to this magnificent mansion. The property, surrounded by fourteen hectares of impeccable gardens – stables included – neighbored a beautiful and exclusive golf course, far from the Big Apple's noise, when he was not skiing in New York or New England. These ski tracks would lead him, in one of his journeys, to the path of business, to continue with another branch of which he would have never dreamed: politics.

Fernando did some works for a publicity communication firm, besides from Grolier and Crosby. The director of this firm,

Figure 19 *MARIE OTIS, CHARLES BARRON OTIS, HELENE DARCEL, FERNANDO PRUNA AT THE HARWYN IN NEW YORK CITY.*

Murray Ross, a great friend of Fernando, invited him to ski. In the free slalom that the slopes gave him, Fernando didn't notice that someone admired his sports deeds.

"Hey, my friend, I've seen you ski! You are an ace!"

"I'm not that good, but thanks. Thank you."

"I would need someone like you."

"To...?"

"To give me skiing lessons. Would you be interested?"

"To teach you how to ski? I am not an instructor. Let's say I do the best I can."

"You do it very well," the stranger interrupted. "By the way, my name is Jeff Walker."

"Fernando Pruna."

"So, you are not from here, I mean, you are a foreigner?"

"Indeed, I'm Cuban."

"Amazing, a professional skier from a snowless country and you speak English as if you were born here."

"I don't know if professional is the word, but something like that."

"Well, then. How much for the ski lessons? Of course, I'm going to pay you."

"It's just that I will only be here for a few days."

"That's all right," the individual finished.

"Why not? Let's go for it."

If he got paid for an activity he enjoyed, he would give it a try?

"What do you do for a living?"

"I'm an architect, and I live and work in New York City. What about you?"

"I sell encyclopedias and work for a publicity and communication firm. I attend night courses at Columbia University in New York. Tell me, architecture. A happy coincidence that we have met now. I am very interested."

"Why, are you interested in architecture?"

"I've been dreaming for a while about a project that would be viable in my homeland — building a motel in Cuba."

"Interesting. If I can do something to collaborate in this project, I am willing and able."

"Great, we could discuss it after a couple of runs?"

Jeff and Fernando liked each other, while they discussed business and real estate projects on the ski slopes. A few days later, they saw each other again in New York. The project was presented in several meetings and began to take form. One evening, Fernando pronounced a phrase that synthesized this collaboration.

"You take care of the drawings. I will promote the idea and try to find financing."

"There won't be any problem if we reach an understanding at a financial level."

The young man didn't take long to find the possible financing, thanks to the contacts made at New York's elegant nightclubs or the beach parties in Long Island. It was during one of these parties when he met Jack Stewart, a successful real estate broker in Long Island, who put him in the right track.

"I know a lawyer who heads the prestigious legal firm of Rosenberg & Burris in Miami Beach. Their office is on Lincoln Road. He has

Figure 20 *MOTEL CASINO FOR EAST HAVANA DESIGNED BY JEFF WALKER, ARCHITECT. Circa 1957*

many contacts in the business world. He will surely have some clients interested in the operation."

Jack Burris, a lawyer with long experience in investments in the tourist sector, admitted that he liked the project.

"I know someone who will be pleased with this project, the lawyer added. So, no more talk."

"Who do you have in mind?"

"E.M. Loew."

"Loew! Yes. With E.M., you can take the project to a higher level."

Jack Burris' client was up to the project.

He alone was a considerable financial heavyweight, which gave a glimpse of a pharaonic project.

New York, end of 1956

Fernando was getting ready for a great evening with his group of friends. They often went out together at night. They were friends from the University. There was Peter Roome, William Lane, and Paul Robinson, one of his best friends from Columbia; They were fraternity brothers.

"Boys, tonight, we are doing the rounds of the great dukes. I buy. Everything is on me."

"Pruna, what are you after?"

"Fun! Lots of fun. I'm taking you all out for dinner in Greenwich Village. Later, we're going to go to Jimmy Ryan's and Eddie Condon's for a small jazz session."

Nothing else?"

"No, there's more. Afterward, we are going to watch and listen to a beautiful singer."

"Your singer!" Robinson exclaimed.

"Explosive Denise Darcel's sister?" Another one asked.

"Who is she?"

"I don't know. The Cuban has had so many conquests."

"Don't you see it is serious this time?"

"Yes, Hélène Darcel. I have already told you about her. I even introduced her to you. "

"Not to me. I've never seen your lady!"

"You bastard. You beautiful bastard. You also dated the actress, Denise, didn't you? Come on, tell us all about it!"

"Hélène is singing at the Waldorf Astoria Hotel, at the Starlight Roof. I have never listened to such a beautiful voice. You will fall on your backs, boys. However, no touching. Ok? Also, please, don't ask indiscreet questions."

That night their first stop was at Eddie Condon's, which was named after the owner and was a jazz temple on West 3rd – whose owner, Eddie himself, would welcome them – with an elegant bow tie and slicked hair, looking like a movie star from the thirties. A young crowd spent delicious moments there, listening to the magic sounds of clarinets, saxophones, and guitars. In Greenwich Village, there was good jazz too, like at many fashionable clubs in New York City: at Birdland, the Five Spot, or the Metropol Bar. The most significant figures used to play at these places, among them, Miles Davis and John Coltrane. Charlie Parker was missing for having disappeared too soon, destroyed by drugs.

"I want to have a super night before I go…with my dear friends. In the "future, I expect to often go to Cuba for business. I have a project on hand."

"Is that it? Do you have your motel thing in your pocket already? What about your nightclub project in Havana? "

"If it were only that, the opportunities are many."

"What do you mean?"

"Fellows, I intend to get involved in politics too. In one year or two, there will be elections in my country."

"What elections? Are you kidding?"

No, not at all! At least, not immediately. There is plenty of time: they will take place at the end of next year or the following year. However, I sometimes think (?)

Hey, fellows: Pruna president! Pruna president! Pruna president!

"It's the legislative elections for the Congress," the young man explained.

"Pruna senator! Pruna senator!" the boys shouted in fun.

Batista, without a doubt, would place himself once more at the head of the country but would put someone close to him in the presidential chair.

For the moment, in the full halls of the Waldorf Astoria, the ambiance was rather cheerful, but, above all, sophisticated.

In the velveted ambiance of the highest floor, in the exquisite Starlight Room, Hélène was ready to sing.

"I'll go backstage for her," said Fernando.

The young couple reappeared. Hélène was introduced to everybody, and they were all seduced by her charm. She took some time off since she was fatigued. A few minutes later, she sauntered to the stage, microphone in hand. Her performance was delightful. The boys were awed. They all fell in love with her.

For the happy group, the night was not over yet. It was their night before Fernando's departure. A sort of "goodbye party."

"Ok, guys, now I will take you to an exceptional place. I will take you all to the Gold Key Club! It's my turn now to show you my performance."

The building consisted of four brownstone floors on 28 West 56 Street. It was a private afterhours Club, but Fernando was a member, and they all entered as Fernando's guest.

The friends sat comfortably on sofas. The saloon only had sofas, no chairs — a low table in front of each couch. It was elaborately decorated in a classic way that gave a deep sense of luxury.

"Fellows, we have had too much to drink, but there is still room for a little more."

"What a place! How classy!"

A scantily dressed young beauty delivered a couple of bottles of whisky, glasses and ice and placed them on the table in front of the boys. The bottles had the name "Mr. Pruna" handwritten on them in bold letters. It was a prerequisite to go around the New York City liquor laws. The liquor had to belong personally to the member.

Do you want to be a member?

Fernando asked a clerk for a membership application form. One of his friends became a member right then and thereby paying out the sixty-dollar membership fee. It was for Paul Robinson.

"Hey, guys, now another one of us is a member of the club already. What do you say to that."

Two weeks later, the premises investigated by the "police and New York prosecutor, Frank Hogan, ordered the appropriation of all registration cards. The investigation caused the disruption of members who ignored that two floors above, some girls offered illegal special services, while customers engaged in illicit games of chance under the cover of a gambling hall. It was an excellent anecdote to be able to tell later. On the other hand, when Fernando called Paul, a month later, they were still laughing at this story.

"Paul, I called you to say goodbye. I am going back to Cuba, but I will return to New York from time to time. I will let you know. Keep in touch."

"Have the best of luck with your projects, amigo!"

"Thanks, brother, don't worry, everything will go very well. It's almost a done deal."

Pruna soon departed to new adventures. Dollars. Politics. Would there be opportunities in Cuba?

A strange story circulated at the Waldorf Astoria about a Cuban troupe. The troupe in question was made up of a considerable number of stars and dancers from the Tropicana nightclub of Havana.

It was a good publicity stunt, organized by Martin Fox, the owner of the Tropicana. It was said that an individual had suddenly emerged out of nowhere, armed with a gun and shouting: "Down with Batista!".

But it was only an isolated case. The inconvenient rebel was immediately subdued, and the party went on. For Fernando, who had never heard of this incident, what mattered was the great evening with his friends during his last moments in the Big City. Paul Robinson, Peter Roome, William Frye, Hammafstrom, Rudolph Wurlitzer, James Cahouet, and William Lane were a litany of names that were very nice to the ear because they associated with delightful memories. None could imagine for a minute that those were names that would appear one day in a list that would weave a weak link between New York and Havana, to share other moments. The worst, since Damocles' sword, was just waiting for a signal to fall on Fernando's head.

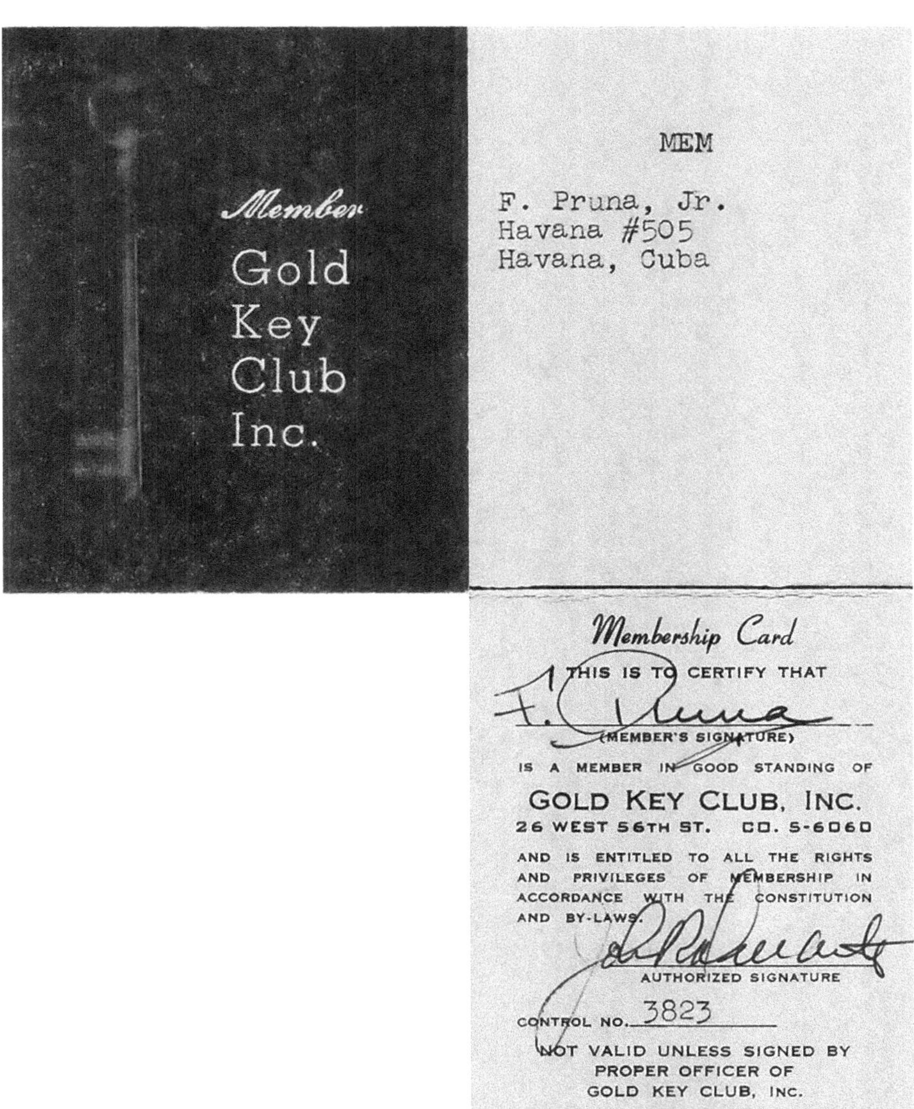

Figure 21 *FERNANDO'S GOLD KEY CLUB MEMBERSHIP CARD*

Figure 22 HELENE DARCEL

 10 

BLAME DESTINY

Who knows
One never can tell whose fault it may be,
But forgive our love,
Blame Destiny. FP

"Marry me."
"What?"
"You've heard me. Marry me. I mean it."

Hélène's face saddened.

"No, be quiet. I know what you are going to say."
She would repeat that she was too old for him.
"What will people say?"
"I couldn't care less. All I know is that I love you and that I want to marry you."
"But..."
"Shush! Please be silent!"

He placed his fingers lightly on the young woman's lips. He was barely twenty years old, and she was seventeen years older, but still full of youth. Her exotic and penetrating beauty reflected her exquisite grace and refinement; there were tears in her eyes.

He had told her he would soon be going back to Cuba.

"What are you going to do there? We are so happy here in New York. Why go at all?"

"I have told you that I have some business projects in mind. And, possibly, later, in a more distant future, there will be elections, and I might consider politics and perhaps Congress."

"Do you want to run for office?"

"It is crucial for the future of my country that honest, decent people, run for office. It is a consideration. Regarding your concerns, what happened in Tropicana was an isolated event."

No doubt, it could become dangerous. During New Year's night, a bomb exploded in the bar of the nightclub, and a woman customer had lost an arm. Everyone was talking about it.

"Who is behind all this?"

"Who do you think it could be? The answer is the terrorists — a faction of the revolutionary movement. Terror is a form of war. They want to instill fear on the People. They don't want people to go to nightclubs and to enjoy life."

"So, what do they want? What is their objective?"

"They want to stop the People from living a normal life as if nothing is happening. They have taken it out on the ones who run the casinos. They want to kick Batista out. They want to take over. A sort of - I want to kick you out so that I can take your place."

The explosion had caused panic at the Tropicana Cabaret, and people feared that there could be a second bomb hidden somewhere, ready to explode. The club owners, Martin Fox, and his wife had not been the victims or witnessed the scene. Fortunately, they were not present because, George Raft, the actor, invited them to the Capri Hotel for a little get together.

"There is talk about those revolutionaries who hide in the mountains, Hélène continued. Or even worse, they could be hiding in the cities."

"They are only a few hundred, at the very most. There is no reason for concern. Batista will know how to keep them at bay. The bearded ones will not get our skin in any case, not the skin of tourists. And even less the skin of beautiful women. And, particularly, the skin of a lovely French lady with a divine voice."

He shouldn't have made Hélène worried about anything by announcing his departure to Cuba to her. After all, these events had different options.

"Please, everything in its own time. First, it's that project in Havana. I have to feel out my contacts. Later, if I can't return to New York, I will invite you to revisit Bellavista. There you will be like in your own home, and you know it. You could also bring Denise with you if you wish. She needs the rest. You know very well that you can both come to visit as many times as you want and for as long as you wish. Bellavista is your home in Cuba."

Even though the Pruna's lived in the city on workdays, in their beautiful apartment, they almost always spent the weekends at their countryside home. It was a superb farm with a lovely chalet that Dr. Pruna had made, built with the most beautiful woods. He chose, at his discretion, the precious wood that he needed, provided by his father in law, Don Leopoldo Gonzalez, the owner of the largest sawmill in Havana, Gonzales & Brothers, not to mention his ownership of the biggest towel factory in Cuba: Telva.

In the very heart of Havana Province, geographically centered, the Bellavista estate was a show for the eyes. This vast one hundred-sixty-acre property was forty-five minutes away by car from the center of downtown Havana. Perched on the heights, atop high hills, it offered an unencumbered panoramic view of two seas: the Caribbean Sea to the south, and the Gulf of Mexico, to the north. South, overlooking an immense valley of Palm Trees, it offered a clear view of the Gulf of Batabano. North, you could devise the silhouette of the city of Havana with its tall buildings and huge neon signs, and beyond, the sea, the deep blue Florida Strait. The estate could only be named Bellavista. It was impossible to dream of a better view or a more picturesque place. Always a fresh, clean breeze caressing life.

It was a fascinating place, and the young man still recalled that anecdote his father used to remember proudly. When President Fulgencio Batista himself had visited the Bellavista Farm, he walked around the surroundings of the "batéy" and stopped to look at the views.

The president, too, owned one of Cuba's most beautiful farms. He had spent millions of dollars to beautify his property named Kukine. Then, Batista told Doctor Pruna:

"Dr. Pruna, this is, without a doubt, the most beautiful farm in Cuba."

"Why, thank you, Mr. President."

"Of course, but…"

"But what..?

"Mine is the best!"

They both laughed together.

One morning, in Bellavista, the young man found Hélène standing next to a well, holding a garden hose. She raised her head and said:

"Good morning. I'm washing your car. I hope you don't mind, Cheri?"

And Fernando could not help thinking that Hélène might be the ideal wife. She fit perfectly into the Cuban way of life with her natural simplicity. Behind her image of a sophisticated singer at the world's most elegant halls, the lady could blend naturally into the environment of a countryside home – and to top it all, Hélène was also a magnificent cook — a fantastic chef. Hélène's **coq au vin** was unrivaled – besides all of that, she was also capable of following the agitated discussions on Cuban politics from a distance, when she was not washing the car.

As time goes by, when I look back, I can objectively appreciate that Helene Darcel was a woman of extraordinary qualities. of exemplary decency and impeccable honesty. She was the epitome of modesty and simplicity. Extraordinarily talented, with a brilliant voice and an flawless interpreter of a music internationally identified as 'feeling'. Her very presence exuded a contagious and dazzling sensitivity. Her memory and her absence still disturb me acutely.

Figure 23 *Helene Darcel and Fernando at Bellavista Farm, Nazareno, Cuba.*

"Do you think that the newspapers are telling the truth? That the Castroists are being adamant about Batista? There are sabotages. They have set cane fields on fire and placed bombs in public places in the cities. They are terrorists."

The New York Times announced that Batista was in a weak position.

"In any case, it seems that Castro is alive and well. Or was he killed, as Batista attested after the Granma landing?"

A picture showed Batista with his assessors studying a map of the Sierra Maestra Mountains, pointing out the strategic objectives and planning how to harass the fugitives of the recent Granma invasion. Earlier, the reduced number seemed practically ignored. Batista even claimed having annihilated the revolutionary invaders and, in fact, had a significant number of the armed opponents executed and possibly Fidel Castro also killed. Batista did not clarify the situation. Soon, the head of the rebels finally dared to defy him openly.

The fantastic power of propaganda

Unexpectedly, another phenomenal weapon fell into Castro's hands. The good fortune that accompanied his political existence throughout his life once again came knocking at his door. This time it was in the form of an American journalist and editorialist of the New York Times, probably the most influential newspaper in the United States. His name was Herbert Mathews.

In 1957 Ruby Phillips, the Bureau Chief of the New York Times in Havana, arranged for Matthews to interview Fidel Castro in the Sierra Maestra. Before coming to Cuba, Mathews had covered the Spanish Civil War for two and a half years. His reporting manifested his ideals as a heartfelt sympathizer to the socialists and the communists in Spain.

Prudently avoiding Batista's troops, Mathews managed to reach the Sierra Maestra and personally interview the man that Batista had reported dead, Fidel. The articles had such a repercussion that it reduced fire to ashes. The name of Fidel Castro returned to the spotlight like a ghost that had risen from the dead. His picture crossed the oceans and made the entire world aware of a revolution in progress that most had ignored.

Figure 24 Hubert Mathews interviewing Fidel in the Sierra Maestra Mountains

It showed Fidel in good health, smoking a Cuban cigar, surrounded by his men who showed off their rifles as well as what would be their trademark, their beards. A horde of armed bearded men dressed in camouflage uniforms. The American journalist nicknamed him the Robin Hood of the Forests of the Sierra Maestra Mountains.

Fidel, making great use of his propagandistic talents and his undeniable capacity to manipulate deceit, managed to convince the sympathizing New York Times journalist, Herbert Mathews, that he ruled over a rebel army of thousands of men. In reality, there were hardly a hundred guerrilla fighters in the entire Sierra Maestra.

Fidel created this illusion by skillfully moving the same men from one place to another in the dense forest, pretending to count on scores of ambushes strategically located in different parts of the Sierra. The journalist, an acknowledged and spontaneous sympathizer of the underdog, fascinated to the point of infatuation with Fidel Castro, was the man who invented, politically speaking, Fidel Castro. Nothing or no one did so much for Fidel Castro during the entire rebellion as the three top-story articles published by the New York Times signed by the naïve and romantic leftist journalist, Herbert Mathews.

Even after the takeover of the Cuban Revolution, when voices started to accuse Fidel Castro of fostering a Communist Revolution, which Castro vehemently denied, this is what Huber Mathews had to say:

"This is not a Communist revolution in any sense of the word, and there are no Communists in positions of control... Even the agrarian reform, Cubans point out with irony, is not at all what the Communists were suggesting, for it is far more radical and drastic than the Reds consider wise as a first step to the collectivization they, but not the Cubans, want."

A student killed and a martyr born to the Homeland

In parallel, in the heart of Havana, two steps from the luxury hotel Sevilla-Biltmore, confusion had taken over. Endless speculations resurfaced after an attack on the Presidential

Palace. There had been a frustrating attempt to put an end to Batista's life.

Had Castro left the mountains to infiltrate the capital? Fidel had nothing to do with this bold revolutionary action. Furthermore, he criticized it since it cast a shadow on his absolutist aspirations. He did not want to be outdone by any other subversive organization.

Everyone knew that the Revolutionary Directory, headed by José Antonio Echeverria, fought far more actively to overthrow Batista than the July 26 Movement. A student underground cell had neutralized the radio station, Radio Reloj, and a vibrating announcement had invaded the waves:

"People of Cuba, at this moment, the dictator Fulgencio Batista has just been revolutionarily executed. The People of Cuba have gone to settle the account inside his lair at the Presidential Palace. And it is us, the Revolutionary Directory, the one who, in the name of the Cuban Revolution, has delivered the final blow to this disgraceful regime."

"Armed men broke into the palace! Have you heard? Batista is dead."

Some feared the worst. The bullet impacts shattered the palace façade. Amazingly, Batista had miraculously escaped alive. Echeverría did not know this and thought that Batista was dead, and therefore he pronounced his public announcement. But the attackers of the Presidential Palace had failed in their attempt and paid with their lives.

The great discourse ended when the regime took the transmitter out of the air. It was then that José Antonio left the premises and got in a car driven by Chino Figueredo to the University of Havana. Arriving at the University, he accidentally collides with a police patrol car coming in the opposite direction. Echeverría gets out of his car, intending to kill the policemen in the patrol car.

One of the police agents, Fernando Rodríguez Vega, crouched in the patrol car, observes that Echeverría is coming to kill him raises his machine gun and opens fire, killing Echeverría in self-defense.

After the triumph of the Revolution, Rodriguez Vega faced trial. When judged, Echeverria's mother had the civility of refusing to accuse Rodriguez Vega, stating that the accused police were justified because they acted in self-defense. However, the Revolutionary Court sentenced policeman Fernando Rodríguez Vega to 44 years in prison, 20 for firing a firearm, and 24 for manslaughter.

In retrospect, it is impossible to deny that Echeverria's death was an irreparable loss for Cuba's future. Jose Antonio Echeverría was a true patriot with impeccable credentials and a clear vision about the way the Cuban revolution should move towards representative democracy. His death was of great benefit to Fidel Castro. It dismissed the competition of a revolutionary leader who would undoubtedly have overshadowed Fidel's totalitarian ambitions. When Echeverría died, Fidel must have remembered that medieval saying ***"La tua morte (è) mia vita" (your death is my life)***

The attack on the presidential palace of Cuba, on March 13th, 1957, had a single purpose: to kill Fulgencio Batista, the President of Cuba. It was planned and executed by Cuban students under Jose Antonio Echeverria, a devout catholic, a university student, and an anti-communist. Other participating leaders were Carlos Gutierrez Menoyo, who directed the military attack, Menelao Mora, and Fructuoso Rodriguez. Approximately 80 individuals participated in the plot, but only the first wave of attackers got into the presidential palace. These first waves of attackers managed to get to the second floor of the Palace, but Batista moved to the third floor where, with the help of bodyguards, had all the attackers killed. It was a close call for Batista, even though he had intelligence of an imminent attack, he did not of the date it was going to take place. There were forty people killed and eighteen wounded in the attack. The only student that got away was Faure Chomon, who eventually managed to get to the Escambray mountains, where he joined the rebellion. Later he backed Fidel Castro and became an essential member of the communist government until his death. In short, a student died, and a Cuban martyr had been born.

It is interesting to speculate on what would have happened if Echeverria had been successful in assassinating Batista. Certainly, Fidel Castro's guerrilla initiative would have become meaningless and consequently the course of Cuban history would have taken a totally different venue. Of course, a lot would have depended on whether Echeverria had lived to become the leader of the revolution or if other political factors would have come into play. A silly exercise of the mind responding to the eternal question of what if.

Figure 25 FERNANDO PRUNA - circa 1958

11

THE QUEST FOR WEALTH
AND POWER.

"The best things in life are free.
The second-best things are very, very expensive."
— Coco Chanel

Despite the significant political irregularities and the brewing uncertainties sensed by guerrillas opposing the government in the mountains of the Sierra Maestra, the vibrant financial activities of foreign investors in Cuba, mostly from the United States, overshadowed the weakly felt resistance of the opposition. Havana was thriving financially, and the infrastructure of the tourism business continued to develop on the Island without apparent restraint.

Havana was a marvelous place in which to live, and its vigorous financial growth palpable everywhere. Impressive high-rise buildings were sprouting all over, and the government itself had undertaken the development of a new gigantic Civic Center. The center was surrounded by modern buildings that would house ministries and government offices which included a sprawling Justice Building that was an architectural work of art. The square was dominated by the Jose Marti Memorial, which featured a 358ft tall tower and a 59ft statue of the Cuban apostle. The National Library, many government ministries, and other buildings, located in and around the Plaza. The end of 1958 showed the completed construction of the Civic Center and the José Martí monument. All these projects were started and realized during Batista's government. It was an impressive architectonic feat that beautified the city of Havana immensely.

Batista's presidency fostered capitalist enterprises, and perhaps the tourist industry evidenced the most impressive financial growth. Cuba, as always, was a magnet for American business interests. Meyer Lansky started a new project contemplating vertiginous dollar numbers. It was now or never. Fernando had not forgotten the seductive big-dollar phrase pronounced by Jack Burris some weeks before: "I know someone who will love this project. Nothing more needs to be said. It's E.M. Loew".

Jack Burris, an established Miami Beach attorney, was the legal advisor of a film industry magnate. The well-known multimillionaire Elias M. Loew. (the press said that the M stood for "Money") – Burris assured everyone that E.M. would immediately detect a good investment in this Cuban initiative, and he was right. E.M. loved the project.

E.M. was the owner of E.M. Loew's Theatres, Inc., the largest movie theater network in the United States since the thirties. Later, he launched himself into the drive-in theaters and had more than one hundred, but he had investments everywhere and in multiple fields. In association with Lou Walters, he owned one of the most famous nightclubs, the Latin Quarter, created in Boston twenty years earlier. With a particular Paris Moulin Rouge environment, it was an original myth. Later on, he opened the Latin Quarter in New York and then in Miami, near Al Capone's famed mansion in Palm Island. E.M. also owned hippodromes, like the famous Foxborough Bay State, and hotels in Las Vegas and Miami, and shares in a ski resort. That's why when one knocked on E.M. Loew's door, one's heart went a mile a minute. E.M. symbolized the Twentieth Century's entrepreneurial spirit. An Austrian Jew immigrant arrived in the United States and proceeded to find El Dorado, at the beginnings of the century, with the European immigrant wave. He worked as a waiter and errand boy, but he was soon fascinated by the movie theaters. Little by little, he placed himself at the head of a small movie theater empire in New England, embodying a social success model in Boston, the city where he invested in his first movie theater.

"He fell completely in love with this city," Jack Burris recalled. To the point of making a passionate statement: "He was the one who electrified Boston and other cities along the East Coast. There is only one problem. You will have to persuade him to go to Cuba".

"Why?"

"E.M. has a terrible fear of planes! He's never flown on a plane."

It was in 1956 that I returned to Cuba after leaving New York City. I immediately started to look for business opportunities in Havana. Before leaving, I had discussed with a good friend, Arnold McKee, the possibility of importing quality used cars to Cuba. We had become friends through our mutual business association with Peter Crosby, Denise Darcel's ex-husband. Arnold's father owned a major car dealership in Washington, DC, "McKee Pontiac," and learned the trade through his father. Shortly before leaving New York City, Arnold invited me to visit him at Camden, Maine. I drove up in my Oldsmobile convertible, stopping only in Boston briefly to see a friend. Camden was then a fashionable small town with rolling hills overlooking the Atlantic Ocean. The coastline was breathtaking, with fierce waves smashing against the rocks and exploding. It was beautiful in the Autumn, with the dying leaves' multi-color patterns from the autumn cold. He had a lovely home. It was a vast property that he had just purchased named "Undercliffe," with five acres of land and a stone wall in front of it. Arnold had a beautiful family, wife, a charming lady, three sons, and two daughters. I particularly remember his son Jim, who later attended Hebron Academy on my recommendation.

I especially recall an unusual incident that occurred during my visit. Jim, who was still a young boy of 13, was riding his nice looking mare named "Sugar" in front of his home when the animal unexpectedly panicked and ran away at full gallop with the boy on top. The horse ran crazily out of control. Arnold saw the situation, ran to my car, parked in front of the house, and got behind the wheel. I had left the keys on the ignition switch, and he started the car while screaming at me to join him, which I did. The top was down on the convertible. Jumping inside, I sat on the back of the seat while steadying myself by holding to the top of the windshield frame. Arnold stepped on the gas hard, and the Olds took off like a rocket, wheels screeching and lifting a cloud of dust and gravel. We raced after the runaway horse, and in seconds we caught up and positioned the car parallel, right next to the galloping animal. Standing on the seat of the car as best I could, I was able to pull Jim off the saddle and lift him into the vehicle safely, sitting him next to his father. Without further consideration, I decided to jump onto the saddle and recapture the galloping horse's reins. Shortly I was able to control the horse, which I rode back to the house. I had ridden horses all of my life, and this was not the first time a horse had run away with me. I knew how to control it. Arnold was delighted and told everyone that would hear what the crazy Cuban had done. That night we celebrated with good Scotch whiskey and fantastic Maine lobster dipped in butter. Arnold used to boil the lobsters along with seaweed and some seawater. He told me that was the real Maine way to cook lobster. I believed him. It was superb.

During that visit to Maine, Arnold agreed to start a little business with me importing used cars to Cuba. In Havana, I began to see how to set up the business. I met a great car salesman that worked for a big car dealership named El Relampago. It was in the Luyano area. His name was Orlando Camacho, and we immediately hit it off. I explained what I had in mind, and he liked the idea, but he had no capital to invest. I did not have much either, but I had brought the Oldsmobile convertible to Cuba, and I told him that I was willing to sell it to get some capital, plus some savings that I had. We proceeded, and he sold well the Oldsmobile; I hated to see it go. It was a beautiful car. But I realized that sometimes you have to sacrifice something to make other important things happen.

We created a corporation, Autos Campru S.A., a combination of our last names, and proceeded to rent an attractive showroom in the Vedado section of Havana, on 3ʳᵈ. and 6ᵗʰ. Streets. It was the base floor of a lovely new building, and it had the space necessary for a great showcase. I asked my brother Andy to decorate it, and with the help of Charley Lee, a great artist, and a close friend, they painted a beautiful mural on the largest wall. Orlando got the owner of El Relampago to provide us with some new cars, mostly Fords, on consignment. But our real interest was the used car market. Arnold McKee had moved to the Fort Lauderdale area of Florida, and he started to buy some cars at auctions or wherever he could get them at a reasonable price. He would send them to Key West and ship them on the Ferry that traveled continuously from Key West to Havana Harbor.

When the cars arrived, I would pick them up at the dock after paying Customs Duties, which were pretty steep. Although I had useful contacts in Customs, I still could not get a good deal from them. The head of Customs was making a fortune.

I agreed to pay McKee one hundred dollars on top of each car's cost, and he accepted. He purchased the cars with his money, including freight to Havana. We paid for Customs and took the cars. We had a few days to pay him back his investment plus the agreed fee. He sent us a batch of vehicles and would wait until we paid him to send us another set. He had limited capital, and I understood the situation. I would tell him the cars to buy and not to buy according to the Havana car market. Eventually, we were moving between fifteen and twenty cars every month. The business was making money. I started to drive a brand-new 1957 Ford Edsel, 2-door hardtop convertible, which was very lovely and functional. It was a new experimental Ford product.

The business flourished and allowed me to dedicate my time to other business ventures that I was trying to put together with E.M. Loew and Jack Burris. These business initiatives with the American Investor and the Miami Beach attorney were the real reason that I came back to Cuba. However, while working on these deals, I still had to make some income, which I did.

*Arnold flew in **Aerolineas Q** from Key West to Havana, which was very inexpensive. He would leave this car in Key West and then drive back to Fort Lauderdale, where he had rented a house. The purpose of flying to Havana was to pick up his money in cash from our car sales. Arnold had chosen to operate only in hard currency, which was fine with me as long as he came to pick up the money. The operation worked very smoothly for more than a year until Arnold called me up and told me that he would send his younger brother, Richard, to pick up the money. The moment that I met Richard McKee, I had the impression that he was not trustworthy. By this time, it was a pretty substantial amount of cash, and I understood that it was our working capital. So, I decided to call Arnold directly from our dealership's office before handing the money over to Richard. Richard was waiting outside my office. I expressed my concerns to Arnold, but he told me not to worry about it. Arnold insisted that his kid brother was a sincere and reliable guy. I asked him again if he was sure that he wanted me to hand him all the cash. He said yes, so I called Richard into my office with Arnold still on the line. I then pulled the money out of a drawer, where I had it nicely organized in one thousand-dollar stacks. I asked Richard to count the money, which he did by just counting the stacks. I still had Arnold on the line and told him that at that very moment, I was handing all the cash to his brother. I then had Richard get on the phone with Arnold to confirm receipt of the money, which he did. Richard walked out* *of my office with about twenty thousand dollars in cash. Richard told me that he was going directly to the airport.*

One day later, Arnold calls me to inform me that his brother had not returned to Florida. He was concerned that something could have happened to him. That perhaps someone robbed him. I immediately put into action all my police contacts to find Richard in Havana. I also started to look on my own, going to different night clubs and gambling houses. To make the story short, Richard had not left for Florida as planned, and he remained in Havana for three days. In those three days, he visited multiple bars, casinos, and whore houses. When Richard got back to Florida, Arnold took several days to locate him; they finally found him in a bar, still drinking. By the time Arnold found him, he had blown all the money. Richard had gone on a drinking and gambling binge, and they had cleaned him out of his cash. When Arnold found him, he was broke and drunk.

The Richard McKee debacle ended my business relation with Arnold McKee. Not because he had any differences with me, but simply because he did not have any capital left to continue buying cars. Richard's binge hurt us both badly, no doubt about that. I soon sold my part of Auto Campru S.A. to an investor that was Orlando Camacho's friend, and I moved on to other ventures. My payoff was a new white 1958 Edsel 4-door sedan and some money. After that, unfortunately, I never talked to Arnold McKee again, though we parted as good friends. He was a nice guy, and we got along great[33].

Despite his youthful looks, Fernando's energy and determination awed E.M. Loew when the young man told him about his hotel project.

---

[33] Several decades later when Fernando returned to the United States, he got a hold of Jim McKee, only to discover that Arnold had passed. They reviewed the story of the runaway horse and Jim had a clear recollection of the incident. He simply said: "How could I forget."

"Bingo!" E.M. Lowe exclaimed. "Go to Cuba. Pave the way. We can do business together. A motel project does not entirely convince me, but we need to start making contacts. Find good sites. Prepare conditions for me. You will be my eyes in Cuba."

His fears soon vanished after studying Fernando's projects. After a while, he showed up in Cuba. It was the first time that he had flown on a plane. Jack Burris couldn't believe it.

"I dreamed about your motel project, though it is not exactly what I want. I prefer a hotel. We will add a casino. A hotel with a casino is something that makes me enthusiastic."

"I'm not against it, all the opposite."

"Are you able to get a gambling license from the government? With your father's contacts – He could perhaps discuss it with Batista. We need the permit. It is essential. Do you understand? We require that license."

Fernando nodded calmly and smiled.

"A gambling license should not be any problem. I am quite sure of that. My father could sort it out directly with President Batista if it were necessary. But the size of the investment meets the legal requirements for a gambling license. It is within the legal guidelines for the tourist industry. We will automatically get a gambling license, and should there be a problem, my father can solve it. Count on it."

It was nothing but a mere formality; the government provided big investors and prominent promoters clear guidelines. Batista did his best to facilitate investments in Cuba. Two years before, the General had approved a law aiming at easing regulations on tourist business investments. There were functional financial bank structures in position and financial considerations when

Figure 26 ELIAS M. LOEW

it came to foreign investments. Obtaining a license when a new hotel represented a minimum investment of no less than a million dollars or an original nightclub cost at least 500 thousand dollars was feasible. Of course, there were particular expenses to cover individual requirements. The result was that hotels and casinos sprung like mushrooms.

E.M. remained silent for some seconds before addressing the young man with a challenging smile.

"Tell me, why don't you enter politics? Aren't you interested? With the contacts you have."

"I have considered it. At least, my father has raised the matter."

"You have everything a young Cuban can wish for to succeed in politics. You are young, ambitious, and educated. You studied at Columbia, a prestigious University. You speak English perfectly, and you understand business. You have an attractive personality, and you look pretty good. It's a winner."

After a pause, he continued, "I am sure that you will succeed. I think that you must get involved in the political life of your country. You know the importance of political influence; it can save you a lot of problems. Even in the United States, political power is enormously essential to make big things happen. And for the casino licenses and all the complications that are part of this game, it is a must."

"Maybe I can run for the next elections to Congress. I will talk to my father."

"Do it. I can help you if you want me to. I will make a financial contribution to an eventual candidacy."

E.M. seemed to be leapfrogging, but Fernando already had the answer.

"There are six provinces in Cuba. I think I can eventually present a candidacy to represent the province of Havana in the elections to the National Congress for the Democratic Party[34]."

"Good, we'll talk about all this again when ready. We already have a bun in the oven."

While he waited to get involved in politics, Fernando devoted his time to elaborate on the real estate project initiative. His hotel sketch's skeleton became a massive hotel-casino complex with a truly dizzying cost: between twelve and fourteen million dollars. The young man also dreamed about constructing an apartment building; in Cuba, they were called Horizontal Properties. The apartments were not for rent but for sale. It was at the Havana Yacht Club where he met Mr. Álvaro Velasco y Montalvo. The Velasco family, a family of lineage and prestige on the Island, owned a massive extension of inherited lands, mainly in East Havana. Fernando thought East Havana was the perfect area for a new luxury hotel and an apartment building. Even though these lands were undeveloped, they had acquired an immense potential value after construction of the Havana tunnel, mainly for their proximity to the heart of the city. In addition, because they were located behind the El Morro Fortress and overlooking the sea, their perspective from a real estate viewpoint was incalculable. The meeting promised to be fruitful.

"I want to inform you that I have another real estate project," he confessed to E.M.

---

[34] The Democratic Party was part of the coalition of parties that supported Andres Rivero Agüero's candidacy for president of Cuba in the presidential elections of November 3, 1958. At the time it was led by Francisco "Panchín" Batista, brother of President Fulgencio Batista. The Democratic Party in Cuba was Ideologically conservative and anti-communist, it favored US investments in Cuba.

"A very modern building of apartments to sell. It consists of two twin towers, and each tower will be twenty-seven (27) stories high. Here I have part of the architectural drawings. I had them designed by the prestigious Cuban firm of architects and engineers: Maza and Lorenzén. I got them interested in the initiative. What do you think?"

Fernando had managed to convince the architect Maza and the engineer Lorenzén. He had met them thanks to his association with another engineer, Horacio Núñez de Villavicencio, a great friend of Dr. Pruna. They agreed to design the project and draw all the architectural plans for its construction in East Havana. Maza, as well as Lorenzén and Núñez, had bought their apartments in the giant FOCSA building. The building was built in the Vedado area of Havana. They were delighted with the innovative concept of horizontal property. All the apartments of the FOCSA building sold almost immediately, all of them!. Fernando's idea was to do something similar but in the area of East Havana. The Maza and Lorenzén firm completed all the drawings for the future building conditioned on being assigned the contract to construct the project. Fernando agreed.

To better conceive the configuration of the building, Fernando held several meetings with the two top salesmen. They sold almost all the apartments of the FOCSA by themselves. They discussed with Fernando and with Maza and Lorenzén the difficulties they had confronted when selling the units of the FOCSA. They analyzed and suggested, according to their experience as salesmen, the apartment's distribution. How many should have two bedrooms and how many should have three. Based on these suggestions, Maza and Lorenzén developed the architectural drawings for the future building.

Fernando had already thought of a way to get E.M. Loew interested in this project. He explained the concept to the

Figure 27 THE PRUNA BUILDING DESIGNED BY MAZA & LORENZEN, circa 1957-58

salesmen, as well as to Maza and Lorenzén. They discussed that the FOCSA had built a two-floor private club named **La Torre**, which included an excellent restaurant on the very top of the building. That's where they got the idea to construct a structure consisting of two twin towers joined by a bridge on the top floor, converting the bridge into a spectacular nightclub that would captivate E.M.'s imagination.

When shown the project, E.M. frowned for some instants. Then he looked up at Fernando with a shine in his eyes.

Fernando continued. "As you can see, both twin towers are joined on the top by a sort of bridge, and it is my idea that the bridge will host the most extraordinary nightclub of America, not to say the whole world."

"Interesting. Two towers joined on the top by a bridge."

"A bridge!" The young man repeated slowly.

He had realized E.M. was fascinated by the idea.

"Yes, a bridge that would be a nightclub, a spectacular nightclub with a panoramic view of the sea and Havana; Mr. Loew, I am picturing Cuba's Latin Quarter. What do you think of the idea? I had you in mind when I conceptualized the bridge-night-club idea."

After Boston, New York, and Miami, the fourth version of the Latin Quarter would be in Havana. Fernando shuddered. In collaboration with E.M. in person. As part of the story, Loew's ex-wife's reputation should be considered. Sonja, a Czechoslovakian former beauty queen, had met on a trip to Europe when he was recruiting staff for his club. E.M. took her to the United States and married her. Sonja Loew was the queen of mundane organizations, and she orchestrated the glamorous universe of all Latin Quarter's shows and decorations.

"Quarter's dancers of today are the Hollywood stars of tomorrow. Lou Walters my associate, who runs the New York Latin Quarter, has many contacts which allow him to bring in the best musical productions in the world. On the other hand, he dreams about the Folies-Bergère. So, Fernando, without any further formalities, I am willing to give you up to one million dollars for the bridge, and we will build the Cuban Latin Quarter. It will also still be "your" building!"

The vast amount of green bills reflecting on the eyes of E.M. made Fernando dizzy. When he returned to Havana, he feverishly displayed the plans. He could already sense how his castles were coming together.

"The area of East Havana is presently in the process of development, but it's still virgin territory. The tunnel has opened the doors to this vast, beautiful zone: it is right there where we will settle. What do you think?"

Dr. Pruna nodded with a smile. His son went on developing the idea of his building with an unstoppable fever but without neglecting the Hotel-Casino project. E.M. had been delighted by the financial perspectives he had discovered in Cuba. He was willing to invest his money on the Island. He was captivated by Fernando's initiatives.

For the Hotel-Casino, E.M. had preferred to buy the lands closest to El Morro Castle, a symbol of Havana, suspended on a knoll. The fortress had been built by the Spanish conquerors in the XVII century to guard the city. If you approached by sea, you could see it from miles away. Any building built in this zone would stand out, visible to any ship approaching Havana Harbor.

The company that owned these lands was the Cuban Bay Land Company belonging to Pedro Grau y Triana and his wife, Lucía Victoria Bacardi y Cape, known by the nickname "Mimín," a woman of great artistic talent, heiress of the Bacardi family. The lands of the Cuban Bay Land were the first private ones neighboring the State-owned lands belonging to the El Morro and La Cabaña Fortress. E.M. fell in love with the first lots Grau Triana had parceled in the sketches; the lots ended on the sea. Fernando personally negotiated with Pedro Grau y Triana at his expansive mansion in the Miramar District. E.M. was willing to buy two entire blocks. They agreed to a price and signed a letter of intent.

"Congratulations, my son. Do you see how perseverance bears fruit?"

"The good thing is that we can also count on an excellent piece of land for our real estate investment. In return, we will pay the Velasco family with finished apartments in the same building that we are going to build on their land. They have already accepted my proposal, an innovative one for them, but very profitable at the same time. The Velasco's attorney, with whom I met in an ancient but well-furnished office in Old Havana, as well as the three Velasco Montalvo brothers, Álvaro, José and Carmen, approved the proposal with enthusiasm. They are willing to contribute the land I need in exchange for my paying them, at a pre-agreed price, with finished apartments at market prices. Imagine, this building will be the first one built on their land, which is still desertic. Our initiative will also benefit the property owned by the Velasco family's neighbors, the one owned by the Cuban Bay Land Company. When you emerge from the other side of the tunnel and enter East Havana, you first see the land owned by Bay Land and then, immediately after, the property belonging to the Velasco family."

"The building will open the doors of real estate to them; their surrounding land price will rise like foam. Anyway, the price they are giving me is a very reasonable one and very attractive to me since they contribute the land without asking for any amount of money in advance. When I speak about donating, I mean that their contribution is like a capital investment that they, the Velasco y Montalvos, are making in my project."

Fernando continued, "With this capital investment in land and the sale of the cabaret to E.M., I will have all the funds that I need to obtain the total financing that I require to complete the construction of the project. The project, of course, meets the financial parameters of FHA[35]. Besides, long before constructing the building, when we break ground, we will start to sell apartments at attractive pre-construction prices. I am putting together the sales structure as we speak. What do you think, father?"

"I think it's impressive. You have clairvoyance for business, son. This area is the future of Havana. I agree with you; this is Havana's most promising zone. It is a virgin zone that has gained immense value because of the finished tunnel. All this land is only minutes away from the Capitol Building, which is the Center of Havana. And you are one of the first to take part in its development, or maybe the first one with two big projects."

The director of the BANDES[36] Dr. Rodríguez y Rodríguez, could not repress positive surprise when he spoke to the young man who was accompanied by E.M. Loew, Jack Burris, and Dr. Pruna, who he knew very well.

"Dr. Pruna, I am delighted to see you. I will prepare your dossier."

"Oh, I am here only as a lawyer."

"I am afraid I don't quite understand."

---

[35] FHA: Fomento de Hipotecas Aseguradas.
[36] Banco de Desarrollo Económico y Social.

"It is not me that you need to address. I am just the legal representative for Cuba. It is my son who is in charge of this project. We both have the same name. The dossier is in his name. Fernando Pruna Bertot."

"Oh, I see. I wouldn't have imagined it."

"This boy has a golden touch," E.M. interrupted with a tranquilizing smile and sparkles in his eyes.

"Everything he touches turns into gold," Burris added. "It is enough to listen to him speak to realize it."

"Tell me, then, how have you managed to promote businesses of this magnitude at your age?"

"Trust him," E.M. concluded.

"In this case, I can only congratulate you."

Dr. Rodríguez y Rodríguez gave the green light to endorse the operation with a loan guaranteed by Bonuses of the BANDES. E.M. Loew's portfolio would make up 25% of the total investment. He would complete his part with a direct personal cash investment. He was willing and able to invest immediately no less than three million dollars in his Hotel-Casino Project in Cuba. The last words of the magnate were the most gratifying Fernando could have expected.

"For the efforts you have made and your initiatives, you will have a participation of 49% in the enterprise. You will be my partner in this hotel project."

E.M. Loew kept 51% for himself, and Fernando would receive 49%. Of his percentage, Fernando would share half with his partner, the Miami Beach attorney, Jack Burris, with whom he had an agreement, keeping a little more than 24% at the end. When the deal closed, Fernando was twenty-two years old, and

Figure 28 Celebrating deal to construct Hotel-Casino in East Havana. May, 1958

he would soon own a quarter of the Hotel project. Twenty-two and already worth on paper a few million dollars.

Financially speaking, Cuba was on a roll. You could feel abundance in Havana. Tourist activity was buzzing, restaurants were full, and in downtown Havana, the large department stores flooded with goods and buyers. Cuba had ample capacity to produce food for its people; the markets loaded with top quality merchandise. Cuba did not need to import food, as was then the case for many other central and south American countries.

There was a giant construction boom, an authentic architectonic revolution. Buildings competed in craziness, greatness, and beauty. Santos Trafficante, who already owned the Comodoro Hotel with its casino, opened a new one, the Deauville, on the Malecón Walk. The Capri Hotel, a colorful, ultramodern building with a swimming pool on the roof, was opened with an explosion of fireworks, music, and stars. The establishment belonged to Charley White, who also managed the busy casino, but the actor George Raft officially ran it. With Raft on the front line, fiction and reality came together. He played the roles of gangsters for the Hollywood studios with Humphrey Bogart and James Cagney; in real life, he shared the poster with the kings of the underworld, and he had the General himself as buddy and backer in the process. George Raft's vision on how the Capri should work guaranteed the best publicity. Meyer Lansky wanted to hit even more substantial: he proudly opened his hotel-casino jewel on the Malecón Walk. The futurist, bold, and architectural mastodon Riviera Hotel had twenty-one floors. It exhibited hundreds of rooms with incomparable views of the sea, besides he showed off that it was always fully booked.

Lansky liked to line up numbers. 21 floors. 385 rooms. 14 million dollars. Havana exhibited a record number of tourists, and a new hotel joined this competition of excess and extravagance, the Havana Hilton Hotel in La Rampa, at 23 and L Street in the lovely Vedado section of Havana challenged the Riviera Hotel. Its budget rose to 24 million dollars, and it opened its doors for Christmas 1958. Fabulous loans were still on course. In the outbid, the shadow of a new tower appeared in the dollars-overflown horizon and inaugurated another dream flame. Meyer had a crazy project baptized as the "The Havana's Monte Carlo," a disproportionate hotel with high-range infrastructures. Whenever it seemed the height of culmination had been reached, it turned out that it wasn't.

Fernando embraced passionately a piece of the future planned for the glittering city of Havana. He was about to break ground on a new building, his hotel-casino complex, that was in the drawing rooms of a world-renowned architect who had built the Fontainebleau Hotel in Miami Beach. Besides, this time for himself alone, the twin-tower 27-floor apartment complex with the bridged colossal nightclub-casino on top. The apartment building would announce his name in big letters: "Pruna Building." His accomplishments gave him a shot of adrenaline and boundless energy.

Nevertheless, with his time distributed between Toronto, New York, and Havana, Fernando's encounters with Hélène were gradually spaced, while the shadow of a legendary dancer was about to flutter around into his life.

HELENE DARCEL - FERNANDO PRUNA - DENISE DARCEL

 12

I FERNANDO "ASTAIRE," PLAYBOY, MAMBO AND MAFIA

"She can wiggle her ass,
but she can't sing a goddam note!"
Meyer Lansky, referring to Ginger Rogers

Havana December 1957

When he picked up the phone, he heard a weary voice on the other side of the line.

"Hello, Darling."

There was only one person who called everyone "darling" with so much affection.

"Denise, how are you?"

"Very well, my love. Hélène is well too. On the other hand, I think she would like to visit you in Cuba soon. I have called you because a good friend of mine is in Havana at this moment, at the Riviera Hotel. Also, I would like you to do something for me, or, better said, for her. She is playing in a musical review for Lansky at the Riviera Hotel. I just talked to her on the phone five minutes ago. She will be in Cuba for a few weeks. I know for a fact that she is feeling lonely and I would like you to call her. Take her out for dinner. Be gentle to her. You understand what I mean, I am sure. I have told her you would get in touch with her. I hope you don't mind."

"No problem, Denise. I will be pleased to take care of her."

"Thanks, you are a sweetheart. I knew I could count on you: a kiss, Darling. I look forward to seeing you soon too. Keep me in mind."

Fernando could not believe it. The Broadway and Hollywood indisputable diva of dancing, of clap waltz, going through swing, and tap dancing! The one whose tapped steps flew and swirled in the young man's memory. Incandescent blond, with infinitely long legs and peerless grace. A mermaid of the music-hall that had illuminated his teenage years with her eternal accomplice of rhythm and music, the elegant Fred Astaire. A duet of unique chemistry that had revolutionized the thirties. She had just premiered a new show with songs and dance, conducted by the renowned choreographer Jack Cole, for the opening of the Havana-Riviera Hotel on the corner of Paseo and Malecón, in Vedado. The show was on a billboard for several days.

"Miss Rogers?"

"Yes."

"Hello, I am Fernando Pruna, Denise Darcel's friend."

"Oh, how are you, you have been so kind as to call me! She has told me so much about you, and I expected your call.

"Denise told me you were performing in Havana. It would be a pleasure to accompany you and be your guide. I am at your service."

"Thank you so very much. That's so sweet! Look, come to see my show. Denise has talked to me about you in such praising terms. You are such a helpful gentleman. If you which I'll meet you tonight at the Riviera. I am performing at the Copa Room nightclub. I will make a reservation in your name, and I will order a bottle of champagne for you. You'll be my guest."

"Thank you so much, I look forward to meeting you."

The advertising read:

"On the 10th of the current month – the opening of the Hotel Havana Riviera - with the superstar, Ginger Rogers, in-person and her great show. The hotel cost 14 million dollars and has twenty floors".

With an enormous advertising effort of glamor and dollars, the stores announced the arrival of the superstar. When Fernando walked into the Copa Room, he gave his name to the maître d', who immediately led him to the best ringside table in front of the stage. He shuddered at feeling entrusted with such an important and exciting mission: to provide all kinds of delicate attentions to a Hollywood legend. Fernando felt a guilty pinch in his heart when thinking about Hélène, who was singing in New York now, but, suddenly, the curtain lifted. When she appeared on stage, he was a little taken aback. Even though her dress was magnificent, Ginger Rogers was not the same as in her youth, the one with whom Fernando had fallen in love in films when he was still a child[37].

Nevertheless, the star honored her age. However, as soon as the first notes sounded, the beautiful legs of the dancer began to move. That night she worked her magic. Ginger Rogers danced as if she were on Hollywood Boulevard, but on this occasion, under the Cuban velvet stars as a stole. Her lamé dress highlighted her body and cast sparkles. Surrounded by three elegant gentlemen dressed in dark suits. When she began to sing the first notes, her voice sounded a bit weak, lost in the immensity of the hall. Ginger Rogers wasn't, actually, a singer. She was an average singer rather than a good one. Ginger's voice wasn't even remotely close to Hélène's magnificent voice. However, she danced with

---

[37] Ginger Rogers was 45 or 46 years old when she performed at the Habana-Riviera Hotel in Havana.

total, almost magic, grace. Her vocal lack didn't go unnoticed to the owners of the place where she performed. Meyer Lansky didn't hesitate to state:

"She can wiggle her ass, I'll give her that, but she can't sing a goddam note!"

Suddenly she was standing in front of Fernando, who was still sitting at the table.

"Good evening. Have you enjoyed the show?"

"Yes, you have been sensational."

In the Copa Room, Ginger slides on the floor like a feather in my arms. Fantastically and graciously. I realize that despite the years she is in great shape, and, above all, I find her very sexy. Her longish blond hair frames her high cheekbones and falls on her beautiful neck.

Tonight, I feel a little like the soul of Fred Astaire. Many men would love to be in my place. So, I make the best use of the present moment. Ginger seems to be delighted. For a second, I was about to hold her waist and make her turn in the air as in those devilish choreographies I had seen in her movies. I am in heaven arm in arm with a divine dancer.

Heaven.... I'm in heaven
And my heart beats so that I can hardly speak
And I seem to find the happiness I seek,
When we're out together dancing cheek to cheek.
Dance with me! I want my arms around you.
The charms about you
Will carry me through to-
Heaven

Those days were left behind, and Fernando wonderfully fulfilled the mission Denise had entrusted him. He was the best of guides for Ginger, who had discovered Havana and its distinctive charms.

Ginger was radiant. She was so much fun, always laughing or smiling. She had incredible strength. Energetic. Healthful. She returned to the hotel very judiciously, without letting Fernando accompany her to her bedroom. During the day, they went to the beach, almost always to Santa María del Mar, some 20 miles from Havana. In the evening, they had dinner together in different restaurants before or after her show. Hélène was always in Fernando's mind, but Ginger was part of his daily life for most days and, almost, every night. They did nothing wrong, but Hélène would have died with jealousy. I don't know if Denise was completely reasonable on nearly pushing him to the arms of such a divine dancer, though she could have almost been his mother. Fernando never asked her about her age. A gentleman should never ask a lady about her age. They were like two old friends and mostly drank champagne. However, she loved the burning sensation of straight Añejo Cuban rum, and the smoothness of Aguardiente made of sugar cane. A kiss or a hug at certain moments but no more. She did not want to miss anything Cuban. Yes, those days have been left behind and lost in the distance of time.

"I will take you to *Bellavista*, my parent's farm. You'll see it, it's magnificent! The view of the Gulf of Mexico and the Caribbean Sea is spectacular."

They were alone. Ginger surrendered to the charming views and the intoxicating Cuban landscape covered by majestic royal palms dancing in the wind. She felt she could allow herself to do anything she wanted to do. He thought that he could maybe conquer everything too. So on a starry night of December, the dance of their bodies left traces on the large bed intimately wrinkled, of Dr. and Mrs. Pruna.

A terrible sacrilege. If Fernando's parents had found out, they would have killed him.

Yes, I collected conquests. It was more durable than me. I like women, and I'm not sure that I can praise myself for it. I am sure that I did not accomplish more in my life because I invested an enormous amount of time in the pursuit of lovely ladies. There are show girls, models. I muse: What other dance steps will I not have executed between my sheets!

The Greek-French singer Rita Dimitri performed on Broadway, in the musical comedy Cancan, by Cole Porter. She made a tour in Havana. I picked her up every night after the show; we had something to eat or drink, and then I took her to her suite at the Nacional Hotel for her to relax. She was fascinated by Cuba and the Cuban's hospitality.

One night, Hélène went to Washington, to sing. Denise performed in Las Vegas. I was all by myself at the New York apartment that we shared. I invited two models — sublime girls, who posed in the magazines for swimming suits and underwear. We had planned to go out. They purse their lips like little girls and say they have nothing appropriate to wear. Then I open the Darcel sisters' huge, Xwalk-in closet. They opened their eyes like plates.

Their only worry was to choose, like in the most elegant of New York's boutiques. On the street, they place themselves at each of my sides, each of them wearing sumptuous fur stoles that wrapped their princely necks. We go out for a drink and men X stare in astonishment, watching those magazine creatures. Sexual bombs of white ermine covering their silk dresses. Such deliciously beautiful women! Dressed "like a million dollars."

Some were unforgettable and left indelible traces in my memory. Like the precious model Caroline Kahler, whom I met when I studied at Columbia University, and she was barely 18 years old. As tall as me with blond hair and blue eyes. She dazzled everyone when we went to the Starlight Roof of the Waldorf Astoria for dinner and wine and to dance. She looked like a fairy princess with her white ermine overcoat, courtesy of the Darcel sisters, covering her from neck to knees. Under the coat, she was only wearing an elegant blue silk dress that enveloped her body like a glove, and nothing else. It was snowing when we walked along Park Avenue for a while after dancing the whole evening until we took a taxi that drove us to the apartment. Sublime! I wonder what became of her, her life? Many years later, I tried hard to find her. I failed. Perhaps it is better to remember her the way she looked that morning we parted.

One day, Denise called me to entrust me with a divine mission: To have lunch with Joan Collins! We ate at the Plaza. The conversation was amicable, and the encounter came to a happy ending around a table at the Plaza Hotel. Just a 'piscolabis.' Indeed, a beautiful lady.

I was like a cocky cockerel swaggering in the exclusive henhouse of its dreams. I could have even conquered the rival of Marilyn Monroe at the time, Jayne Mansfield! For sure, she had the necessary attributes to convince the producers. I met her when she was a deb and had only obtained a couple of small parts in some movies. She dated a friend of mine from Columbia University, and we were together at the Artists and Models Ball, in Greenwich Village. A little bit afterward, she had a massive success on Broadway.

I confess I like American women, whether they are plump or slim. I caress them with my eyes, with the tip of my fingers. I slap their curves. They vibrate, they purr. They are rutilant and hot. Their bodyworks leave me hypnotized. They are named Lincoln, Cadillac or Chrysler.

I could talk about French women in the same terms when they turn around for me - and the Cubans - not one word more - Cuban women are the non-plus ultra: a volcanic miracle.

When I was not swaggering in New York, I got together from time to time with my friend Eddie in Havana. His father was no other than Senator Eduardo Suárez Rivas. Curiously, Mr. Suárez Rivas was involved in the American Mafia issues. Trafficante, Lansky, Luciano, and the others came to him to make their respective enterprises legal. When the United States deported Luciano to Italy, the Sicilian boss organized a good bye party with the Mafia big names in New York. Suárez Rivas, who frequented Lansky, was also there. That's how they met. When Luciano entered Cuba clandestinely, he got in touch with Suárez Rivas and did everything in his power to bribe him. He even offered Mrs. Suarez Rivas a Chrysler that cost the frippery of forty thousand dollars! There were rumors that the Senator got sucked into cocaine trafficking, but I do not believe this to be true. His business passed through a small air company in Key West, which allowed him to evade the US customs. Suárez Rivas laundered and multiplied his fortune in the real estate business, among other endeavors; I know that he owned an impressive apartment building across from the Nacional Hotel, where he lived in a beautiful apartment which he shared with his wife and family. He had another studio in the same building where he housed his mistress of the moment, one of the dancers of the Nacional Hotel nightclub. I secretly dated one of her friends, also a dancer at the hotel, in this beautiful apartment. Suárez Rivas somehow found out and was pissed off out of his mind; he screamed at his son, Eddie: "Tell your friend never to come here again if it is to bring his whores to fuck."

As for the kings of the US underworld, I never really got to know them that well. There was a generational barrier between us. I was nothing but a boy, and those guys had indestructible nerves, running tens of businesses and packing their convoys of suitcases full of greenbacks, to travel out of the country.

However, I have often frequented them. I wandered about their dens. XCaptain Arsenio Labrada was the first to introduce them to me. Arsenio Labrada was one of the Secret Military Intelligence (SIM) chiefs in Cuba. The secret service of Fulgencio Batista's government. He was a personal friend of the President from way back when Batista directed his first coup d'état. He constituted a solid pillar, since he was, at the same time, the gambling official inspector and supervisor in Havana. Labrada was one of Batista's most trustworthy men and had the rank of Captain. Even though such a position could have made him a wealthy man, he was unquestionably honest and incorruptible. I dated his daughter, Josefina, whom I called "Fina," for a short time. A charming young lady, she was my date in multiple proms and cadet graduations at the Mariel Naval School as well as the Military School in Managua. She was an excellent person, and I held her in high esteem. We were good friends. All I remember is that she married a Canadian and moved to that country[38].

Labrada appreciates me. Sometimes, he uses one of his paternal phrases to describe me when he introduces me to someone. He is indeed a close friend of my father.

"This one is like a son to me."

We are at the Riviera Hotel. Captain Labrada pats my back and takes a look around. He raised his voice a little as if he wanted everyone to hear him. A man looked up to me. He is wearing his inseparable felt hat, with a broad black silk ribbon. His presence impresses me. I haven't had any champagne yet, but I can already feel its bubbles. I greet the great chief. He doesn't open his mouth, but I imagine what he is thinking: "if Labrada considers this young man as his son, I can only welcome him. "After nodding to me as if saying hello, he adds:

"We will serve you something to drink. What do you want?"

---

[38] In 2019 (more than 60 years later), I received a call in Miami from Josefina "Fina" Labrada. She was still living in Canada. She thought that I had been murdered in a Cuban prison and she mourned me for years. Her daughter informed her that I was still alive and provided her with a phone number for me. We speak on the phone often, always talking about the past. A wonderful, good friend.

"A glass of champagne is all right."

I am a little over six feet tall, and he looks like a dwarf next to me. However, I feel tiny. I know that I am standing next to a mighty man. He always wears a suit; very elegant. It is also true that I don't find him classy at all. He speaks badly, with horrible manners. Anytime I see him, we keep a friendly conversation; after all, he is the indisputable advisor of the Mafia. Meyer Lansky himself, standing before me. Dusty Peters is also on these sites. He is Lansky's right-hand man. He regularly takes care of the shipments between Cuba and Miami. At least that was what I was told.

When I don't run into Lansky, I run into Trafficante at the Sans Souci. He makes a gesture so that I get served something to drink.

"Let us set the table for you," he says.

Figure 29 *Santos Trafficante Jr. at the Sans Souci*

I am the son of Dr. Pruna, the lawyer of Batista and other personalities, and I know very well, Captain Labrada; this, inevitably, opens many bottles of champagne to me. However, our conversations, though polite, don't usually get any further. They are all bosses except for some lieutenant that is also around. I only sit at the table provided. Mostly, with a lovely company.

"Good afternoon, young lady, I do hope you are enjoying the club."

With an elegant maneuver, Trafficante takes his hat off after having put it on before. Bowtie, white handkerchief in his jacket pocket and a cigar between his lips. The guy comes to spend the evening in one of his "houses." Nobody moves. There is always this difference between him and me: To him, I am a kid. However, dealing with Santos Trafficante, even without knowing him well, was at least practical. I remember one night, at the Sans-Souci. Of this relation, besides opening a bottle of champagne for my guest and me, it also opened his wallet. I was with my date of the moment, the daughter of former Mexican ambassador in Cuba, Lilian Reyes Spindola, a charming and refined seductive brunette. That evening, at the club, I must have spent more money than I had in my wallet. Besides, my brother Andy was with me, and he was courting a beautiful and talented young lady named Georgia Gálvez, who sometime later became a well-known singer. I ran short of money and needed to cash a check.

"Please wait a minute, Lilian, I'll be right back."

I went to the office, and I found Santos Trafficante there.

"Mr. Trafficante, I am afraid that I need to ask you to cash a personal check for me. I have run short of cash. I hope you will accept my check."

To which Santos Trafficante replied: "Not a problem at all. After all, you have business with E.M., don't you? That is a good sign."

Figure 30 Lilian Reyes Spindola with Fernando Pruna at the Sans Souci in Havana

I didn't personally know Santos Trafficante, but he was aware of my business with E.M. Loew and Jack Burris, and that I was going to sit on the dollar mine of my real estate projects. Yes, at the young age of 22, I, Fernando Pruna Junior, had the unusual opportunity to have my check cashed by Santos Trafficante, an indisputable giant of the underworld.

If there is a brothers' connection that I knew very well, it was the McLaney brothers. Michael and William, of the American Irish Mafia. Arsenio Labrada frequented the Nacional Hotel to supervise the gambling there on Batista's behalf, and he had introduced them to me. I also went there frequently on my own and once I encountered E.M. Loew and Jack Burris there; they were all sitting together at a table. The McLaney brothers had reached an agreement with Jake, Meyer Lansky's brother. He ran the International Casino of the Nacional Hotel. When the McLaney brothers took control over gambling at the casino, Jake Lansky put himself in charge of the casino at the Riviera Hotel owned by his older brother Meyer. That's how they distributed the market so that everybody had their share. From time to time, I had a drink with the McLaney brothers, particularly with Mike. He was a very natural guy and enjoyed a good conversation. They were pleasant individuals, and they treated me with familiarity, often picking up my tab. They ran a very smooth operation at the Nacional. The shows at the cabaret were fantastic, and I was dating a couple of the chorus girls there. By the way, the girls were American and needless to say, gorgeous. But at the same time, really lovely and friendly. They were nice American girls that worked for the brothers.

"What's up, young man! How is business?"

"Smooth sailing up to now. My hotel project is taking shape. We will place the first stone in a few weeks."

"It is a promising deal, the one we signed," gargled E.M. Loew.

"Then, let's drink to your future success!"

It is like the trailer of a film noir playing before my eyes, with a background of bars full of smoke and lounge music in the style of Julie London. Nightclubs, crimes, secret agents, cops, hitmen, femme fatales. Such was, from time to time, my world. I feel well in these padded corners, where the fingers of pianists caress the piano keyboards. Velvet singers sing Billie Holliday's standards. James Cagney-looking guys throw cards on the gambling tables. Eligibility criterion: to show dollars and spend them. Some challenge each other by dint of dollar rolls to poker, protected by the timba; afterward, they tell some good stories over a drink. There are lucky women. Sometimes, there are ephebe-looking, slicked-haired young men, sitting on the other side of the bar. They know they are beautiful. They have money, mainly after realizing how profitable being a gigolo can be.

Figure 31 Denise Darcel and Fernando at El Morocco, New York City.

When I am not dancing the mambo in Havana, I dance jazz in New York. I often go, with Hélène and Denise, to the mecca of mundane life, El Morocco. Denise, always smiling, and exuberant, knows many people. She introduces her friends to me. Actors. Actresses. Singers. Wives of Beautiful people. This lair of champagne and music is often attended by two young ladies who come together to have fun. I met them through Denise. One of them is a divine beauty: Linda Christian. A Mexican cinema star who gravitates in the US film studios and one of the most beautiful actresses we are allowed to watch. Very handsome young men fly around her, wrestling in actress hunting. They are elegant. Mundane. Maybe a little bit gigolo, or refined pimps, as we Cubans say. Italian Americans, sons of New York's or international upper class. "They jump on anything movin." They tell me. I would like to know if she is up to her reputation. After all. Isn't that the one that Brazilian millionaire Pignatari called "the best hit of all times"?

Sometimes, I dance with the other young lady. I wonder why she comes with her friend, Linda. She is married. She seems very sensible. Quiet. Distinguished. Different. Her husband is a US Senator, and he is often absent. In these moments, he is taking part in some mass meetings. She is a regular customer at El Morocco.

"May I have this dance?"

"Yes, with pleasure."

On the floor, in the arms of this beautiful brunette woman, I could feel many pairs of eyes on me. She was seductive. I dance with her several times while launching a loving smile to Hélène, who was sitting on a striped armchair. I wonder why a beautiful woman married to a known politician comes to this place for fun. She must feel bored at home. I am sure this married woman likes to be in my arms to dance with me because I am an excellent dancer; it is my Cuban blood. Denise tells me: "You dance like a Matador!".

"Thanks for this exceptional dance," she told me.

"Hopefully, we'll dance again," I replied.

When she is not holding a long discussion with the writer Truman Capote, I would like to dance with her again.

"Of course, with pleasure," she says.

"Hasta pronto, Jackie. It's been a pleasure to see you again."

"Muchas gracias, Fernando."

Yes, Jackie's husband must do authentic acrobatics. Even more in Cuban territory! Regarding a short stay of the senator in Havana, during which he gave himself to the pleasures of the flesh to satisfy his active libido, maybe even helped by Lansky or Trafficante, who would know how to provide him well. So, in return, I could have attracted Jackie to my Cuban soil. Its only a thought.

I look back to when I was moneyless. That was long before meeting Solange, Hélène, Denise, and the others. Before making a better living. When I was still a student at Hebron and broke, by chance I had the good fortune to meet Martha Playford at the Nacional Hotel. She and her sister Jane were in Havana for a vacation with their parents. A superb girl, blond with green eyes like emeralds, just gorgeous. Beautiful outside and inside, with a distinctive personality. Her father, Harry Playford, was the president of a bank in Florida[39]. Harry married the rich heiress of an industrial empire, Elizabeth Coates, a lovely, sophisticated lady. Playford was a simple bush pilot at the time and had no fortune of his own, but his mother-in-law, who appreciated him sincerely, had given him an excellent financial push in business. He moved from airplanes to the banking industry. I was very much in love with his daughter. She was a beautiful, wonderful girl, a superb human being, with a

---

[39] First National Bank.

radiant spirit and, besides, a great sportswoman. Her father had a horse stable in Saint Petersburg, Florida and she could ride a horse like an Amazon. I was sure that, in the future, she would be my wife. That was my aspiration, and she felt the same way.

Mr. Playford appreciated me too, and he often invited me to spend my vacations by the sea, in his beautiful house of Snell Island[40], in Saint-Petersburg, Florida. He once came to New York to close the sale of a radio station (WNEW) he had acquired at the beginning of the fifties, pocketing a four-million-dollar contract in the process. He was very happy with the deal he had just closed and wanted to celebrate. I spent the whole week with him staying at his suite at the Ambassador Hotel in New York City. He had the reputation of being the last of the big spenders and, let me tell you, that he was.

"Come, we are going out tonight, Fernando proposed with his usual cunning air. We're going to a place where there are beautiful women to buy and sell, and there is also good scotch."

"No," replied Playford, "I'm the one who is taking you to a first-class, charming place. A lovely place."

"Where are you taking me?"

"We're going to the Embassy Club."

Playford's looks were quite the opposite of a playboy, but he said that with deep pockets, you could always manage. Besides, he was likable and hilarious and charming, one of those guys loved by everyone.

"Come, Fernando," he told me when the time came to pay the bill, "You sign the check."

"What? I don't have any credit here!"

---

[40] 415 Brightwaters Blvd. Snell Island, St Petersburg, Florida.

"Well, from now on, you do, and anytime you come, you'll be able to. "

"You want me to sign! I'm afraid I don't understand." Playford just burst out laughing.

"They owe me a lot of money in this place. You are with my daughter; I know that you love her, and you are likely to marry her, so you are like a son to me. Sign without any worry. Do not pay for anything! When you come with your friends; you are authorized to sign the check on my behalf. I will tell the club administration at the hotel. It's something I want to do for you."

Harry Playford's generosity with me was impressive, and the affection and friendship that grew between us was something uncommon. I highly respected and admired him. His daughter, Martha, was just wonderful and I sincerely cared very much for her. I loved Martha, and Mr. Playford was, as Cubans say, one in a million.

So that's how I became a regular at the Embassy Club of the Ambassador Hotel in New York City. Without spending one dollar, just using the account put at my disposal by future father-in-law, Harry Playford, at will. I regularly invited good friends and, of course, lovely ladies, I offered whatever they wanted to them, and it was Playford who finally paid the bill. Everybody knew me at the Embassy Club and frankly treated me like royalty. The magic of Mr. Playford's limitless generosity.

The wedding project with Martha sadly dissolved when I returned to Cuba, and my life got complicated for political reasons. Whims of fate. Perhaps karma. Even though many girls have come and gone, she was, in every way, the one and only; unique. In truth, I have never stopped loving Martha.

Later, when I toured New York's fashion nightclubs, with Denise and Hélène, I made them know what would be from then on, one

Figure 32 **MARTHA PLAYFORD**

of my favorite dens and also theirs. They liked the Embassy Club, the same in which Chauncy Grey's metals and saxes or my friend, José Quintero's Latin band still make me shudder when I remember that unforgettable music that sank deep inside Solange and me: "Something's gotta give."

Years later, even though my heart belonged to Hélène at the moment, I liked women too much. I loved them all a little. At least, for an instant. Even those who seemed to be entirely out of my reach in my wildest dreams. I have attracted those inaccessible, incredibly gorgeous women to me. Denise was the perfect passport to enter this beautiful world, to close the gap with the Hollywood stars. Denise reached out, laughed with everyone, joking with her funny French accent. On nights when she addressed the most sparkling of stars, my heart began to beat faster.

Her dress flutters away from me in my memories.

I have often seen her at the Embassy Club, arm in arm with Joe DiMaggio, the baseball player. Every time, the couple comes to our table to say hello. They never sit with us, but we always exchange some courtesies. Sometimes, it was us who, on arrival, before going to our table, went to the sitting couple to chat for a while. She has a prodigious sensuality. Unfortunately, I never danced with her as I had done with her brunette rival Jackie. However, I was dying to dance with her. One dance. Just one. Maybe had the occasion arisen if Dimaggio had not always been present jealously watching his prey. It was common knowledge that he was jealous. Even after their divorce, in society, he never abandoned his goddess as he would never leave his baseball bat on the playfield. I'll also say, without hesitation, that, when the planetary explosive blonde was around, the Darcel sisters urgently sought for my company. So, from the lack of one dance with the sex-symbol at the Embassy Club, I always had to be satisfied with the usual conversations, sitting next to Denise and Hélène, which is a lot and certainly enough.

"I've seen you in your last film. You were sensational."

"Thank you. You are so kind."

"We wish you a lovely evening," DiMaggio rushes to say. "I wish you a beautiful evening, Miss Monroe."

I was still a young man. I was twenty-two, and everything was hunky-dory for me. We were at the starting block. We had bank loans. Signing with the Bay Land Company to start the works was imminent. My young professional life was starting with fabulous numbers. I would soon begin to build two towers with a disco between them, suspended on the top. The building would have my last name. The "Pruna Building," and its neon lights would illuminate the Havana evenings.

I also owned a quarter of a fabulous hotel project that had a 12-million-dollar budget. It would be even more splendid than Trafficante's Capri and more phantasmagoric than Lansky's Riviera. More spectacular than his Monte Carlo project in Havana. I felt a little like the young king of Cuban investments, surrounded by the most beautiful ladies in the world. I danced with the American queen of musical comedies. I also danced with John F. Kennedy's beautiful wife. I would maybe end up marrying the sweetest of women. I drove my beautiful convertible along the seawall drive of Malecón and walked on the elegant Fifth Avenue in Miramar, with the cigar between my lips. What more could I want? What other horizon could replace this one, but another even more shining star like the candidacy for congressman in the next elections? No, no earthquake could destroy my dreams. Yet, sometimes, thought and reality do not match.

Solange had arrived in Havana and was staying at the Nacional Hotel, a block away from Fernando's apartment.

"Fernando, I don't feel at ease having to see each other like this, hiding."

"We have done nothing improper! I wanted to see you. Aren't you happy to see me?"

"Of course. What kind of question is that! But, our actions will end up bringing us trouble. It is a strange, senseless game. It is challenging for me to be close to you. You know that."

"Perhaps... my brother could take David submarine fishing. And,"

"And what?"

"We could put an end to this 'strange game' as you call it." "I'm afraid I don't understand. Submarine fishing is hazardous and."

"Precisely. Yes, accidents happen."

Solange woke up startled. She looked around and breathed a sigh of relief when she saw the sun reflection in the pool of the Nacional Hotel; she had dozed off. She had been dreaming. But what a horrible dream. Did she feel in her subconscious that her husband was getting in the way of her most intimate desire? She opened her eyes, startled, quickly wiping those ugly thoughts from her mind. Andy was standing in front of her.

"Good morning, Solange, so sorry to wake you up."

"Oh, Andy... Good morning. I must have dozed off. But what are you doing here?"

She empathized a lot with Fernando's brother. He limited himself to admire her.

"I came to tell you that my brother wants to see you."

"Where is he?"

"He is in the basement of the hotel. He is waiting for you at the entrance on 23rd Street."

Solange took her towel and rose immediately. To see Fernando again, behind David's back, always filled her with a strange feeling half excitement and half malice. That sensation one feels when breaking the law—the danger of what is forbidden and then the sensitive waves of pent up desire.

When they met, they embraced tenderly. They couldn't help it. Solange had not seen Fernando since that Christmas in 1955. She just had to kiss him, and she did.

"It has been an eternity. Much too long. It is beautiful to see you, Fernando."

She had not seen him since December 1955, and it was now December 1958. Three long years had passed.

"I feel the same way, Solange. You are more beautiful than ever."

"I told Andy to go with David to a restaurant near the Capitol and to stuff themselves with oysters," said Fernando. "They have fantastic fresh oysters there. David will undoubtedly enjoy it. He is a gourmet."

"Sounds fine to me."

Solange sighed. Her nightmare had faded away.

"Afterward, they will have a banana daiquiri close to Cathedral Square. So, we'll be able to spend some hours together, alone, you and me. Is that agreeable to you?"

"Sounds fine. Then, are we only going for a walk, or do you have something else in mind?"

"We are doing whatever you want, anything you want. Whatever your mind and your body desire. I want to please you. Pleasing you gives me great pleasure."

One day, Solange had naively wanted to believe they would take a walk on the beach. When she saw Fernando pay for a room at the inn in Miramar, she lost it. She simply was not prepared for it. It was different when they met in New York City. It was more natural. Beautiful. Perhaps being in Cuba, a foreign country, made a difference. She often thought about it, but now she realized that she saw things differently. Perhaps she had matured.

"Very well. Fernando. But don't try to change the world- possibly the world will change you."

"Yes, I agree, whispered Fernando," still embracing her, and then he kissed her again, softly.

13

THE GATHERING STORM

The worst possible mistake that President Fulgencio Batista can make at this point of his mandate is to hinder the fulfillment of fair, honest, and impartial elections on November 3rd,. – Fernando Pruna

1958: A Perspective.

Terrorist acts perturbed the New Year's Eve celebrations coming into the year 1958. Rebels set off bombs in movie theaters in Habana. That was the time of the most contradicting hypotheses.

"Manuel Urrutia will be the new president after Batista leaves!"

Fidel Castro called to boycott the elections scheduled for June 1st, 1958– the presidential elections as well as the parliamentary ones. Defiantly, he anticipated a revolutionary victory and announced the name of the man that he would place as President of Cuba after overthrowing Batista. Some news cables later, on United States soil, this proclamation was seen as a threat. The conspiracy of the great Soviet octopus agitated its red tentacles each time closer. Moscow Radio trumpeted its support for Castro.

Throughout the year, the revolutionaries tried to make use of every opportunity to be in the spotlight. They wanted to get as much publicity as possible, as demonstrated by their actions.

On February 23rd, 1958, in downtown Havana,[42] a group of revolutionaries kidnapped the Argentinean ace of car racing at his hotel lobby in the eve of the Havana Grand Prix taking place in the city. It was an audacious coup that dampened the event significantly. Fangio was going to be the star of the show. The races had to go on without him. A few hours later, the race car driver was finally released. Still, the kidnapping was a clear signal of strength and a significant publicity stunt as well as an embarrassment to Batista's government.

I watched the Grand Prix car racing event from the comfort of my parent's apartment on the 17th floor of the Someillan Building. We had a Birdseye view of the exciting and colorful races as well as a superb view of the Gulf of Mexico and the Malecon Drive. The races were to last two or three days, and the apartment was full of friends invited by my parents. Drinks served, and a well-stocked buffet table refreshed continuously. Amongst the friends was a well-known Cuban newspaperman, who was accompanied by a delicately beautiful European young lady who was one of the stars of the Folies Bergère troupe visiting Cuba on tour. Introduced, later, she voluntarily provided me with her telephone number. We soon started to see each other and eventually we got to know each other quite intimately. She preferred to meet me at her small but well-furnished apartment, courtesy of the newspaperman, in Linea Street in the Vedado section of Havana near the Miramar tunnel. After our meeting, I visited her often. She was delightfully attractive and a very charming woman as well as a very private person. Her name was Trudy. When I can't see her, I feel satisfied looking at the beautiful picture she gave me. She is naked, with a flower in one ear, and she poses, with a hat in her hand, as the only

---

[41] Juan Manuel Fangio, nicknamed El Chueco or El Maestro, was an Argentine racing car driver. He dominated the first decade of Formula One racing, winning the World Drivers' Championship five times.

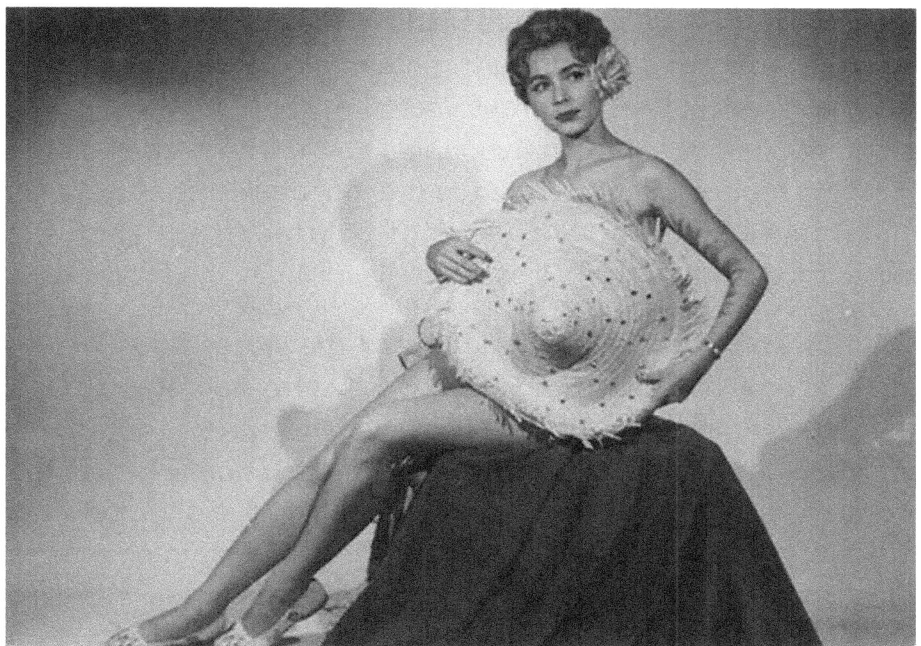

Figure 33 TRUDY, a star of the Folies Bergère

piece of clothing, covering her body from her upper thighs to her shoulders.

I remember how frustrated I felt about Fangio's kidnapping. We were all looking forward to seeing Fangio's performance, driving his sleek Maserati 300S. A year before (1957), Fangio won the first Cuban Grand Prix with the same car, and everyone was sure that he would win again in 1958. His kidnapping certainly dulled the Party. Nevertheless, the races went on without any other interruption except for the fact that a driver lost control of his Ferrari and crashed into the crowd injuring several dozen people and killing seven bystanders. This unfortunate and tragic accident led the government to stop the races a few minutes later. Fangio's kidnapping and the horrible accident spoiled the charm and excitement of the sport, better known as the Havana Grand Prix. The settings for the races could not have been more spectacular or beautiful.

Months later, by clandestine radio, Fidel Castro ordered Batista, again, to resign, to prevent a threatening civil war. Some days later, a couple of rebels broke into the Habana Hilton Hotel, which was not yet open to the public, as the workers gave it the finishing touches. They climbed to the roof and threw thousands of fliers in all directions that the wind would take them. The flyers called for a general strike. The general strike never happened.

Tourists walked the streets and visited the stores as usual; the streets were not desertic. Since Fidel Castro had appeared in the Herbert Mathews articles published by The New York Times, the rebel leader had become a well-known figure all over the world. A consummate narcissist, he delighted in the publicity. But there is no doubt that the effect of the articles in one of the most important newspapers in the world, above all a United States newspaper, had an immense psychological impact on the Cuban people, particularly in the college-educated and the upper-middle class.

Although Cuba was an independent republic with its government and ways of life, it is essential to remember that the United States represented the almighty big brother only ninety miles away. The Cuban people sublimated the United States. It was almost a mystic belief. A major and highly respected American newspaper publishing three articles that depicted Fidel Castro as the Robin Hood of the Sierra Maestra and classifying Fulgencio Batista as a tyrant, had a tremendous impact in detriment of the Batista government. It is difficult to gauge with precision the enormous influence that the socialist-leaning Herbert Mathews had on the eventual fall of Batista and the overthrow of his government by Fidel Castro's communist revolution.

On March 10th, in Paris, two rebel sympathizers wanted to commemorate, in their style, the March 10th, 1952 coup by Batista, which to them marked the end of Cuba's democracy and the trashing of the 1940 Cuban Constitution. They displayed a big red and black flag from the Eiffel Tower to protest against the regime.

Easter was tense. A rumor began to circulate: the rebels were supposed to have distributed weapons all over Havana, awaiting a signal to launch an offensive. It turned out to be a deceitful rumor. Nothing happened, and the U.S. investors behaved just as if the Castroist revolt did not exist. They tried to reactivate the luxury tourism that had not been so much affected anyway. Batista affirmed that there were no rebels in the Sierra Maestra Mountain Range, and he inaugurated a Shell service station in the outskirts of the city. After having ruled in Cuban politics for almost twenty-five years, with his comings and goings, he stated that, nevertheless, he wouldn't run again for the next elections and that he would transfer power to the candidate elected by the people.

Fernando asked his father, "Who will run to take over as new President?"

"Maybe Andrés Domingo Morales del Castillo. I believe he has the best chances."

Mr. Morales del Castillo had secured the internship of the presidency during the month the General had to abandon the presidential palace to run for elections in 1954. He was a close friend of Dr. Pruna. Morales del Castillo had different positions in Batista's government: Prime Minister, Minister of Justice, of Housing, of Foreign Affairs, and Defense. He was one of the politicians who had the best chance to be elected in the next elections. Batista considered him to be one of his best collaborators in advisory councils. He was always a precious help, mainly during Batista's exile. "Are you running for the next elections?" his supporters asked him. But Andrés Domingo only smiled. The opposition was agitated, shouting loud and clear that the scrutiny would be, beforehand, full of irregularities to secure Batista's man victory. The revolutionaries doubled their efforts aimed at destabilizing the pre-election period. The elections, due to take place on June 1st, according to the Constitution, were postponed until November 3rd. The anti-establishment Castroists who called for a strike and carried out armed actions had, partially, gotten away with it, because they caused the postponement.

"And you, my son," continued Dr. Pruna, "what are your projects for Cuba's Congressional elections?"

"If possible, I'm going to try to be a candidate for the Congress for the Democratic Party."

"Let's take care of that, shall we? Let us talk to Reyes Spindola to help us organize it. Let us take advantage of his being in Cuba at this moment."

"Yes. Let's ask Lilia's father to arrange a meeting with Panchín Batista for us."

Fernando was determined to participate in the race for the legislative elections. Surrounded by advisors, he was going to propose his candidacy for the primary elections to the Party. Once the primaries concluded, the elections to the Congress would have to take place on the same day as the presidential elections, on November 3rd. He would be the youngest candidate in Cuba's history to run for a Congressional seat; he was twenty-two years old.

"Youth is of the essence to represent a country because it contributes new values, new perspectives," Dr. Pruna ended.

Hélène and Fernando had grown apart by time and distance, though there was still something beating between them. The same happened with Solange, who had moved to Canada to be with her husband at the University. Lately, for some time already,

Fernando was frequenting a young lady with a pretty nickname, Lilia. The young lady was a presumptuous brunette, very seductive, polished, and refined. The affair was torrid but ephemeral. The most important thing about Lilian, who everyone called Lilia, was the fact that she was the daughter of Don Octavio Reyes Spindola, Mexico's former ambassador to Cuba. Mr. Spindola was a distinguished gentleman who had been with his lovely and intelligent wife, Lila Cardenas, for many years. Without a doubt, he had an impressive personality. His inseparable ornate walking stick provided him with an aura of prestige and elegance. His wife, Lilia Cardenas, who was almost thirty years younger, had been a close friend of Argentina's first lady, Evita Perón. For this reason, her daughter Lilia was Evita's goddaughter. At that time, Don Octavio was Mexico's ambassador to Argentina.

Mr. Reyes-Spindola cultivated a social relationship with Dr. Pruna. Still, he was quite fond of Fernando, whom he got to know through his daughter, and, at the same time, he was a close and dear friend of the President's brother, Francisco Batista, nicknamed "Panchín," the governor of Havana Province. A strategical position to promote his candidacy and launch a campaign under the best auspices. To top it off, the Democratic Party, the second-largest Party after the President's Party, was also presided by Panchín Batista.

Finally, Morales del Castillo didn't run for President. Batista proposed the candidacy of Andrés Rivero Agüero, one of his protegees and an adept from the beginning. Several parties constituted the National Progressist Coalition. They were: the pro-government group, which included Batista's Party (the Progressive Action Party), of which Rivero, the Prime Minister at the moment, was intellectually the leader; the Liberal Party and the Democratic Party, as well as Alberto Salas Amaro's Party, the Cuban Union Party. Several opposition parties also ran for the presidential elections. Finally, these were the official candidates that were running: Andrés Rivero Agüero, from the official National Progressist Coalition; the former President Ramón Grau San Martin, through the Authentic Party; Carlos Márquez Sterling, from the Free People's Party, and Alberto Salas Amaro from the Cuban Union Party. During that pre-election period of 1958, the debates developed with a good rhythm in the opposition headquarters, revolutionary or not. Rivero, Márquez, Amaro, and Grau, the four of them had received death threats from the revolutionary underground movement.

"Castro has asked Cubans to boycott the ballots by staying home. Anyway, with this tension, the elections have been postponed. We have then enough time to set our projects in motion."

"One can only hope one thing: That the elections take place with absolute transparency, because, if any of the opposition candidates win, as they should, that will stop Castro's revolutionary movement dead on its tracks. Castro anticipates this possibility, and therefore he is against the elections. The outcome could ultimately work against his political interests."

"Do you think so?"

"Yes. A defeat of the opposition would mean that the elections were fraudulent. If the polls are honest, I am sure that Márquez Sterling will be elected President. The unpopularity of anything related to Batista secures the triumph of the opposition. Besides, Márquez Sterling is clean, and his credentials make him, unquestionably, the best and most capable among all the candidates."

For his part, Dr. Pruna had a personal conversation with General Batista. He dared to give him some advice. The meeting took place at the Presidential Palace in downtown Havana.

"Mr. President, I believe that you should take the necessary steps to ensure that the elections take place with absolute normality, total transparency, and impartiality. However, it may mean defeat for the Progressist Coalition."

"What do you imply?"

"To your benefit, you should let Carlos Márquez Sterling win, as he should if the elections are impartial."

"Dr. Pruna, why do you think that this is so important?"

"Because if we have honest and impartial elections and the opposition, specifically, Dr. Carlos Marquez Sterling receives the majority of the votes from the people, it will automatically frustrate the very reason why Fidel Castro is in the Sierra Maestra mountains. Castro will be without motivation, without a moral right to be doing what he is doing."

"Dr. Pruna, what makes you think that Dr. Carlos Marquez Sterling would get more votes than Andres Rivero Aguero?"

"Mr. President, with all due respect, the people of Cuba desire a change of government. It is my belief and my understanding that Marquez Sterling will undoubtedly win the elections if you guaranty fairness and impartiality."

"Dr. Pruna, there are many interests involved. It is a very complex issue. Not an easy one to resolve. You must understand this."

"Mr. President, I respectfully ask you to weigh my advice carefully for the alternative might translate into the end of representative democracy in Cuba, as we know it, and as decreed by the 1940 Constitution of our Republic."

Batista did not comment; the advice remained unanswered.

Fernando didn't stop repeating the same thing.

"Do you think so?" E.M. asked him during one of their business meetings.

"Yes. I am convinced. If these are honest and transparent elections, Marquez Sterling should be elected. In any case, it would be the right thing. He is trustworthy, capable, and respected. He has no liability or links with the past. His election will stop the revolutionary initiative, above all, Fidel's ambition, who, if he succeeds, will take the totalitarian path to Fascism or Communism, without a doubt. According to Captain Arsenio Labrada and according to Batista's intelligence services, in which he works, the path of Fidel's Revolution is communism. There is evidence and confirmation that international communism has a marked interest in Castro's victory. If Márquez Sterling obtains a clean win in the election, his success would ultimately frustrate the guerrilla initiative. There would be no reason for the existence of the rebel army and no place for them to hide. They would have to come down from the mountains and would have to surrender their weapons; they would have no alternative. Besides, there are not so many of them. We are talking about Castro's troops as if he had an army in the Sierra Maestra Mountains, but we know this is not true. In the Sierra Maestra Mountains, there are, maybe, some hundreds of rebels, I can assure you there are not even five hundred of them."

Fernando continued to explain, "Consequently, Batista should not keep Márquez Sterling from winning the presidency and the candidates from his Party elected from assuming their positions. On the other hand, we should understand and accept that Batista has no popularity at this point. We all know this. The time has come for a qualitative change. The opposition party will obtain a great win in the elections if conducted with total impartiality and justice.

Let me make it clear to you that Andres Rivero Aguero is an honest and most capable person. He is a self-made man of humble origin with impressive credentials. Indeed, he would make a good president. But, unfortunately, he is profoundly linked to Batista and this is an unsurmountable problem. His links to Batista unfortunately disqualify him. From my point of view, it is time for Batista to abandon power. At this stage of the game nothing related to Batista has public backing. It is an unfortunate reality, but indeed a reality.

Furthermore, we know how Marques Sterling thinks. He believes in a democracy; he believes in a capitalist financial system and will not bring any hidden surprises to his government. He is a firm advocate of the 1940 Constitution.

"Why? Why is Batista so unpopular?"

"The people of Cuba have many different reasons. Some reasons are justified, and some are not. Believe it or not, what I think is an important reason is that he is a mulatto. Unfortunately, it is no secret that Cubans are racist. Additionally, Batista and his subordinates have made countless mistakes. They are deeply corrupt, with very few exceptions. There has been a lot of bloodshed, much of which is unjustified. They have killed many; the repression has included illegal torture. They have caused human damage; they have hurt the people's sensitiveness. Corruption is deeply rooted, and the worst thing is that this corruption has reached the democratic armed forces. The soldiers and classes are not corrupt. Still, the elite of the Armed Forces is dishonest, and they have turned the war against Fidel's rebels into a highly profitable business. It is an endless war. It is continuous because the military elite doesn't want it to end; it is not in their best interest to stop it. Otherwise, it is inexplicable, not to say, shameful, that a republican army of forty thousand well-trained and armed soldiers, with a modern air force, has not been able to demolish a few hundred rebels hidden in the Sierra Maestra Mountains. The only explanation for it is named corruption. But I repeat one and a thousand times, the biggest mistake this "soft" dictator could make would be not to conduct clean and impartial elections. To keep Carlos Márquez Sterling from cleanly winning the presidential elections would become political suicide for Batista. It will also expose the Republic to a revolution that is philosophically inclined to change the entire system of government. In other words, a terrible threat to a system based on representative democracy. The leaders of the Revolution have embraced the idea of a socialist government mirroring the Soviet Union or other communist governments. The perspective is quite terrifying.

"And why do you call him a soft or pseudo dictator? You have used the word "soft."

"Because Batista is not an absolute dictatorship in the full sense of the word, but what we Cubans call a 'dicta-soft.' Batista has always wanted to leave behind, historically speaking, a democratic legacy, although, indeed, he effectively carried out a coup d'état in 1952, therefore trashing the 1940 Cuban Constitution. This single act is what classifies him as a 'dictator'. But he has tried to amend this. You must remember that the people fairly elected him in July 1940 for a period that ended in 1944. Again in 1954, he was elected in a general election, and now Batista has committed to realize a general election in 1958, precisely four years after being elected to office. There is no doubt that he is trying to correct his actions. And, in doing so, he is distancing himself from being a hardcore dictator. And this is his predicament and his contradiction. You are a dictator, or you are not. You cannot be a little of both. Initially, he imposed himself by force. Now he lacks the energy and the determination, not to say the courage or even the moral integrity to make the proper use of the armed forces to sweep that group of communist led rebels that are hiding in the Sierra Maestra Mountains.

He wants to appear democratic before the People of Cuba who, to be sure, will never look at him that way. Mistakes require corrections, and he and his repressive followers have made too many, and they keep on making them. The man is soft because he lacks nerve, or he is merely tired of it all. In other words, for whatever reason, he is a weak president, or rather a weak dictator. If you are going to play the dictator, then you need to be tough. We have baptized Batista's government as a "dicta-soft." That is the closest I can come to describing his government."

Thank you, Fernando. Wow, very eloquently explained."

"Yes, indeed, Mr. Loew, it's as sad as it sounds. How many times have we heard people refer to him as: "That fucking nigger, that black son of a bitch"? The word "nigger" is demeaning.

"I understand what you mean."

"I say what I say. And what I know is that here in Cuba, I repeat, people are racist. But beyond racism, Batista is, politically speaking, a dead man. Beyond the racial factor, people want a radical change. The people are angry and frustrated, for lack of a better definition.

"In any case, it seems to me that Batista is on the edge of an abyss, isn't he?" E.M. concluded.

"I am profoundly worried about the situation. Honestly, I think the country's political stability is in danger. The very structure of the system is in danger. We have to make essential decisions on the purchasing of the Cuban Bay Land Company's land. Besides, the BANDES demands that we make a required multi-million-dollar deposit to go ahead with the structuring of the financing for the Hotel-Casino. I want to ask you that we delay the purchasing of the land as well as the upfront deposit to the BANDES, at least until the November elections take place. We won't have to wait too long now. Once we have the result of the votes, we can make a definitive decision. The election result will be our thermometer."

"But this will significantly delay our project, don't you think?" E.M. asked.

"Yes, indeed, and it hurts me deeply to have to ask you to postpone our plans, but I don't want us to put your money in danger. You have believed in me, and I want you to keep on believing in me[42]," Fernando replied.

"It is a matter of credibility. I will always tell you what I think and, believe me, what I think I hardly dare to say. But listen, E.M., if the November elections are not honest and impartial, and Batista's candidate is elected President, then I'm afraid that we will have to freeze our projects indefinitely or, at least, up to next year's presidential swearing-in, which is in February."

"Well, we'll do as you say. I completely trust your judgment." E.M. concluded.

ON STANDBY

By putting the Casino- Hotel projects on hold, Fernando was voluntarily conspiring against his pocketbook. He felt that he did not have any other choice. The good commissions that he was due to earn on the Hotel-Casino project would not become valid for the moment. The different initiatives, including his building, was automatically also put on standby. The front money required to kick off the project was purposely not delivered. It was very frustrating for him, but there was nothing that he could do. He did not want to take E.M.'s money if there was any chance of risk. Standby did not mean that he would stand still.

---

[42] The postponement of the financial investments that E.M. Loew was required to make, even though they worked against Fernando Pruna's personal financial interest, saved Mr. Loew from losing several million dollars. E.M. Loew did not lose one cent in the Cuban initiative thanks to Fernando's decisive advice.

Another imaginative business initiative that caught my interest was a rum factory. My father had a close friend, who was an avid entrepreneur. His name was Pedro Montequín. He was an extremely nice guy with a severe personality but very amiable when you got to be his friend. He lived in a town next to the Havana International Airport named Rancho Boyeros. Although he was my father's age, we got to be good friends, and once he invited me to have lunch at his home. After lunch, he told me that he wanted to show me around town, and Pedro took me to a nearby warehouse where he introduced me to his father-in-law, an older Spanish gentleman whose name was Guillermo Suarez Rubiera[43].

In this warehouse, Suarez had a rum factory. It was a small business, but he had it well organized. Suarez was a self-made chemist who focused on making an excellent rum. He made all three types of rum; white, gold, and aged, which is called "añejo". There were several large oak barrels. When I demonstrated my interest, he insisted that I taste different samples from different barrels to see how I felt about the color, the taste, and the mellowness of his rum. I was immediately impressed by the quality. It was exceptionally smooth, and it had a very slight taste of sweetness that was very agreeable to my taste buds, and I told him so. He intimated that one of the ingredients was honey. I was impressed. The problem that he was having was in marketing. He simply did not know how to sell his rum. Then I became interested and told him so. I had Pedro Montequín's blessing. I think that was why he had invited me for lunch, to introduce me to his father-in-law and see if a deal could come out of it.

After a couple of drawn-out meetings with Guillermo Suarez at his warehouse, from where I usually left a bit drunk from tasting

---

[43] Guillermo Suarez Rubiera, born in Oviedo, Spain on April 10, 1883 and died in Rancho Boyeros, Cuba on December 23, 1969. His grandsons Antonio Garcia Suarez and Felix Montequin verified my information for the anecdote and provided me with the photos of the Rum label, for which I am grateful.

his excellent rum, we agreed that I would handle sales, and he would manage production. The deal was uncomplicated; I would get exclusive rights to sell his rum. He could not sell to anyone else. He would put a price on the finished product unbottled but charge an extra fee for him to bottle it, but I would provide the bottles, the labels, and the corks. The rum would be named **"Ron Montequín,"** *but the name of* **Guillermo Suarez** *would also appear on the sticker. We were starting very modestly, but it was a solid plan, and he agreed to it. Pedro Montequín, whom I playfully called "the Pirate" because he was missing an eye from an accident years before, gave his blessings to the deal I made with his father-in-law.*

I talked to my brother, Andy, about the initiative. Still a teenager, Andy was already an upcoming painter and a student of one of the world's best Art Schools, San Alejandro. I wanted him to help me design a unique presentation for marketing rum. I told him that I wanted a different bottle and an attractive label. We talked about it for hours, and we came up with the idea of painting the bottles. We decided to paint the bottles to match its content. The result was a silver bottle, a gold bottle, a bronze bottle; silver for white rum; gold for gold rum, and bronze for aged añejo rum.

The three brands would be:

- *Ron Montequín Plata*
- *Ron Montequín Oro*
- *Ron Montequín Añejo*

However, we left on each side of the painted bottles a quarter-inch vertical stripe clear from the top to the bottom of the containers to determine the level of rum left in each bottle. We carefully analyzed different bottles and finally agreed on a wine-like bottle that was shorter than the regular wine bottle. It was a beautiful bottle with gracious curves. Andy also designed a new label, and we proceeded to go into production and marketing.

Because I enjoyed Havana's nightlife and was acquainted with most of the owners or managers of nearly all nightclubs and bars in the city, I decided to start my marketing in this area. My marketing plan was pretty straightforward, and I simply offered the rum on consignment. I also decided to do it personally. So, I borrowed my father's Chevy station wagon, loaded it with cases of rum, and started to canvas the product. Many of the owners and managers of these night places knew me pretty well, and it was hard for them not to accept my consignments. They had nothing to lose if the rum did not sell. They agreed to pay me when they reordered. I said, fine.

I also started to visit different clubs to talk to the bartenders. I had friendly conversations with them and tried to get them to give me an opinion of the rum and the presentation. It was a learning experience. Some did not like the idea of the painted bottles. They said that people liked to see the transparency of the fluid. Everyone had a different view, but they did agree that the rum was top quality.

I also had a real boost from some friends and acquaintances. Mike McLaney, who ran the gambling at the Nacional Hotel, ordered fifty cases of rum from me and paid in cash up front. He was having a big party with free drinks, and he would tell his bartenders only to serve Ron Montequín. The owner of the Centro Vasco restaurant, Juan Saizarbitoria, who was a dear friend of my family and owned my favorite restaurant in Havana, ordered a bunch of cases and would invite friends to try out the rum. I talked to Charlie White, who was my neighbor, and owned the Capri Casino, and he too helped by buying a few cases. In a short time, I had placed the rum in every famous waterhole in Havana, to the delight of Guillermo Suarez. The only problem was the fact that I initiated this venture a bit late in the almanac. It was only a few months before the end of 1958 that I started this business, which seemed very promising. It abruptly came to an end with the coming into power of the soon to be a communist revolution. Sadly, I never possessed the chemical

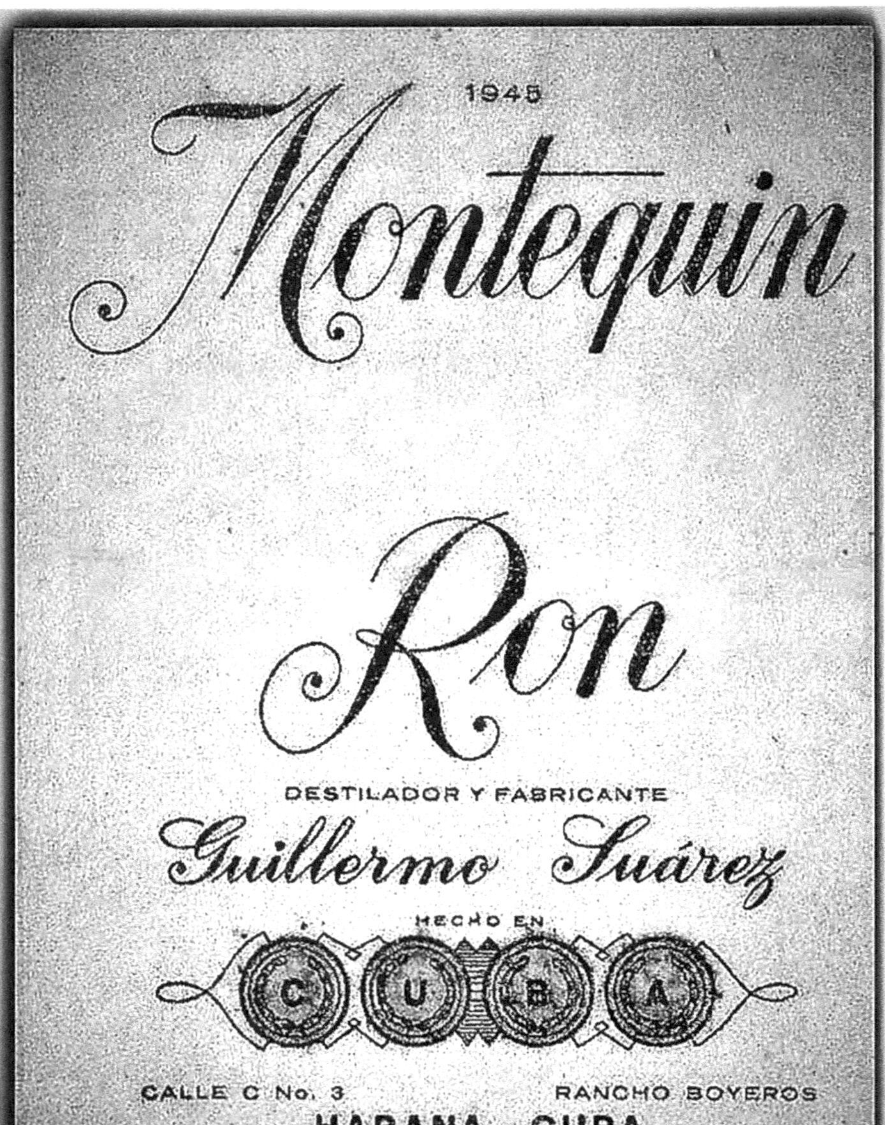

1945
Montequin
Ron
DESTILADOR Y FABRICANTE
Guillermo Suárez
HECHO EN
CUBA
CALLE C No. 3
RANCHO BOYEROS
HABANA - CUBA
GRADO 40 A 15

formula of the rum made by Guillermo Suarez. Frankly, it did not even occur to me to ask him for it. The vertiginous changes that took place in Cuba at the time clouded not only my mind but my existence. Everything came to a stop for me with the arrival of Fidel Castro. I felt castrated by this horrific event. At the time, I felt unable to understand how a communist sympathizing terrorist and outlaw could have gained total power in my country.

The saddest part of the Montequin Rum factory story came to me many years later, when Felix Montequin, Pedro's youngest son, updated me.

A few months after the Cuban Revolution came into power, they started to confiscate all small business enterprises without paying for them. They simply seized the business. Unexpectedly, government agents would knock on your business door, come in and just notify you that the company was no longer your property, that it now belonged to the Revolution, and that you should leave the premises. Straightforward robbery. It happened throughout the island, it happened to Guillermo Suarez, who was now an older man. He owned the business for several decades. Losing the company to the government without justification or retribution was deeply disturbing to Suarez, to the point of affecting his health. Nostalgic, he would walk by the factory a few times a week merely curious about what the government was doing to his precious old factory. By now, he was walking with the aid of a cane and shuffling along the familiar street. Then one day, while walking on the other side of the road, he saw a group of men taking the huge, sealed oak barrels where he aged the rum for years out of the warehouse. Once the barrels lined the street, they took axes and started to destroy the barrels. The rum spilled and disappeared in the drains. Witnessing what was happening to his sweet rum shocked him so much that at that very moment, he lost his eyesight. The psychological effect of seeing the destruction of his life work was so devastating that it blinded him instantly. He never saw again; he never recuperated his eyesight and died a blind broken man sometime later.

Some local communist leaders decided that the Revolution no longer wanted this liquor factory and decided to convert the facility into living quarters for workers and families. Without further consideration, they did what they do best; destroy.

Panchín Batista had been appointed Governor of Havana Province by his brother after the coup d'état of 1952. Later, in 1954 he had been elected Governor of Havana. He was the head of the Democratic Party since 1955. Batista had just announced that he wouldn't run for the presidential election with the coalition party, but he would cede the candidacy to whoever was elected. The meeting between Fernando and the President's brother took place on the farm owned by the Governor of Havana.

The four of them had lunch together: Mr. Reyes Spindola, Panchín Batista, and the Prunas, father, and son. Panchín had always been nice by nature, friendly, and very pragmatic, a pleasant person.

"Very well, boy. I can still call you a boy, given your youth. How old are you?"

"Twenty-two, Governor."

"Very well," Panchín went on. "Up to now, we have few of influence, from the upper class, in Congress. We need young men like you who support our country. Some say that the Rebels knocking on our door sound more threatening each day. But that is not wholly true, and we have the means to reduce those men. The Castroists are not so numerous. What happens is that we get spokes in our wheels all the time. Some organized groups are operating in the mountains. Young men. We need other young men to confront them. To fight them with their fists, if necessary. I believe that you have that nature. But we have nothing to fear. The secret services keep us informed of their moves. I know that their number is insignificant. I will talk to my party leaders about your candidacy anticipating the primaries. I will propose Pruna Bertot as a candidate for the Democratic Party for the upcoming general elections. By the way, I believe that you are a friend of my son Mañy; he called me to ask me to help you with your aspirations. I just wanted you to know, and yes, I will do my best to further your political career."

"I believe that you will be the youngest candidate to the Congress in Cuba's history," Mr. Spindola concluded.

"It is true," confirmed Panchín.

While waiting for the November 3rd elections, Fulgencio Batista ordered the police and the army to reinforce security at the airports, the railroads, and the main highways. The rebels kept pushing back, particularly the cities' underground movement, given the upcoming election date. Their threats and actions became more violent. Rumors spread that some of the candidates that were running for the legislative elections suffered death threats. Fernando often recalled his mother's conversations with President Batista.

"What do you think about these armed groups that are in the mountain and carry out an armed struggle against you?"

"They are terrorists. We will defeat them. It is all propaganda. Be sure that we will overcome any form of Revolution, mainly if dyed in red," the General assured.

Despite my concerns about the elections, I was very much in the dark regarding the overall risk level that existed nationally. I wrongly thought that although things were not too good, there was no chance for the rebel military to topple the government anytime soon. In 1958 I still believed that Castro did not have an opportunity to militarily take over the island, although I had grave concerns about the political situation. I was merely ignorant of what was going on militarily speaking.

Such was my blindness that when a group of American investors came to talk to me about putting together a financial study to build a cement plant in Cuba, I immediately agreed to work on it. I started to look into it and make some essential contacts to study the feasibility. It would be a multimillion-dollar foreign investment that would enormously benefit Cuba's economy, and besides, I found it to be an exciting endeavor and a challenge.

The most important chemical components of Portland cement are calcium, silica, alumina, and iron. Calcium, derived from limestone, marl, or chalk, while silica, alumina, and iron come from the sands, clays, and iron ore sources. I talked to several experts familiar with a cement plant that already existed in Cuba in Mariel, Pinar del Rio. I discovered that there was a landowner near Gibara City, which was in Oriente Province in North East Cuba, about 480 miles from Havana by road. The city itself was next to the sea, but a few miles to the east, there were mountains of limestone that contained the principal components to make Portland cement. I got a lead to the owner of a large property that included mountains of kaolin clay ideal for making Portland cement. I got his number and was able to call him up. It seems that he had been approached before with the same objective. However, the deal had soured because of the revolutionary turmoil in the area. Nevertheless, he told me that if I wanted to talk business with him, he was interested and that we should meet.

I called Rodolfo Castillo, who was my chauffeur at the time, and told him that I wanted him to drive me to Gibara on a quick trip. He told me he would love to go. I then called my friend and assistant, Engineer Horacio Nuñez de Villavicencio, and shared my plans with him. He immediately agreed to accompany me to help me assess the potential of the kaolin clay mountains. Finally, I called Irene Martinez, a lovely young lady I was seeing and invited her to come along for the trip. She was delighted, having never traveled to that area before.

I told Rodolfo to prepare my 1958 Edsel, 4-door sedan, and be ready to leave for Gibara at daybreak. And so, we embarked on a ten to eleven-hour trip stopping only to eat or gas up. I confess that it never entered my mind that this was a dangerous trip. It was early in October 1958, less than a month before the general elections that were going to occur on November 3rd. 1958.

We were going into enemy territory. If by chance, some rebel contingency stopped us, I would have probably been shot on the spot, considering that I was a running congressional candidate for the Democratic Party and part of the Government Coalition, therefore an official enemy of the rebel initiative. But in fact, this did not happen. Instead, when we were already in Oriente Province, close to Gibara, we passed a critical army post at high speed, and a patrol ordered us to stop. Floodlights turned night into day, and a group of army soldiers and officers quickly surrounded us with machine guns. They searched the car and asked us to go inside. There was no problem because I quickly identified myself. Everyone was very cordial to us as of the moment that they became aware of my identity. However, they were very much surprised that I had chosen to go on such a dangerous trip. I sat down to talk to the officer in charge and asked him a few questions. He was very straightforward.

I learned for the first time that the Cuban army did not train for counterguerrilla warfare. The role of the military was fundamentally to protect the population from sporadic rebel guerrilla attacks. Oriente had around fifteen thousand well-armed soldiers[44] guarding the cities, towns, and villages of the Province. The role of

---

[44] According to First Lieutenant Hugo Sueiro, the Cuban Army was armed at a level equivalent to the American Army in the Second World War. The rifles they were using were Springfield's. In the last year 1958 one single battalion started exercising some proactive guerrilla tactics. They were also armed to the level of the United States Army during the war in Korea. They had M1 Garand rifles. This battalion was under the command or Colonel Angel Sanchez Mosquera, who fought bravely against the communist rebels until he was wounded in battle.

the army was principally managerial and defensive. There was not a proactive sector of the military in the offensive. No commandos or special forces were going after the rebels that holed up in the Sierra Maestra Mountains. Commandos did not exist at the time in Cuba. This discovery left me speechless. It began to answer the question as to why Fidel and his rebels had not been wiped out and were able to survive since the landing of the Granma on December 2nd, 1956 as well as in October 1958, the day I drove to Gibara. Fidel and his rebels had managed to survive and increment their numbers without any severe interruptions for almost two years. But, in those two years, he had only managed to put together just under five hundred guerrilla fighters. That was the totality of his forces in the Sierra Maestra. The guerrilla activity was mostly sporadic attacks on small towns or villages throughout the Sierra Maestra protected by a small group of soldiers or rural guards. They would hit these places, create as much turmoil as possible, and immediately pull back and return to their hideouts. It was mostly a terroristic strategy; hit and retreat with the least casualties possible. There were no significant battles. They never happened. The crucial actions that later, when in power, they talked about, was a figment of their imagination. It was merely the systematic propagandistic effort of the communist apparatus to reshape history to their convenience. It had nothing to do with what happened in the mountains of Oriente Province.

I went on to Gibara, arriving late at night. We slept in Gibara and met the landowner early the next morning. We drove to his property, and indeed we discovered that it fulfilled our needs. But by then, I realized that it was impossible to put the deal together under the present military-political conditions. I did not tell him this, but after he clarified what he wanted, I said that we would study his conditions. I told him that I had to get back to Havana, and we left at that very moment. But instead of driving directly back to Havana, I told Rodolfo to go to Varadero Beach in the Province of Matanzas, where I would invite the group to a couple of days of relaxation. We drove back without any impediment, and the group was thrilled to stay and relax at a Varadero hotel next to the water. Everyone had a wonderful time in Varadero, and the food was delicious, mostly fresh seafood. I decided to dedicate all of my time to lovely Irene, who preferred that we stay in our room all the time, which meant that we did not even have the desire to take a swim in the transparent blue waters of that magnificent beach, although we remained there for three days.

Leaflets decorated Havana's streets: Fernando Pruna Bertot had never posed with so much solemnity for a photograph. His elegant tie and his white handkerchief highlighted his dark suit. His look was thoughtful, but, thanks to a natural frowning, it was impossible to overlook how the seducer poured through his skin. After all, running for elections was, somehow, like going to a dance and drawing the weapons of charm. Meeting the star of the show in which even some hidden actors perform wearing a mask.

"I will call Denise and Hélène. They will be proud of me," Fernando thought.

November 3ʳᵈ, 1958

Fulgencio Batista, dressed in white and displaying countless smiles for photographers, next to Marta, his wife, deposited their votes in the ballot box. The voting conducted in the middle of certain tension caused by the threats of the rebels. For security, the electoral offices guarded by the army. The Party of the General had, once again, won the election. Batista's mandate would expire on February 24ᵗʰ, 1959 and then, he would hand the presidency to Andrés Rivero Agüero, who had just won over his two main adversaries: Márquez Sterling and former president Grau San Martín. The losers immediately challenged the results. Grau San Martín claimed Rivero's victory had been

DEMOCRATA
REPRESENTANTE
15
Fernando Pruna Bertot
PANCHIN - Gobernador
RIVERO AGUERO - GODOY

due to fraudulent scrutiny. He signed a petition to have the elections annulled. Marques Sterling also denounced the corrupt elections. Fidel Castro spoke about the "electoral farce," and his partisans assured and complained of ballot boxes stuffed with false ballots.

That was all that the rebels needed to fuel their anger and justify their struggle. Overall, the people felt cheated. Batista allowed his collaborators to manipulate the elections, and the result was the defeat of the opposition. This permissiveness was the kiss of death for Batista. His political blindness rather than his political myopia doubtlessly confirmed. The elections were neither impartial nor honest, and for the People of Cuba, this turned out to be unforgivable. However, what the People of Cuba were still not aware of was that the results of this elections would radically change Cuban history in the most negative way for a long and unforeseeable future.

Fernando celebrated his twenty-third birthday with a golden Real Estate contract with the American millionaire E.M. Loew and with a probable seat in Congress won in the elections. In a few weeks, there will be much to celebrate for the New Year. Fernando will be a flaming and worthy congressional representative in Havana. The official scrutiny not yet tabulated, yet there were pretty accurate estimates off the record. Of course, there was no doubt about the presidency. Andrés Rivero Agüero elected President of the Republic of Cuba with a narrow victory. But there was nothing precise confirming other candidates. Given the legal opposition's challenge to the election results and other formal complaints and accusations, the officially confirmed results unknown until early January of the next year.

Congratulations, Dr. Pruna, said while clinking his glass with the young man's. You are now a Congressman, the youngest in Cuban history, to obtain a seat. Spindola called me to congratulate you.

He said Panchín had called him to confirm your success. What else can I tell you, my son?"

"Father, your congratulations are premature. We still don't know who has been officially elected, except for the President and some senators. And that only because the victory has been significant. We should accept it; these elections have been a farce. They are a mockery to the People of Cuba. I confess I regret having taken part at this moment, and I never thought Batista would be so shortsighted as to allow this electoral comedy to happen."

Fernando was disturbed. His apparent victory didn't make him as happy as he had expected. And it made sense since he understood that the triumph of the pro-government candidates had been one of Batista's biggest political mistakes. The electoral farce of November 3rd, 1958, opened the doors to the Castro brothers' Revolution. Even worse, to a communist totalitarian dictatorship. It was now a matter of time, of little time, for the curtains of darkness to fall on the country: the dice cast — political damage of incalculable proportions challenging to gauge at the moment.

Fernando immediately understood that his presumed electoral triumph was fleeting and that it would never come true because he envisioned that Batista's government wouldn't stand much longer. Deep in his heart, he instinctively perceived, with dreadful certainty, that there would never be a swearing-in in February of 1959.

The year was coming to an end. Fernando received an unexpected phone call from Solange.

"I am in Havana at the National Hotel. Will I be able to see you?"

"What a surprise, of course, you will see me. Tell me, are you alright? I have many things to tell you. When shall we meet? It has been an exceptionally long absence."

"Yes, much too long. Soon, very soon, please."

"Alright, call me when you are ready to see me. I am only a couple of blocks away. We'll take a walk on the beach or whatever you want to do. Chao."

Yes, 1959 would be, by force, a year of expectations. Would it be the year of political, social, and economic success? Of love success? Solange and Fernando wished each other all the happiness in the world. She was stunning and luminous, like in magazine pictures. They both felt well; they walked and talked, without doing anything compromising, though they indeed wanted to. Merry Christmas! Happy and prosperous New Year!

In the same instant, a sinister Santa Claus dressed in red and a black beard decided to wish Fulgencio Batista a Merry Christmas, but in his way. On December 25th, 1958, after an offensive attack that had been corruptly purchased by the rebels, Cuba, the island, was, geographically, almost split into two parts.

14

FACTS AND EVIDENCE

"Facts are stubborn things; and whatever may be our wishes, our inclinations, or the dictates of our passions, they cannot alter the state of facts and evidence." – JOHN ADAMS[45]

The fragility of Truth

"Twenty thousand dead is the tragic balance of Batista's regime."

The Cuban Revolution began with a blatant lie. Colonel Ramon Barquín, a highly respected Cuban military historian, hostile to Batista, affirms that the casualties in the insurrectionary process against the Batista government (July 26, 1953 – January 1, 1959) were a total of 2,495, of which 968 belonged to the Armed Forces and 1,527 to the opposition side. Of the latter, most of the fallen corresponded to the clandestine cells of the different revolutionary movements. It means that Fidel's guerrilla losses in the Sierra Maestra were insignificant compared to the deaths suffered by the Frank Pais' clandestine organization in Oriente Province or the University Student Directory[46] underground movement led by Jose Antonio Echeverria in Havana. Various reliable sources of information from different Cuban parties and organizations agree and confirm these statistics.

---

[45] **John Adams** (October 30, 1735[a] – July 4, 1826) was an American statesman, attorney, diplomat, writer, and Founding Father who served as the second president of the United States, from 1797 to 1801.
[46] Directorio Estudiantil Universitario (D.E.U.)

Accepting that these numbers are correct, and we should, 2,495 casualties in a civil struggle that lasted almost five and a half years, does not rise to a level of catastrophic bloodshed when compared to other extreme historical statistics. Yet, all the political factions involved in the battle and, above all, career mid-level United States officials in the State Department made it sound as if the world was coming to an end. It is essential to digest this information to understand the years of rebellion better. What took place from the year 1953 to 1959 during the presidency of Fulgencio Batista in Cuba.

Deceitful Publications

Miguel Angel Quevedo y de la Lastra (July 31, 1908 – August 12, 1969) was the **owner, publisher**, and editor of **Bohemia Magazine**. He inherited Bohemia from his father, who founded the publication in 1908, the most popular news-weekly of its day in Cuba and Latin America, known for its political journalism and editorial writing.

Mr. Quevedo was a firm believer and admirer of Fidel Castro. Under his direction, Bohemia Magazine did everything in its power to further the interest of the Cuban Revolution, and Fidel Castro before and after the Castro brothers gained control. In many cases, the magazine's partisan articles disregarded the truth. Such was the case when, on January 1959, excited over the fall of Batista; they published the deceitful headline with a long drawn article worshipping the Revolution and accusing Batista of all sort of atrocities:

"Twenty thousand dead is the tragic balance of Batista's regime."

Bohemia Magazine, Year 51, Number 2, January 11, 1959, page 190-210

It was a shameless lie published by Bohemia Magazine.

Quevedo, like a vast majority of the Cuban population, believed that Fidel Castro was an ardent defender of the 1940 Cuban Constitution and, therefore, a firm believer in the principles of a democratic government duly elected by the people and a progressive capitalist state with a deep concern for expected social justice. Fidel Castro masterfully masked his intentions of converting Cuba into a Soviet Union satellite with a communist system of Government. As a result, a significant number of rebels, some of very high standing and merits, eventually turned against him and accused Fidel of having betrayed the Revolution. This sense of betrayal was, to a great extent, ill-founded. In Fidel's previous speeches, one could quickly identify his socialistic inclinations, not to mention that his two top lieutenants, his brother, Raul Castro, and the Argentinian Ernesto "Che" Guevara, openly identified themselves as communists. Indeed, the Ambassador of the United States in Cuba in 1958, Earl E. T. Smith[47], as well as the director of the CIA for the Caribbean, were quite sure that, unequivocally, Fidel Castro was a communist and not merely a "fellow traveler." Furthermore, the BRAC[48] and the SIM[49], the two top intelligence agencies during the Batista presidency, proved, beyond the shadow of a doubt, that the Communists had deeply infiltrated the 26th of July Movement and that the principal leaders of the organization were communist, including Fidel Castro. The Central Intelligence Agency of the United States was aware.

Ironically, it took more than a year for Quevedo, who was not communist, to wake up to reality. Soon deception set in. He realized that Fidel Castro was a tyrant that wanted to convert

---

[47] The Fourth Floor by Earl E.T. Smith.
[48] BRAC – Buro Para Represión de las Actividades Comunistas.
[49] SIM – Servicio de Inteligencia Militar.

Cuba into a Communist State to perpetuate his power. His awareness came a bit too late. Quevedo sought political asylum in the Venezuelan embassy in Havana in 1960 and arrived in Miami on September 7, 1960. Bohemia magazine was confiscated, without retribution, by the Communist Government of Cuba and all other newspapers, magazines, radio, and television stations in the entire country. All news and information were monopolized and controlled by the communist state. All stolen, not paid for. Sadly, before, and for a short time after the coming to power of the Revolution, many publishers, like Quevedo, as well as newspapermen and radio commentators, became, unwittingly, tools of the communist propaganda machine. They unintentionally helped Castro cut off their throats.

On August 12, 1969, Quevedo, a bankrupt, disillusioned, and broken man, committed suicide in Caracas, Venezuela. He shot himself in the right temple with a 38-caliber revolver.

About Cuba

In 1958 Cuba's population was 6,880,728 people, and the country geographically divided into 6 Provinces[50]. From west to east, the Provinces were Pinar del Rio, Havana, Matanzas, Las Villas, Camaguey, and Oriente. Cuba, officially the Republic of Cuba, is a country comprised of the island of Cuba as well as the Isle of Pines, presently named *Isla de la Juventud*, and several minor archipelagos. Cuba is in the northern Caribbean, where the Caribbean Sea, Gulf of Mexico, and the Atlantic Ocean meet. The country occupies an area of 42,426 square miles. To have a better idea, Cuba is approximately the same size as Florida in the United States. However, the conformation is different. It resembles an alligator, extending 760 miles West to East and about 55 miles North to South.

---

[50] Years later the communist government of Cuba geographically divided the country differently adding provinces, etc.

The Sierra Maestra

The Sierra Maestra is a ***mountain range*** that runs westward across the ***south*** of the old Oriente Province in southeast ***Cuba***, rising abruptly from the coast. The Sierra Maestra mountain range is approximately 150 miles long and 19 miles wide. Within the Sierra Maestra mountain range is the Pico Turquino Mountain, the tallest in Cuba with 6,476 feet.

In the Sierra Maestra, Fidel Castro hid and organized his guerrilla, named the July 26 *Movement*, after his failed attack on the Moncada Military Barracks on that same date in the year 1953.

After the Granma invasion's disastrous military landing on December 2, 1956, Fidel Castro took refuge in the Sierra Maestra mountain range with 17 other members of the landing raid that managed to survive out of a total of 82 invaders. The rest of the invaders were killed, apprehended, or deserted. It was here that he remained until December 31, 1958.

Fidel Castro remained in the Sierra Maestra for 759 days (about two years), and from there, he organized his rebel army, which according to pretty exact figures, numbered slightly less than 500 fighters[51]. It took Fidel two years to put together a five-hundred-man force.

The Sierra Maestra rebels did not fight any significant battles against the Constitutional Army. The strategy was to hit and run.

---

[51] Alfredo Mustelier Nuevo was a First Lieutenant in Fidel Castro's rebel army in the Sierra Maestra Mountains. When the revolution turned communist, he was arrested for counterrevolutionary activities and sentenced by the Revolutionary Court in La Cabaña Fortress (1969 Case Number 564) to 25 years in prison and forced labor. Fernando Pruna asked Mustelier how many men conformed the rebel army on December 31st 1958. His answer was: "I was in the Sierra Maestra until the last day of December 1958. We were only about five hundred men. In the Sierra Maestra and the Sierra Cristal we numbered just under 700 fighters."

They chose to attack weakly protected villages with few or no soldiers guarding it. They never held onto any territory. If they took over a town, they would give it back a few days later to the Cuban Armed forces. Their strategy was mostly terroristic. Bomb roads, bridges, and railroad lines to destroy the economy of the country. Burn sugar cane fields and destroy sown fields and crops to terrorize the landowners from which they demanded tributes in exchange for protection. If they paid, their farms would be left untouched. In this way, the rebels raised significant amounts of money. In the cities, several clandestine political organizations tried extremely hard to terrorize the general population by bombing public places, particularly movie houses, theatres, and other open businesses where people gathered. These terroristic acts mutilated dozens of guiltless bystanders and killed innocent people.

On the other hand, the Cuban Army, better known as the Constitutional Army, was more administrative than a proactive force. Its fundamental function was to protect cities, towns, and villages and vital business interests instead of actively going after the rebels in their hideouts. Unfortunately, it was also plagued by corruption, particularly on the part of individual high-ranking officers. There are credible reports that some officers sold arms to the rebels from their stockpile. Some senior officers considered the war to be a very lucrative business and therefore did not want the fight to end. When the situation got worse, some soldiers defected and joined the rebels. The demoralization of the constitutional army resulted from psychological factors that came to play in the relationship between the Cuban Government and the Government of the United States. It will be analyzed in-depth in the next few paragraphs.

The territory in which the rebels hid was not so vast as to make it impossible to discover their location. In fact, on more than one occasion, top army officers, having established precisely where the rebel's high command was, accepted significant bribes to direct their forces to the wrong area.

Corruption on the part of the Government weakens the very structure of its foundation. There is no doubt that President Batista enriched himself greatly through graft and corruption and his direct association with the American Mafia that ran the gambling business in the country. But it is also fair to say that corruption has historically been an endemic plague of Latin American politics, and Cuba was not an exception. Factually, Cuba's prior President, Carlos Prío Socarras, was able to amass a fortune of close to one hundred million dollars[52]. He was able to deposit his money in American Banks without any legal complications.

Jose Manuel Aleman, a minister of Education in Cuba during the Presidency of Ramon Graw San Martin, performed the most extreme case of corruption in Cuban history. Just the day before Grau left the administration[53], on October 9, 1948, José Manuel Alemán personally entered the Ministry of Finance and stole 147,000,000 pesos in cash (the Cuban currency then had parity with the dollar)[54]. To perform the robbery of the Treasury of the Cuban Republic, he used several trucks from the Ministry of Education and filled them with the cash. That same day, he chartered a plane bound for the United States and appeared at the Miami airport. When Customs officials searched his bags, they immediately detained him; they had found $ 19,000,000 in cash. But, Alemán, who was an old fox, knew perfectly well what he was doing. No law prohibited the entry of money from Cuba, whatever the amount, so, after informing Washington, the airport authorities released him.

---

[52] To get an idea of what would be the equivalent value today adjusted to inflation, the answer is 11 times more. Therefore, one hundred million converts into over a billion dollars today.

[53] The end of his term as President of Cuba.

[54] Adjusted for inflation, $1.00 in 1948 is equal to $10.98 in 2020.

In Cuba, the scandal was colossal. Senator Pelayo Cuervo put together Judicial Case number 82. He formally accused Aleman and his co-conspirators, ex-president Grau San Martin and his wife, Paulina Alsina, for the theft of the Republic Treasury. But, nearly two years passed, and none of the defendants were legally prosecuted. On July 22, 1950, all the evidence and documents gathered on the case stolen from the courthouse. A colossal robbery in the history of Cuba went unpunished. Corruption is the disease of Latin American governments.

Jose Miguel Aleman moved to Miami with his family, deposited his stolen millions in American Banks, and became a highly respected entrepreneur and investor. He remained in Miami until his death.

Alemán, for his part, stayed in Miami living life; although for a short time, since he would die of leukemia on March 24, 1950. When he died it was considered that his fortune was between 60 and 100 million dollars, and that almost all the money came from the colossal robbery carried out on the Treasury of the Republic of Cuba that he had been taking out of the country in various ways.

Elena Santeiro, his wife, inherited, in addition to a huge amount of cash, large investments in Cuba, Venezuela and Miami, including several of the most important hotels in Miami as well as the old Miami Stadium.

Ex Cuban President Carlos Prío used a significant part of his fortune to help overthrow Batista. He provided Fidel Castro with money, arms, and ammunition and men to join the rebel forces. These deliveries executed by private planes flown from Miami, Key West, Venezuela, Costa Rica, and other countries and landed in clandestine airfields within the Sierra Maestra. The flights, originating in the United States, were able to take off without a problem thanks to the U.S. Customs Department's tolerant eyes and the sympathy of the Caribbean Division of the State

Department. Prio's contributions to the rebel initiative were so significant that President Batista considered him his most dangerous adversary. In doing so, Batista underestimated the importance of Fidel Castro. It was one of Batista's grave mistakes. Prío was another extraordinary personality that was duped by Fidel Castro. It must have been a very bitter pill to swallow when he realized that Fidel was a communist tyrant and that all his efforts and money had only benefited the wrong person.

Carlos Prio returned to Cuba in 1959 after being exiled in Miami, Florida, since March 1952. He enthusiastically returned to his country with high hopes for the Cuban Revolution, at which time he supported Fidel Castro. Disenchanted, he broke with Castro, asked for political asylum, and went into exile once again in 1961. He lived in Miami, Florida, until he committed suicide at the age of 74 on April 5, 1977. A self-inflicted bullet wound from a 38-caliber pistol ended his life, a single shot to the heart. The motive for his suicide was never clearly explained.

Batista was able to retain power in Cuba as long as he did due to three fundamental reasons. First and most important was that Cuba enjoyed a robust economy. For as long as Batista governed the country, his economic policies highly benefited the people of Cuba, who were better off than at any other time in Cuba's history. In 1957 Cuba reached its best financial results ever, with a national income of 2,397 million[55] pesos. At the time, the peso was at parity with the U.S. Dollar[56]. In 1956, the United States Department of Commerce issued a report named "*Investment in Cuba*," which said, "*Cuban national income has reached levels that give the Cuban people one of the highest living standards in Latin America.*"

---

[55] As per figures compiled by the International Monetary Fund, May 1952, Vol XV, No 5.
[56] Adjusted for inflation, $1,000,000.00 in 1957 is equal to $9,310,652.17 in 2020.

The second reason Batista was able to hold on to power for as long as he did was that he pretty much had complete control of the armed forces and the National Police for most of his governing years. Having risen from its ranks, he enjoyed uncontested popularity and loyalty from the armed forces.

The third reason was that he had the backing of all the labor organizations and their leaders.

Cubans adored the United States before the Revolution.

It is of utmost importance to understand how the Cuban people felt about the United States of America only ninety miles from its shores.

Simply said, the Cuban people idolized the USA. They loved the American way of life and tried in every way to copy it and make it their own. American influence was everywhere in Cuba. Cubans only purchased cars made in the USA, openly imported to Cuba without any restrictions. Cubans loved to see American movies, shown in all the movie theatres scattered throughout the country. Cubans loved American music as much as they loved Cuban music. Most Cubans wanted to learn English as a second language. And the list goes on and on.

Before Castro, the United States was so important in the Cuban people's minds that the American Ambassador was regarded as the second most important personage in the country only after the President of Cuba. He was considered a symbol of power and friendship[58].

No one was more fanatic of the United States than the Cuban armed forces within the Cuban people. And rightly so. Cuba's armed forces organized as a replica of the U.S. armed forces.

---

[57] The Fourth Floor – Earl E.T. Smith, Ambassador of the United States in Cuba from 1957 to 1959.

The Cuban Army used the same uniform as those worn by the U.S. Army. They also used the same arms, the same planes, and the identical vehicles. The only difference was the modernity of the armament. Cuba was using World War II equipment in 1957.

Cuban army officers would pass courses and train in U.S. military installations. Cuban officers proudly manifested their admiration for both the U.S. armed forces and the United States government. Psychologically, this created a dependency on all things American. More like a younger sibling cherishes an older, stronger, and more developed brother. It was an extraordinarily firm reliance that could quickly and severely psychologically impact unexpected changes of behavior.

Cuba chose only one source from where to receive arms, ammunition, equipment, and spare parts. The choice was the Government of the United States. The Cuban Government never prepared for a possible break in the relationship between the two countries. It did not enter their minds that the United States government could shut the door and block the importation of military hardware to defend itself from an internal foe. But this is precisely what happened.

In December 1770, John Adams, who was the second President of the United States but was also a lawyer, said the following words in one of his well known legal defenses. What he said is of such significance for what I will detail that I must quote it.

"Facts are stubborn things; and whatever may be our wishes, our inclinations, or the dictates of our passions, they cannot alter the state of facts and evidence."

Here are the Facts

In the years 1957 and 1958, most United States government officials, in particular career officers, that ran what was known as The Fourth Floor of the State Department, where the Caribbean

Division functioned, had a keen interest in overthrowing the Batista Government. They disapproved of a rightist dictator.

William Weiland, Director of the Office of Caribbean and Mexican Affairs of the State Department (MID Section), firmly believed that Fidel Castro would bring a solution to the "Cuban Problem" if he came into power. With the assistance of John Topping, head of the American Embassy's (in Cuba) political division, they intended to present a document to the State Department that predicted the imminent fall of Batista's Government. Such criteria held by the State Department's career officers were in stark contrast to Ambassador Smith's perspective. It seems that there is often conflict between the beliefs of career officers and appointed officers. These conflictive points of view plagued Ambassador Smith during his entire tenure as Mission Head in Cuba.

Roy Richard "Dick" Rubottom Jr. (February 13, 1912 – December 6, 2010) was a United States diplomat, most notable for being Assistant Secretary of State for Inter American Affairs from 1957 to 1960, a post in which he played a significant role in engineering the United States' response to the Fidel Castro and the Cuban Communist Revolution. In 1957, 1958 and 1959, Rubottom believed that Fidel Castro was not a communist, and through his policies, he did everything possible to overthrow the Batista Government. As late as 1959, when Fidel came into power, the State Department greeted Castro as a "Distinguished Leader." It took Rubottom until the year 1960 to recognize his error, at which time, frustrated by his political blindness and anger, he wanted Castro assassinated. But, of course, it was too late by then. Cuba soon became a loyal member of the Soviet Block.

But it was worse than that, because secretary Rubottom christened Herbert Mathews, the socialist newspaperman of the New York Times, as an "expert" in Cuban affairs. Having Mathews as a political advisor to the Fourth Floor of the State Department gives us an idea of how far this section erred in the department's Cuban policy.

Figure 34   Richard "Dick" Rubottom Jr.

Fidel Castro got his job through the New York Times

We must also include as leverage of enormous influence the progressive press in the United States. On Sunday, February 24, 1957, the New York Times published Herbert Mathew's first vast interview with Fidel Castro in the Sierra Maestra mountains. The title was, *"CUBAN REBEL IS VISITED IN HIDEOUT, Castro Is Still Alive and Still Fighting in the Mountains."* It was the first of three leading articles published by the New York Times and authored by Herbert Mathews. All three extensive articles, written in-depth, with meticulous descriptions and detailed narrative. The pieces detailed with such eloquence and conviction that they converted Fidel Castro into a brave and heroic figure with a profound sense of social justice. Mathews described Fidel Castro as "the Robin Hood of the Sierra Maestra." They also made Fulgencio Batista appear to be a murderous tyrant. Students of history have honestly evaluated the importance of these three articles; the significance of these articles indeed affirmed by students of history. They converted Fidel Castro into an international political personality.

In time humor appeared and inserted the description referring to the effectiveness of The New York Times classified section, in a colorful slogan: "Fidel Castro got his job through the New York Times." But far from being funny, it is a historical tragedy that an eloquent reporter could have had such an impact in helping bring to power a communist tyrant. Unfortunately, the New York Times, the Chicago Tribune, and other vital newspapers in the United States, acted in utter disregard of the truth. They printed stories favoring Castro, and both publications cast their responsibility to the winds and published unwarranted articles about the political situation in Cuba. These articles had the effect of making Castro a hero and helped him gather more and more strength. Only after these and multiple other U.S. publications in 1957 started to print distorted stories slanted in favor of the Cuban Revolution and denigrating the Batista government, Fidel Castro's movement began to grow in size and strength. There is no doubt that effective advertising works. The American press sold Fidel to the people of America and had the ripple effect of selling Fidel to the people of Cuba.

It was not only the press that helped bring Castro to power in Cuba. Jack Paar, a cynical, spontaneous and bright broadcaster whose "The Tonight Show" and "The Jack Paar Program" pioneered the late-night television talk show in the 1950s and early 1960s was a great admirer of Fidel Castro and publicly expressed his admiration for Señor Castro, whom he considered a heroic freedom fighter. He took his camera crews to Cuba to interview Fidel Castro. Mr. Paar, a former comedian, actor, and fill-in host for a mentor, Jack Benny, returned to America as one of Castro's prominent admirers. A skilled improviser and interviewer, he amassed an audience of millions in the United States. He was very influential.

Edward Vincent Sullivan (September 28, 1901 – October 13, 1974) was an American television personality, impresario, sports and entertainment reporter, and syndicated columnist for the New York Daily News and the Chicago Tribune New York News Syndicate. He is principally remembered as the creator and host of the television variety program *The Toast of the Town*, later popularly—and, eventually, officially—renamed The Ed Sullivan Show. Broadcast for 23 years from 1948 to 1971, and it set a record as the longest-running variety show in U.S. broadcast history. "It was, by almost any measure, the last great T.V. show," said television critic David Hinckley. "It's one of our fondest, dearest pop culture memories."

In the New York Daily News dated January 12, 1959, only a few days after Fidel Castro came into power, Ed Sullivan published an article criticizing Earl Smith, the Ambassador of the United States

Figure 35 Fidel Castro acknowledges his gratefulness to Hubert Mathews

in Cuba. The latter had just resigned his post a few days earlier. I will quote the article.

"United States Ambassador to Cuba, Earl E. T. Smith, and his staff missed the boat completely. They swallowed Batista's propaganda, hook, line, and sinker. In Sunday's paper, the White House announced accepting Ambassador Smith's resignation. Our Ambassador should have listened to veteran foreign Correspondents in Latin America. Chicago Tribune's, Jules Dubois, begged Ambassador Smith not to allow the United States Military Commission to train Batista's fliers for bombing forays against the people of Cuba. Pointing out that Castro's bearded Army represented and expressed the deep feeling of the people of Cuba. Our Embassy in Havana ridiculed this interpretation, gave the green light to Batista's bombing of the populace. If the State Department instructed the United States biggies all over the world to contact American foreign correspondents on the scene, get the benefit of their man-in-the-scene street-savvy, we would be spared incidents such as the fiasco in Cuba."

For a man of such enormous public influence like Ed Sullivan to have written such an erroneous article is an embarrassment and a danger to the security of the United States of America. There is no doubt that Earl E.T. Smith was an anticommunist, but he was not necessarily a Batista sympathizer. He did an excellent job as Ambassador to Cuba. Smith tried to be as neutral as possible in his relationship with the Cuban President following the U.S. policy of nonintervention. Despite his position, he could not greatly influence U.S. policy regarding Cuba, which was dictated directly from the Fourth Floor of the State Department.

In the article, Ed Sullivan recommends that foreign correspondents like Jules Dubois should advise the State Department. This recommendation based on his ignorance of Cuban political affairs. Jules Dubois was a distinguished well know newspaperman who profoundly hated Batista and who, during the years of rebellion, tried extremely hard to help the Castro initiative. He, too, passionately believed that Castro was not a communist. On the contrary, as late as 1959, Dubois thought Castro was about to debug the rebel army of communist influence. Of course, he was dead wrong, subjective in his analysis of Fidel Castro and the Cuban Revolution. Dead wrong and ill-informed because Batista never bombed any Cuban city or populace. Simply said, he was misinformed and had no idea of what was going on.

As a result of these highly motivated individuals who thought they knew who Fidel Castro was and who Batista was, the U.S. government, through the State Department, started to put in practice an overly aggressive policy to squeeze Batista out of power. The procedure was a comprehensive embargo applied to the Government of Cuba.

Foreign policy toward Cuba was dictated by the U.S. officers in charge of the Fourth Floor of the State Department. The belief that the policy toward Cuba was that of neutrality and nonintervention in the affairs of another sovereign country is false, as you will be able to judge based on the following legal actions taken by the U.S. government. These measures put into effect step by step, starting almost two years before Batista was finally ousted.

The Arms Embargo or Blockade of March 1958

Here is the list of the legal measures that were executed by the United States Government on March 14, 1958[58].

- Total suspension of the sale of arms and ammunition to the Government of Cuba.
- Refusal to honor outstanding and prepaid orders for weapons from the Cuban Government.

---

[58] Note: The following list was almost textually replicated from the book named "The Fourth Floor", written by Earl E. T. Smith (July 8, 1903– February 15, 1991) a United States Diplomat, ambassador to Cuba from 1957 to 1959. The validity of the source is self-eloquent.

- Total suspension of shipments of all replacement parts, as well as combat equipment, to the Government of Cuba.
- Advising the Department of Defense not to ship to the Government of Cuba controversial military equipment.
- Not fulfilling the U.S. commitment to deliver twenty armored vehicles to the Cuban Government. (*This was a prepaid order*)
- Not living up to the U.S. promise to deliver fifteen training planes to the Government of Cuba. (*This was a prepaid order*)
- On March 14, 1958, the U.S. State Department issued an order suspending a shipment of 1,950 Garant rifles which had been purchased and paid by the Cuban Government and were on the docks ready for delivery by boat to Cuba.
- Issuing public statements that hurt the Government of Cuba and helped the rebel cause. (*Publicizing all the before mentioned measures taken by the U.S. government.*)
- Intervention by innuendo. (*Persuading other governments not to sell arms to the Cuban Government.*)
- Refusing to permit military service officers, attached to the Military Assistance Advisory Groups, to carry out fully their functions as prescribed under the Hemispheric Military Assistance Program. (*Playing down all activities which could be deemed offensive to the revolutionaries.*)
- Bringing pressure to bear on the Government of Cuba by consistently calling its attention the violations of the Military Defense Assistance Program with Cuba, which stated that the use of military equipment for any other purpose than hemispheric defense must have prior consent of the United States.
- Bringing pressure to bear on the Government of Cuba by stating repeatedly that the infantry battalion, which had been equipped through the Military Defense Assistance Program, was actively engaged in suppressing the rebellion in Oriente Province and then attempting to force the Government of

Cuba to break up and retire from active service the infantry battalion.

- Requesting the Government of Cuba to disengage all the Military Assistant Program equipped and trained personnel from the combat area.
- Embarrassing the Government of Cuba by delivering a formal note in March 1958 bringing these matters to their attention and requesting a report.
- Not bringing sufficient pressure to bear on the Justice Department to enforce U.S. neutrality laws.
- Permitting Dr. Carlos Prio Socarras and his supporters to violate U.S. neutrality laws. (*Batista was convinced that Dr. Prio and his agents were the primary sources of supply of arms, ammunition, and bodies to the Sierra Maestra.*)
- Asking the Immigration Department to be lenient on certain Cuban revolutionary exiles and permitting them to prolong their visits in the United States.
- Maintaining friendly contacts with the representatives of the revolutionaries, thereby giving sympathetic audience and comfort to those who were openly advocating the overthrow of the Government of Cuba.
- Permitting Castro sympathizers and supporters in the United States to form groups and organizations engaged in fundraising and overt propaganda activities.
- Embarrassing the Government of Cuba by instructing Earl Smith, the U.S. Ambassador to Cuba, to obtain assurances that the Government of Cuba would not bomb Cuban cities where rebels were situated, with American Military Assistance Programs bombs using napalm bombs.
- Maintaining close contact with Herbert Mathews, of the New York Times, which gave the impression by his editorial conduct of advocating Batista's downfall. (*Mathews was a de facto advisor of the State Department on Cuban Affairs.*)

It is impossible not to understand or imagine the psychological impact that these measures, publicized by the media and the U.S. government, had first and foremost on the Cuban armed forces, the political organizations that opposed Batista and the ripple effect that it had on the general population of Cuba. These measures did more to overthrow Batista than the total rebel revolt that lasted two years in the mountains of Cuba and the overall relentless initiative of the underground movements.

Any military officer in Cuba informed of the measures taken by the United States Government could only conclude that the U.S. was systematically squeezing Batista to provoke his defeat and departure. It also meant that the U.S. government had already chosen sides, choosing the forces of the opposition as their choice to resolve the Cuban struggle. In plain language, the U.S. government wanted to replace Batista with Fidel Castro.

To the rebels in the mountains, it meant that they had the backing of the United States, that they tacitly wanted Batista to be defeated and to abandon power. As one can well understand, this is a morale boost of gigantic proportions to anyone opposing Batista. It also created confusion instability and uncertainty for those that might have sympathized with the Government.

The exiled community was morally lifted to new heights because of the lenient treatment that they were receiving from the U.S. government concerning their illegal revolutionary activities in the United States and the squeeze that obviously and overtly applied to all things Batista.

The eloquence of these measures sent a clear message to the general population of Cuba. The news was that the United States Government was doing everything possible to force

Batista out of power. Considering that the United States is the most powerful country in the world, the fact that they have chosen sides only means that Batista will soon have to relinquish power and abandon Cuba. A noticeably clear message of enormous importance at that particular time in Cuban history. If our powerful big brother in the north is taking these measures, it means, unequivocally, the end of Batista. It is only a matter of time.

15

THE LESSER OF TWO EVILS.

Lesser-evilism is the principle that when faced with selecting from two negative options, the least detrimental one should prevail.

Objectively, Batista did not help himself. Right-wing dictatorships did not have the level of sophistication in treating their opposition that the communist employed. That is giving repression a clean legal appearance when, in fact, that is not the case. Appearance makes all the difference.

A Fair Analysis of Two Different Systems

Our research focuses on an overview of two different systems, a critical observation from the fifties and sixties years perspective. This clarification is essential to know because, with time and experience, systems evolve to meet new requirements, consequently and therefore they suffer the transformational need to survive. It is the dynamic evolution of adjustments to changing reactions. Consequently, it is logical to understand that what was precisely so then, may not be the same today.

Repression during the Batista government worked this way: Initially, the Police detained those who broke the law, politically speaking, and presented the accused to the courts to be indicted and sentenced if found guilty. But because the process was political, many judges who privately opposed the Government simply released the prisoners. Many judges were sympathetic to the political opposition and were, therefore, partial in their judgments. This situation was very frustrating to the police force. They detained a person and presented evidence that proved that the person was guilty, and the judge proceeded to release this person. It created deep police frustration and grew to the point in which the Police decided to become both policemen and judges. Unfortunately, the formula produced extensive political damage.

Eventually, the Police became more aggressive in their interrogation methods, which led to different variations of torture. Then, when the Police finally came to believe that the prisoner indeed committed a serious crime, they were not willing to hand him over to a partial judge that would simply release him or give him a noticeably light sentence. In extreme cases, they killed the prisoner, and they got rid of the body as they saw fit.

Partisanship in politics at the level of civil revolt creates extreme fanatical divisions and fosters intense hate. This reality cannot be understated. The result of this division is quite terrifying. An extreme example of this barbarity took place in Argentina, in what was called the "Dirty War," between 1974 and 1983. The repressive police or military intelligence massively detained members of the opposition suspected of political crimes. They took these suspects, men, and women, to secret detention facilities for questioning. The interrogations included aggressive torture. Guilty or not guilty of political crimes, the methodology was so severe that they felt obligated to disappear them in what eventually became known as the "death flights," a practice initiated by the Military Government, usually after detention and torture. The prisoners were drugged into a stupor, loaded into an aircraft, stripped, and dropped into the freezing deep waters of the Atlantic Ocean to disappear forever.

Nothing like that ever happened in Cuba, but there is no doubt that the repressive groups of the Cuban Police did torture and kill some active members of the opposition that took part in bombings of movie houses, attempts to assassinate, or other terrorist political crimes. Often, they just left the dead body in the middle of a street or buried it in some unmarked tomb. Politically speaking, this has a disastrous effect on the population. A single assassination can be the source of amazingly effective propaganda against the executioner. It transcends and makes its way impacting the general community. If by chance, the Government still allows some freedom of the press, the randomly discovered bodies full of bullet holes photographed and the pictures published for all to see to demonstrate the criminal conduct of the repressive police groups and the murderous actions of the Government. But also, simultaneously, to instill fear on the population and bridle the initiative of the radical opposition.

In the last few years of the Batista government in Havana, the National Police Department kept at bay the underground revolutionary initiative by creating three independent repressive units within its structure. They were the Bureau of Investigations, led by Police Colonel Orlando Piedra Negueruela, the Anti-communist and Anti-subversive Unit, led by Lieutenant Colonel Estevan Ventura Novo, and a particular investigative unit of the Central Division of the Police Department, led by Police Colonel Conrado Carratalá Ugalde. These three units were supremely aggressive in the persecution of the revolutionary underground movement. Although they were very effective and efficient in their endeavor to counter the most subversive activity and terroristic acts from the streets of Havana, they were also rightly accused of committing police crimes. Their police methods included torture, beatings, and murder. These police excesses were criticized and condemned by the general population and, of course, by the rebellious opposition. There is no doubt that police brutality was one of the most critical factors that contributed to the disfavor, disapproval, and dislike of Fulgencio Batista.

Nevertheless, in the case of Cuba, this happened, but it was not a widespread daily occurrence. If the statistics published by Colonel Ramon Barquín are to be accepted, as they should be, the death of 1527 members of the opposition during a five-and-a-half-year struggle should be scrutinized more closely. What I mean by that is that these fatalities include the casualties that occurred in the following warlike confrontations:

- The Moncada Garrison Attack in Santiago de Cuba. (July 26, 1953)
- The landing invasion of the Granma in Oriente. (December 2, 1956)
- The attempt to kill President Batista at the Presidential Palace in Havana. (March 13, 1957)
- The attack on the Goicuría Garrison in Matanzas. (April 29, 1956)
- The two-year-long guerilla insurrection in the Sierra Maestra Mountains. (December 2, 1956 - December 31, 1958)
- The one and a half year-long guerrilla insurrection on the Sierra del Escambray Mountains. (March 13, 1957 – December 31, 1958)
- The six-year underground terrorist initiatives carried out by the Student Directory, the Authentic Movement, and the July 26 Movement throughout all of Cuba. (July 26, 1953 – January 1, 1959)

If you divide the number of fatalities by the duration of the conflict, and the seriousness of the outstanding events in reference, the equation result gives you a more realistic understanding of the intensity of the struggle and the casualties resulting from it.

The communists, as the Castro Revolution showed the world when it came into power, are more sophisticated and subtle in how they treat their opponents. They have a different approach to political crimes. First, they legalize the death sentence and choose the firing squad as the method to be employed in carrying out such a sentence. A revolutionary legal code of law immediately approved by decree and signed into law. Second, they set up military courts parallel to civil courts. An army court judges anything political. The investigation of a citizen detained for a political crime is handled solely by an army intelligence department. In the case of Cuba, the infamous G-2, a structure within the Ministry of the Interior. The inquiries are not limited by time to perform their duties. Military investigations can last indefinitely. There is no such thing as *Habeas Corpus*[59]. It means that they can continue to investigate the detainee endlessly until they get a confession.

During the investigation phase, generally speaking, they do not use physical torture. The communist does not need to do so. They do use highly sophisticated psychological torture. If the investigative body concludes that you are guilty of a political crime, proof or evidence is of relative value. Circumstantial evidence or innuendo are sufficient. When the investigation ends, the standard procedure is to send you to prison to wait for your trial. In the military jurisdiction, there is no such thing as a bond. You go to jail, and you stay in prison until you go to trial. A trial can take as long as they want it to take. You could go to trial immediately after the investigation concludes, or you can go to trial ten years later. They own your time. They have the legal authority to do whatever they want to do. There is no such thing as due process. The military court is also controlled by the Ministry of the Interior, which in turn responds to the highest level of Government. If it is a crucial case, Castro has the last word.

---

[59] Habeas corpus is a recourse in law through which a person can report an unlawful detention or imprisonment to a court and request that the court order the custodian of the person, usually a prison official, to bring the prisoner to court, to determine whether the detention is lawful.

In Military Revolutionary Trials, judges and prosecutors manage the trial, and they are all officers of the Interior Ministry. Officially, all defendants can have a defense lawyer. The defendant can privately hire the defense lawyer, or the court will appoint a lawyer at no cost. The function of a defense attorney is useless. If it is a private attorney, profoundly intimidated, he is usually terrified to defend the accused. Comically, some defense attorneys side with the prosecutor in the accusation. A private defense attorney clearly understands that if he exerts himself in his effort to defend an accused person, he can end up being investigated and possibly charged with a crime[60]. All trials are mock trials. The judges are previously instructed on what the verdict should be as well as the size of the sentence. The conviction and punishment always pre-ordered from above. There is rarely a sentence in which the defendant is found not guilty. The penalties are mostly draconian. If sentenced to death, the prisoner usually executed in a matter of hours. The corpse generally delivered to the family a day later if the family has requested it.

In some cases, if the body belonged to a well-known critical figure, the body is not returned. If they do not want to carry out the death sentence immediately, for whatever political reason, they can postpone the execution for as long as they see fit. I have seen dozens of cases, particularly relating to military personnel that belonged to the Batista government, whose death sentence, placed on hold, was postponed indefinitely. Some of these convicted prisoners died of old age in prison, still pending their execution.

A unique example was the case of Major Felipe "The Chinaman" Mirabal. Major Mirabal had been a top officer of the SIM,

---

[60] Dr. Jorge Bacallao, Fernando Pruna's attorney in the Pinar del Rio political case, was sentenced to three years in prison in a trumped case because of his zeal defending Pruna. He had to serve all three years.

the Military Intelligence Service during the Batista presidency. Brought before a revolutionary court, he was condemned to death by firing squad for certain alleged crimes. His sentence was never executed; he remained condemned to death until he died of old age after several decades of imprisonment. The rumored political reason for the postponement of the execution was that Raul Castro was his bastard son. The result of an extramarital affair between Lina Ruz (Fidel and Raul's mother) with Major Felipe Mirabal. The affair took place when Mirabal was the military commander of the area where the Castro family had their farm. He was called the Chinaman because of his slanted eyes, a trait shared by his alleged son, Raul Castro Ruz.

Those that knew Mirabal personally (like Fernando Pruna and hundreds of other political prisoners) could also attest to the tone of his voice, almost identical to that of his son, Raul Castro, having heard so many public speeches by the latter. A really amazing similarity, according to their observation.

However, the Ministry of the Interior can lift the hold on execution at any time without previous notice. At will, they can fetch the prisoner and take him before the firing squad.

Fernando Pruna was a political prisoner serving time in Gallery number 14 in la Cabaña Fortress with Elizardo Necolardes Rojas, when guards came for Necolardes on Monday, August 14, 1967. On that same day Necolardes was executed by a firing squad in La Cabaña Fortress Prison after having served seven years in prison. A ranking member of the "Masferrer Tigers", a paramilitary anti-Castro organization operating during Batista's government, he had been condemned to death in 1959 for "military crimes." He was shot seven years after he had been condemned.

The firing squad is the most effective terrorizing tool that the communist judicial system can wield.

News is published or unpublished in harmony with the interest of the State. The communist press is controlled and owned exclusively by the Government. Generally, the People don't know anything about arrests, convictions, or executions, unless the Government wants to give an example and publicizes it. A tremendous communist advantage, practically speaking, they believe that what the people do not know will not hurt them. The people lack the information to make a judgment on their Government.

The purpose of this lengthy explanation, comparing the way that a rightist dictatorship represses its opposition versus the methodology of a communist revolution, demonstrates the crudeness of one system and the sophistication of the other. The bottom line is giving the whole judicial process a clean exterior that encompasses an "apparent" legal process.

The U.S. Government has traditionally imposed its foreign policy on governments over which they have leverage. This foreign policy mirrors the human rights principles generally practiced by the American Government and embraced by the American people. Exporting the American way of life and customs to governments under siege is an almost impossible feat for said governments. To start, Comparing the U.S. government to countries in the Caribbean or Central or South America is like comparing apples and pears. It is an impossible comparison. In the case of Cuba during Batista's Government, the U.S. insisted on instituting Constitutional Rights as well as freedom of speech and freedom of the press. Although his Government was under siege, Batista tried very hard to appease the U.S. Government by easing restrictions on press releases and civil liberties. Eventually, he felt compelled to suspend these rights periodically because it weakened his capacity to govern. However, the fact that he instituted Constitutional Guarantees and free press for significant periods allowed for adverse publicity, mainly about political crimes committed. These publications traveled far around the world, and the United States was no exception. News of political crimes in Cuba published by the American press influenced government officials in the U.S. significantly. Strangely, anecdotal stories or photos of mutilated bodies resulting from bombs placed in cinemas or theatres by rebel terrorists still contributed negatively to the Batista government and not consequently to the perpetrators. Terrorist acts like the destruction of bridges and roads, or the burning of sugar fields reflected more negatively on the Government than on the insurrectionists. These types of publications deeply affected the perception of the U.S. Government regarding Cuba.

In this regard, the communist has no concern. The Communist Government monopolizes news and, therefore, only communicates what is harmonious to their policies. Besides, they don't give a damn about what the U.S. government thinks. The best examples that come to my mind were specific quotes and deeds attributed to the well-known comandante of the Revolution, Ernesto "Che" Guevara, who was one of the top commanders after Fidel Castro when the Revolution took power on January 1, 1959.

Published by "Dissident" on March 24, 2015: Forget due process. During the Cuban Revolution, Che condemned to death, many who had never been adequately charged or given a lawyer. The New York Times estimated that in the first two months of the Cuban Revolution, there were approximately 528 firing squad executions. The Black Book on Communism cites a total of 14,000 killings by the end of the 1960s. Che Guevara was quoted in 1962 by the editor of "Revolucíon", Carlos Franqui[61], as saying, "We executed many people by firing squad without

---

[61] Upon the success of the Cuban Revolution in 1959, Carlos Franqui was placed in charge of the rebellion's newspaper "Revolucion", which became an official government publication.

knowing if they were fully guilty. At times, the Revolution cannot stop to conduct much investigation."

Dissenters from the new regime, including unarmed civilians, were not tolerated. Che explained his approach to justice; thus: "We don't need proof to execute a man. We only need proof that it's necessary to execute him." He made no secret of his disdain for conventional legal standards, calling evidence and burden of proof "archaic bourgeois details."

In a speech before the United Nations in December of 1964, Che confirmed his Government's ruthless reputation, declaring, "Yes, we have executed, we are executing, and we will continue to execute."

Guevara's comments in a World Forum eloquently demonstrate his indifference, and therefore his Governments indifference to world opinion, particularly his irreverence of the U.S. Government.

Figure 36 A FIRING SQUAD IN ACTION IN THE SIERRA MAESTRA. PHOTO TAKEN BY OFFICER OF THE 26 OF JULY MOVEMENT UNDER ORDERS FROM CASTRO. CIRCA 1958. ORIENTE PROVINCE, CUBA.

16

CAUSE AND EFFECT

In essence, CAUSE is the thing that makes other things happen. EFFECT refers to what results. A more precise definition would be: CAUSE is the WHY something happened, and EFFECT is the WHAT happened. -Anonymous

The individual initiatives taken by some of Batista's most trusted commanding officers in the Cuban Armed Forces demonstrate the direct psychological effects of the United States Government's embargo on the Batista Government persuasively.

On December 24, 1958, General Francisco Tabernilla Dolz, Commander in Chief of the Cuban Armed Forces, accompanied by his son, General Carlos Tabernilla, Chief of the Cuban Air Force and General Alberto del Rio Chaviano[62], Military Chief of the Province of Las Villas, met with U.S. Ambassador Earl Smith at the United States Embassy building on Malecon Drive. The meeting was requested urgently by the Commander in Chief of the Cuban Armed Forces.

In this meeting, face to face with Ambassador Smith, the two other officers in another room, Tabernilla Dolz, described the Cuban military situation in the conflict with rebel forces, as tetric. He told the Ambassador that the Cuban soldiers had lost their fighting spirit and lacked arms and ammunition.

---

[62] Alberto del Rio Chaviano was a Colonle when the Attack of the Moncada Garrisson took place on July 26, 1953. Later he was promoted to the rank of General.

The real purpose of the meeting was to bounce possible timely solutions off the Ambassador before the Government collapsed into Castro's hands. He suggested the creation of a Military Junta composed of General Eulogio Cantillo, General Sosa Quesada, General Garcia Casares, and a representative from the Navy. He clarified that his motivation was to save Cuba from Castro and Communism. He wanted to give Batista safe convoy out of the country as well as to the top general staff of the Armed Forces and those strongly associated with the President.

General Tabernilla Dolz wanted to know if the U.S. Government would support his plan. Ambassador Smith told him that he would consult the State Department but that a response, if any, would go directly to Batista, because of diplomatic formalities and guidelines. The General would not receive any answer. It was a defeatist meeting on the part of the general, motivated by desperation and total lack of judgment. What Tabernilla Dolz did not know was that too many other activities of prime importance and significance had already taken place for the Ambassador to consider the General's concerns and suggested solutions seriously.

The extraordinary aspect of the meeting was the fact that General Tabernilla Dolz had dared to request and realize this meeting without communicating it to President Batista. Batista did not have any clue that this meeting was going to take place, and it was only after the fact that he went to see Batista and told him what he had done.

The General dared to take this bold conspiratorial step only because his conviction was that the U.S. Government had decided to oust Batista.

While the meeting was going on, the Cuban Intelligence Service notified Batista of the meeting. Consequently, when Tabernilla went to see Batista and recount his meeting with the Ambassador, Batista was already aware.

Batista was furious and harshly reprimanded the General. He seriously considered more drastic measures, but coldly evaluating the current Cuban situation, he just took immediate steps to remove most of General Tabernilla's authority. Prudence dictated softer actions of castigation. Although at first, he had considered demoting and arresting General Francisco Tabernilla Dolz.

The President was no fool. He was keenly aware of significant Army desertions. Informed that the Army's will to resist was waning, Batista was continually evaluating his crisis. The President was conscious that his Government was unraveling. The mere fact that his close friend and highest-ranked General had secretly met with the Ambassador of the United States behind his back amounted to treason and was a clear sign that the General felt defeated, and their cause gone astray.

The day after the meeting, General Alberto del Rio Chaviano deserted. He flew to the Dominican Republic, where he asked for asylum.

I cannot help wondering what Fidel Castro would have done if his top General had done something similar to what General Francisco Tabernilla Dolz had performed. I can only think of one response but I will allow the reader to come to their own conclusion.

What Ambassador Earl smith failed to tell General Tabernilla Dolz was that days before, on the evening of December 9, 1958, the State Department had sent a secret emissary to try to convince Batista to capitulate. The personal emissary was William D. Pawly. The meeting lasted three hours. The man that they sent had been a friend of Batista for thirty years, and therefore it was a meeting in which the participants were friends, trusted, and comfortable with each other. However, Pawly was forbidden to say to Batista that he was an official representative of the U.S. Government, which in fact, he was. This limitation placed on Pawly not to disclose his official role was ordered directly by Ray Rubotton at the last minute as if there was a change of plans about how to present the proposal to Batista. He probably wanted the initiative to fail.

William Pawly proposed as a solution the creation of a caretaker government or temporary Government, basically a Junta, composed of enemies of Batista, but also enemies of Fidel. The list included Colonel Barquin, Colonel Borbonnet, General Diaz Tamayo, and a civilian, Pepin Bosch, Chairman of the Bacardi Rum Company. For the formula to work, all had to be enemies of Batista and also enemies of Castro. This formula would frustrate the motive of the rebel movement. It was a feasible solution. It was also a clear demonstration on how the United States Government was applying direct pressure for Batista to resign.

Batista's Government would surrender, but Batista and his acolytes would be allowed to leave Cuba, and Batista could live in his home at Daytona Beach. They would enable Batista to live safely in the United States. The idea seemed appropriate to Batista and came very close to being accepted by the President of Cuba.

The only reason that the offer failed was that Mr. Pawly was restricted by Assistant Secretary of State Rubotton to say to Batista that if he agreed, it would have the recognition of the United States Government. Instead, Rubotton only allowed Pawly to tell Batista that if he accepted the offer, he, Pawly, would try to persuade the American Government to buy it. Because of the uncertainty of the proposal, Batista turned it down. However, the mere proposition was a clear message to Batista that the U.S. Government wanted him out. Becoming aware of what the United States Government wanted from him must have been a traumatic shock to the President that had always considered himself to be a faithful friend of the United States for several decades. The whole thing only meant one thing: the U.S. government was telling Batista that he must leave. He was no longer useful to the U.S. Government.

To the very end, Batista still believed that he had a standing chance to maneuver, politically speaking, due to the election of November 3, 1958, in which Andres Rivero Aguero was elected President. But Andres Rivero Aguero was never formally recognized by the United States government[64]. It never happened. The State Department refused. Surprisingly, Batista believed that the United States Government would officially recognize President Rivero Aguero. In retrospect, it seems naïve that Batista considered this formal recognition a possibility after the celebration of a rigged election in which the opposition lost. Carlos Marquez Sterling should have been the President-elect, but Batista denied him the chance. Possibly Batista purposely structured the elections to assure the protection of his worldly material interests as well as the heritage of his collaborators. In doing so, however, he accomplished quite the opposite, bringing to power the rebel movement and his leader, Fidel Castro. Batista had done a lot of political magic during his many years in power and had gotten away with it. This time, he failed.

Another thing that Ambassador Smith did not say to General Tabernilla Dolz was that he too had already had a grim meeting with Batista. On the night of December 17, 1958, the Ambassador of the United States in Cuba, Earl Smith, met with President Batista at his small private office adjacent to his library at his country estate, Finca Kukine. Present at the meeting, besides the President and the Ambassador, was Cuba's Foreign Minister, Dr. Gonzalo Guell, and no one else. The meeting lasted two hours and thirty-five minutes.

---

[63] It is ironical that withing 10 days of the Revolution coming into power, the United States government formally recognized the Revolutionary Government of Fidel Castro.

At this meeting, after the usual niceties, the Ambassador told Batista, in no uncertain terms, that the U.S. government felt that Batista had lost effective control of the situation. He continued to say to the President that the State Department of the U.S. would view with skepticism any plan or intention on his part to remain in Cuba indefinitely. Translating the diplomatic language into plain, straightforward English, the Ambassador had just told Batista that the United States Government was telling him that it was time for him to capitulate and leave Cuba accordingly. Ambassador Smith's visit was the second time that the U.S. government was telling Batista to go[64].

Regarding the possibility of Batista residing in Daytona, Florida, where he owned a house, after leaving Cuba, Ambassador Smith diplomatically suggested that he should go and live in Spain for the foreseeable future. Plainly said, on this occasion, the United States Government denied Batista asylum in the United States territory.

In a cut and dry manner, the State Department accepted none of the proposed solutions presented by President Batista at this meeting. Some settlements had feasible potential if addressed promptly. Overcoming the limited options between bad and worse was achievable. A solution without Batista and Fidel Castro was workable. Still, it seems that Assistant Secretary of State, Roy Rubotton, had his mind set on bringing Fidel Castro to power and forcing Batista to capitulate. Perhaps by December 1958, it was much too late to put into motion any other workable solution.

The State Department systematically refused to lend support to any viable answer that would exclude the "dictator" as well as

---

[64] Chronology of the Cuban Revolution - COMPILED BY JUAN O. TAMAYO - NOVEMBER 20, 2008 01:11 PM, UPDATED MAY 08, 2019 01:44 PM - December 1958: U.S. Ambassador Earl T. Smith tells Batista the United States will not back his government or his successor's. He advises Batista to leave Cuba.

the "terrorist." The rationalization for the refusal fundamentally based on the United States' appearance of intervening in the internal affairs of Cuba. A lame excuse when considering that the United States Government indeed interfered in the internal affairs of Cuba when they formally asked Batista to capitulate and leave Cuba.

The blockade exercised by the United States Government against the Batista Government with all its multiple terms and conditions is an implicit intervention in the internal affairs of Cuba. There is no other way to look at it. The sad part is that they were all, possibly unwittingly, encouraging interventions on behalf of Fidel Castro.

In December 1958, the U.S. Government made a feeble attempt to strengthen the position of classic politicians opposed to both Batista and Castro, but that attempt failed to materialize. It seems that some U.S. Government officials started to understand that they could perhaps be facing the possibility of a communist government with the arrival of Fidel Castro. However, this realization came a bit too late. In fact, they had lost control of the whole Cuban affair.

We must understand that Roy Rubotton was not a communist sympathizer in any way. Neither was William Wieland or, for that matter, Dr. Milton Eisenhower[65], whom I mention now for the first time because he was also a significant influence in the Dwight D. Eisenhower administration. However, humans are fallible and therefore make mistakes. These three enormously influential people thought very much alike, and the latter was the brother of the President of the United States and acted as his advisor on Cuban affairs. All three were pseudo-liberals, which means that

---

[65] In 1956, Milton Eisenhower assumed the presidency of Johns Hopkins University.

they believed that their enemies were to the Right and never to the Left. These were the early believers of democratic socialism or socialism without communism. Because of this, they did everything possible to asphyxiate Batista's Government. They truly believed that Fidel Castro was the perfect man to govern Cuba.

We are all aware that it is not the first time, nor will it be the last time, that someone in power makes a terrible mistake. It is not that this person is good or evil but merely that the person is wrong in his judgment. We all know how difficult it is, in matters of religion and politics, to change a person's criteria, beliefs, understandings, feelings about a given topic, subject matter, or perspective. Of course, the result of any political decision is not necessarily immediately apparent. Only time and the natural evolution of events provide us with an objective answer. But even then, objectivity can be warped based on the consideration of different points of view, motivations, interests, and perspectives. Still, hindsight is 20/20. **Hindsight** is an understanding of a past event. When we look back on situations in the past, we see things clearly that were not clear to us at the time.

Despite Batista's harsh admonishment given to the older General Tabernilla, who everyone referred to as "Old Pancho", for his secret meeting with the United States Ambassador, the General, persisted in following a proactive initiative without the President's consent. To this effect, he called in General Eulogio Cantillo, in charge of all the Cuban military forces in the Province of Oriente and ordered him to prepare conditions to realize a meeting with Fidel Castro personally. The purpose of the meeting was to feel out what was on the rebel leader's mind and, at the same time, propose a plan to end the fighting.

General Francisco Tabernilla Dolz was 77 years old in 1958, and some people questioned his fitness to run the Cuban armed forces during such complicated circumstances. It was not only a question of age. Although he did graduate from the Cuban cadet military school as a young man, he never took any army continuing education programs to further his military career. His most significant merit was the fact that he was the first army officer to join and back Fulgencio Batista in the "Sargents Revolt" in 1933 when Batista ousted Carlos Manuel de Cespedes from the Presidency. Since then, he had been a loyal and unconditional "yes man" to Batista, and in return, the President eventually elevated him to the rank of Chief of the Joint Chiefs of Staff. The General was de facto the head of the Army, the Navy, and the Police. From his high military positions, he promoted the career of his three children - Francisco, Carlos, and Marcelo - to whom he conferred the most top ranks in the Cuban armed forces[66].

Rumors existed that the Tabernilla family had become very wealthy by smuggling all types of appliances into the country circumventing import duties. They made use of aircrafts owned by a private company. The company was one of the four existing commercial airlines in Cuba, with the business name of "Aerovías Q" and offices in Paseo del Prado No. 12. The principal owner was Fulgencio Batista, and the other minor shareholders were Francisco Tabernilla, aka Silito, with 8% of the shares and Julio Iglesias de la Torre with 7%. Silito organized the smuggling through the Columbia military airport, which he controlled militarily. The smuggled goods were mostly electrical appliances, which he later mainly sold through Alfredo Zaydén's store, located in Calzada and 14 in Vedado. Aerovías Q, founded on September 28, 1945, by Manuel Quevedo Jaureguízar, operated from Columbia Military Airport, using fuel, spare parts, and other supplies of military origin as the military chiefs used it to smuggle

---

[66] General Francisco Tabernilla Palmero was Chief of the Tank Regiment and Private Secretary of Fulgencio Batista. His brothers Carlos Tabernilla Palmero was Brigadier General and head of the Air Force of the constitutional Army, while Marcelo Tabernilla also held the rank of Lieutenant Colonel.

contraband. The company had national and international routes with Mexico, Haiti, and the United States, where the main one was Key West-Havana.

The Tabernilla Dolz proactive initiative to send General Eulogio Cantillo to meet with Fidel Castro was again a personal initiative done without the knowledge or consent of President Batista. This initiative is in itself a mind-boggling political mistake that Fidel logically interpreted subsequently, believing that it was the act of a desperate crumbling military structure looking for a raft on which to hang on before drowning. But there is much more to the story than meets the eye. Therefore, we must step back and look at all the factors to better understand the outcome.

On December 22, 1958, Colonel Florentino Rosell, Chief of the Army Corps of Engineer of the Cuban Army, who was secretly conspiring to overthrow Batista, met[67] with key figures of the underground rebel movement at a house in the Vedado section of Havana. Amongst those at the meeting were "Comandante" Echeverria and "Comandante" Diego, head of Action, and Sabotage for the July 26 Movement. Colonel Rosell was informing them of an impending military uprising due to take place at precisely 6:00 PM on Christmas Eve. He proposed that the rebels should join this uprising and together march to Havana and take over the Government. He wanted the rebels to join the rebellion and, in order to entice, them was ready to surrender a "fully equipped and crewed armored train" that was under his command, which would soon be on its way to the city of Santa Clara in Las Villas Province. The arms in this train would be distributed to the revolutionaries. If the joint uprising was successful in overthrowing the Batista Government, he proposed a Military-Civilian Junta to take over the Government made up of

---

[67] Winds of December by John Dorschner and Roberto Fabricio.

General Eulogio Cantillo, civilian Manuel Urrutia, Colonel Ramon Barquin, and two others to be chosen by Fidel Castro. At the end of the meeting, Colonel Rosell asked to have a meeting with either Fidel Castro or Comandante Ernesto Che Guevara.

Rosell emphasized in the meeting that General Eulogio Cantillo had his back and was an active member of the conspiracy. Additionally, he stated that his plan had the approval of the U.S. Government. In reality, General Eulogio Cantillo, a Cuban military officer of impeccable reputation, had no idea that this meeting was taking place and was unaware that Colonel Rosell was actively conspiring against the Batista Government. It was true that he had outlined his plan to C.I.A. operative, Jack Stewart, but only received mild encouragement from him and only a promise to pass the information to Washington. In short, Colonel Rosell was name dropping and stating facts that were not true.

Fidel Castro was at his new headquarters at the Central America sugar mill in Oriente Province when he received the report sent by "Comandante" Echeverria describing the meeting with Colonel Rosell in Vedado. When he read the details of the conspiracy and the terms offered by Colonel Rosell, he became outraged. Castro was not interested in any plot that included the United States Government and repudiated any thought of being a part of any Civilian-Military Junta. He interpreted the whole thing as a ploy to make him stop the war and usurp the Revolution from his control. However, Castro saw a potential benefit in the fact that General Eulogio Cantillo was a part of Rosell's military conspiracy. Cantillo had never committed any crimes, and he was in command of all the troops in Oriente, five hundred miles from Habana. Castro logically assumed that if General Cantillo was part of a military conspiracy to overthrow Batista, he, Fidel, could perhaps convince the General to join the rebels with his men in a united front. With this in mind, Fidel, therefore, gave a

Figure 37 General Eulogio A. Cantillo Porras

green light for a personal meeting with General Eulogio Cantillo to take place immediately.

In the meantime, General Eulogio Cantillo, following General Tabernilla's order to arrange a meeting with Castro, made contact with a Jesuit priest in Oriente named Francisco Guzman, whom he considered was a sympathizer of the July 26 Movement and could arrange a face to face meeting with Castro. Although General Cantillo thought it was odd that President Batista had not discussed with him Tabernilla's initiative to meet with Fidel, he took it for granted that the order given by the General had the President's tacit approval, which was not the case.

The priest acknowledged that he could arrange a meeting and promised to do so as rapidly as possible but asked Cantillo if there were any conditions to specify. Cantillo said that his only requirement was that if the meeting ended with an agreement, he would surrender his resignation and would end his military life. The moral impact of this meeting was so significant to the General that it determined and defined the end of his career. The General's academic life had been stellar. The first in his class with straight A ratings during the five years he spent in the Military Academy until graduation. The multiple top-level military courses that he took in the United States, courtesy of the Armed Forces. His spotless conduct as an officer of the Cuban Constitutional Armed Forces. His excellent performance as head of the Cuban Air Force. Resigning was like putting an end to his life, but he felt that this meeting rubbed against his moral grain and implicitly meant a defeat and disintegration of the Cuban Armed Forces.

It is important to remember that Castro assumed, based on communications from his underground movement in Havana, that Cantillo was actively conspiring against Batista. But it is equally important to understand that this was not the case. General Eulogio Cantillo Porras never conspired against Batista.

The meeting approved, Castro waited for the arrival of General Cantillo at the Central Oriente abandoned sugar mill. The reception committee included some of Fidel's closest associates at the time: Raul Castro, Celia Sanchez, Carlos Franqui, director of Radio Rebelde, Vilma Espin, Raul Chivas, and Father Guzman. Cantillo and his pilot, Captain Izquierdo, arrived in a Sikorski helicopter that landed at a designated spot marked by the rebels in the early morning of December 28, 1959[68].

A few minutes later, the meeting started with a long drawn out monologue by Fidel analyzing Cuban historical factors that he felt were relevant to the discussion. There was coffee served by Celia Sanchez and a gift of cigars and cognac from Cantillo to Fidel. The meeting appeared to be going smoothly, but in fact, Cantillo felt utterly out of place. His strictly military education and his career as a professional soldier had not prepared him in any way to face a savvy political veteran like Fidel Castro. He was like a fish out of water, uncertain how to proceed in such delicate negotiations. He did not have the training to cope with complex political arguments from a savvy rebel leader who was a lawyer by profession and who had a clear objective in the meeting. He was a soldier, not a politician.

Tabernilla had instructed Cantillo to present Fidel with the possibility of creating a civilian-military Junta to take over the Government, overthrow Batista and end the war. Cantillo suggested the idea of a civilian-military Junta to Fidel, but he did not dare mention that the initiative came from General Tabernilla. Fidel immediately turned down the idea. So, Cantillo, a disciplined man, calmly appeared to listen to the rebel leader in his unending dissertation. Uncomfortably, he quickly evaluated the rebel leader in front of him and realized the man had a

---

[68] *Winds of December* by by John Dorschner and Robert Fabricio.

dominant personality and that it would be almost impossible to come to any equitable agreement. He quickly understood that this meeting was a waste of time and that nothing positive would result.

At the same time, Fidel had a different interest, and he eventually showed his card. Fidel rightly concluded that if General Cantillo had come to meet him, it only meant that the Constitutional Army considered itself defeated. Therefore, he did not feel hard pressed to come to any agreement. Casto felt comfortable in his position of strength. He then bluntly proceeded to tell General Cantillo that he would not accept any type of a deal coming from General Tabernilla or Fulgencio Batista. Additionally, he made it very clear that he was not willing to take any suggestions or plans that came from the American Embassy. His anti-American position eloquently expressed in his rhetoric.

At this point in the meeting, General Cantillo understood that the initiative and motivation that led him to this meeting was a moot point. He also realized that Fidel's only objective in having the meeting was to see if he could convince the General to join him in the uprising that he was planning to execute at the beginning of the year. Because he believed that Cantillo was a conspirator desiring to overthrow Batista, his conclusion was perfectly logical. General Cantillo suddenly became aware of Fidel's motives and that it was necessary to improvise.

He did more than improvising; he lied by telling Fidel Castro that the military officers in charge of the Moncada Garrison in Santiago were aware of the purpose of the meeting that was taking place. He said to him that they had his back and were much in favor of ending the war. He further informed Fidel that he also had the backing of other top Army officers, like his brother Carlos Cantillo, head of the Army in the Province of Matanzas, as well as multiple officers at the Colombia Garrison in Havana. None of what he said to Fidel was true. He was just trying to leave the meeting amicably and gain some time to perform his duties as a loyal officer of the Constitutional Army.

Concentrating on Cantillo's military rank and position in Oriente and his command of the Moncada Garrison, Fidel told him that the Cuban Revolution would very much welcome an army uprising of the Moncada Garrison. He felt that it would be the right way for the Army to cleanse itself of all its past harmful criminal deeds that had degraded its image. If Batista did not give in to the uprising, then the soldiers of the Moncada Garrison, with all its military might of tanks and cannons, would join the revolutionary forces and together march to Havana to overthrow the Batista regime.

Without further contemplation, Fidel proposed in a definite manner that the uprising was to take place three days later, on Wednesday, December 31, 1959, at 3:00 PM. Cantillo nodded his acceptance. He felt that he did not have any other option but to accept the terms presented by Castro. However, he added that to comply, he would need to fly to Havana to inform his "fellow conspirators." Fidel did not like the idea of his going to Havana, but grudgingly, he accepted. Cantillo felt that he had found an out to his predicament.

In Fidel's mind, he felt that his agreement with General Cantillo was a clearly understood sworn agreement. The terms were straightforward.

- That there should not be a coup d'etat in Havana.
- That Fulgencio Batista is not helped to escape.
- That there be no contact with the United States Embassy in Havana.
- That the Moncada Garrison with all its officers, soldiers and military equipment would uprise and join the rebel forces on the specific set date and hour

Cantillo felt that by saying that his "fellow conspirators" in Havana had not agreed to the terms of the agreement, the deal would become null and void. If the agreement fell apart in Havana, it would not be a betrayal. His reasoning demonstrated that he completely misjudged Fidel Castro's personality.

The meeting lasted four and a half hours when General Cantillo finally stood up as a sign that he was ready to leave while he promised to get back in touch as soon as he talked to his "friends" in Havana.

Later, about two o'clock in the afternoon, when the Sikorsky helicopter landed at the parade ground of the Moncada Garrison, he was immediately confronted by his friend Colonel Martinez Suarez anxiously waiting for him to convey an urgent order directly from President Batista. The order was that he should not meet Fidel Casto under any circumstance. The messenger arrived too late. Fearful of interception, the President had decided to send the order personally, instead of a coded message. Batista did not anticipate that the meeting would take place so rapidly.

Before, on December 25, when General Cantillo flew to the Columbia Military Barracks in Havana, precisely when General Tabernilla gave him the final order to meet with Fidel, he was perplexed by the fact that President Batista had not seen him, as was usually the case. He, therefore, requested a meeting through formal military channels to meet with the President. Cantillo spoke directly to Batista's secretary, General "Silito" Tabernilla Palmero, to schedule the meeting. However, pressing military obligations in Oriente and a very tight schedule had forced him to fly back to the Moncada Barracks early on the morning of December 27 without seeing the President.

Although he believed that Batista must undoubtedly have been aware of the order that he had received to meet with Fidel, he was still puzzled that Batista had not discussed it with him. Before leaving for Oriente, he fortuitously met with his friend,

Lieutenant Colonel Jose Martinez Suarez, and confided him of his mission and his perplexity. He then asked Colonel Martinez Suarez to do his best to meet with President Batista and inform him of the meeting that he was about to have with Fidel Castro.

Concerned that the message to the President could fall into the wrong hands, the loyal and conscientious friend, Colonel Martinez Suarez, ingeniously looked for a way to meet with the President without using the military regulatory conduit. Instead, he contacted Dr. Antonio Lamas, married to the President's niece explaining the urgency of the case without disclosing the message but emphasizing the necessity. They, in turn, located Batista's oldest son, Ruben "Papo" Batista, who was having a late lunch at the Carmelo Restaurant in the Vedado section of Havana.

The Colonel still did not disclose the message that he had for the President, but Ruben Batista arranged an immediate meeting with the President. They left directly from the restaurant to meet the President at the Presidential Palace. Only to Batista, personally, did Colonel Martinez Suarez convey the message that General Cantillo had given him.

Angry and deeply frustrated by the message received, Batista did everything possible to rapidly convey to General Cantillo not to go to the meeting with Fidel Castro. He felt that if Cantillo were to meet with Fidel, it would be an eloquent message to Fidel that the Cuban Constitutional Armey was defeated. It was already late on December 27 that the meeting between the President and Martinez Suarez ended. It also coincided with a report to the President that Colonel Florentino Rosell had deserted[69]. Nevertheless, he ordered a military plane to be ready to take

---

[69] Colonel Florentino Rosell Leyva deserted and arrived in Miami by boat on December 26, 1958. Batista was not informed until one day later, which reflects the observation that the President was not being informed in a timely manner.

Colonel Martinez Suarez to Santiago de Cuba at six o'clock on the morning of December 28. The flight did not take off promptly because of mechanical issues but finally left and arrived in Oriente at about one o'clock in the afternoon.

A curious incident occurred in the early hours of the morning when Colonel Martinez Suarez received a call from "Pancho" Tabernilla's assistant that the General wanted to see him personally. The Colonel notified the request with a call to Ruben Batista, who, in turn, cleared it with the President. So, at two o'clock on the morning of December 28, Colonel Martinez Suarez met privately with General Francisco Tabernilla. The General asked the Colonel if he had heard anything about an order given to General Cantillo. The Colonel responded vaguely, "yes." To which the General then added to tell Cantillo to provide the order given more time; to delay it; no more an extended order, merely an implication.

When Colonel Martinez Suarez encountered General Cantillo just getting off the helicopter from the meeting with Fidel and was about to tell him about his conversation with Batista as well as Tasbernilla's counter order, General Eulogio Cantillo simply said: "Too late, too late."

Colonel Martinez Suarez itemized to General Cantillo every detail of the last days since the General had confided in him the message for the President. Cantillo could not understand why Batista had not put Tabernilla in jail immediately. Nothing made any sense to him anymore. He ordered the Colonel to go back to Havana directly and inform Batista that the order had arrived too late, and the meeting with Fidel had taken place. The Colonel headed to the airport to take the first commercial flight available to Havana. Cantillo told him that he would be flying back directly to the Columbia Military Airport later that same day.

Later, at approximately 9:00 PM. General Cantillo was landing on a C-47 twin-engine Army plane at the Columbia Military Garrison

Airport, where Colonel Martinez Suarez was already waiting for him. He was not to talk to any other officer before being taken directly to meet with President Batista, who was anxiously waiting for him at his country house, Kukine.

Half an hour later, he walked into Batista's private office, where the President awaited behind a small desk. The first item of the conversation was to elaborate on General Tabernilla's treacherous initiatives: the meeting with Earl Smith, Ambassador of the United States in Cuba, and the order given to Cantillo to meet with Fidel Castro to propose the creation of a temporal government or Junta. All done behind Batista's back. He told Cantillo that if he were to stay, he would feel obligated to imprison Tabernilla and even have him shot for treason. But the fact that he mentioned the phrase "If he were to stay" obviously meant that he was already seriously considering leaving.

Probably, when Batista met with Cantillo, the President was pretty much set to leaving the country and abandoning power. In very recent days, some Cuban civic organizations, including the Landowners Association, a compelling financial group with enormous clout in Cuba, had asked him formally to resign. The request was psychologically disheartening to the President because, for years, they had backed him unconditionally. The various treacherous manifestations of treason from some of his top officers and closest friends in the Cuban Army deeply affected him as well, confirming to him his effective loss of power and leadership.

On a personal level, his wife, Marta Fernandez Miranda, with whom he had four sons and a daughter[70], was continually asking

---

[70] (three sons and one daughter): Jorge Luis, Roberto Francisco, Fulgencio Jose and Marta Maluf Batista. Another son, Carlos Manuel, had died in 1969 of leukemia.

the President to resign and leave the country[71]. Her children occasionally harassed at the schools they attended, made her fearful and genuinely concerned for their safety. Ever since the attempt to assassinate Batista at the Presidential Palace on March 13, 1957, which came very close to succeeding, Marta Fernandez lived in constant fear that her husband could die at any moment at the hands of a rebel assassin and that her children were not above harm. This constant pressure from his wife must have been exasperating for the President and must have had a bearing on his decision to abandon Cuba.

Fulgencio Batista was only 57 years old in December 1958[72] but soon to turn 58 on January 16, 1959. He was still a relatively young, vivacious middle-aged healthy man with an extensive family. Besides his children with Marta Fernandez, he was previously married[73] to Elisa Godines y Gomez, with whom he had a son and two daughters. There is no doubt that he loved all of his family dearly and took good care of them. Besides, he had been able to amass a considerable fortune of several hundred million dollars during his many years in power. Most of this money was safely tucked away in foreign banks and investments outside of Cuba.

---

[71] Josefina Labrada, daughter of SIM officer Captain Arsenio Labrada, and a personal friend of Fernando Pruna was a very close friend of the Batista family, and conveyed to Fernando the enormous pressure that Marta Fernandez submitted to her husband in her passionate desire for him to resign the Presidency of Cuba and leave the country. Her deepest concern was the safety of her yourg children.

[72] Batista was born on January 16. 1901.

[73] Batista married Elisa Godinez y Gomez (1900–1993) on July 10, 1926. They had three children: Mirta Caridad (1927–2010), Elisa Aleida (born 1933), and Fulgencio Rubén Batista Godínez (1933–2007). By all accounts, she was devoted to him and their children throughout their marriage, and their daughter remembered them as a "happy, young couple" until their sudden divorce. Much to her surprise, he divorced her in October 1945 against her will in order to marry his longtime mistress, Marta Fernandez Miranda.

There is no exact estimate, but in today's dollars, for sure, he would rank as a billionaire[74]. His enormous wealth must have influenced his decision to abandon power. He had mostly been in a position of significant political power from 1933 to 1958, except when he went int exile (1944-1948). It is conceivable that he had become weary of the never-ending complications that are part and parcel of power—probably disillusioned by the ungratefulness he attributed to many friends and associates that had now turned against him or conspired against him.

Undoubtedly, the Batista of 1958 was no longer the hungry young, ambitious military Sargent of 1933. He was now a rich gentleman, a genuine bourgeois, giving preference to economic materialism and hedonism. Such a man no longer possesses a will to fight and to sacrifice. Risking his life for a new political or military adventure was no longer part of his plan. These traits, lost in time, led him to find a way out of the political complexity that he was facing. He was no longer up to the task.

Batista probably came to realize when it was too late that he was the creator of his predicament—imposing his will on an election (November 3, 1958) that could have avoided a catastrophic end by only allowing it to be honest, transparent and impartial. Militarily, he had surrounded himself appreciably with yes-men, cronies, and lackeys, men without professional military skills, with few significant exceptions, that were not willing or capable of sacrifice or true loyalty when things soured. And then there is the greed theory—corruption at multiple levels. Turning the rebellion

---

[74] There have been many estimates about Batista's wealth but it was probably about 300 million dollars. $300,000,000 in 1958 equals $2,714,514,084.51 in 2020, which would make him a billionaire in today's dollars. This estimate do not include multiple businesses, including a mayor sugar mill and plantation that Batista owned in Cuba and that were confiscated by the Communist Government.

into a profitable business by creating extraordinary defense expenditures, a way to milk money from the Government. These various reasons jointly created the perfect storm that eventually destroyed the Batista Government. A political phenomenon of such social complexity cannot result from one single explanation; it has multiple components.

Besides, topping the list, the United States Embargo, and the systematic opposition of the Caribbean Division of the U.S. State Department bent on ousting him from power.

On the night of December 28, 1958, while meeting with General Eulogio Cantillo, after the General detailed his meeting with Fidel Castro, the President said the following words to Cantillo,

"I am surrounded."
And minutes later:
"I am thinking of leaving."

Although General Cantillo did his best to convince him that from a strictly military perspective, all was far from lost, it was apparent that the President had already made up his mind.

Objectively, from a strictly military evaluation, there was no decisive reason for him to relinquish power. In the east of Cuba, the principal focus of the rebellion, the three most crucial military strongholds, Camaguey, Holguin, and Bayamo, as well as Moncada in Santiago de Cuba, stood unmolested and adequately equipped for battle. These military forts had remained unaffected by the revolt. Only in Oriente, the Army had close to fifteen thousand soldiers perfectly able to continue the fight. We must recognize that there were moral issues to overcome and desertions to deal with, but nothing that could not be surmounted by forceful disciplinary decisions and effective leadership. The Constitutional Army was still in control of the island. The provinces of Camaguey, Matanzas, Havana, and Pinar del Rio were still under the total control of the Army and the Police. Only the city of Santa Clara, in the Province of Las Villas, was about to fall in the hands of the rebels in significant part because of the treason of Colonel Rosell who delivered to the insurgents a train full of arms and ammunition in exchange for a hefty payment negotiated with Ernesto Che Guevara.

In the meeting with Cantillo, Batista never said that he would leave. His exact words were, "In case we have to leave." His statement inferred the possibility of having to go and the need to prepare for such an event if it became necessary. The President and the General parted after agreeing to meet again on December 31, 1958.

Colonel Florentino Rosell Leyva

For historical reasons, the story of the Colonel's betrayal should not be left untold. Here is an accurate description of the object of the disloyalty, as described by Ramon M. Barquin in his book, "Las Luchas Guerrilleras en Cuba."

The armored train, a combination of two locomotives and seventeen freight and passenger cars, containing 373 soldiers and four million dollars[75] worth of munitions and provisions for two months, departed Havana on December 23, 1958. It arrived in Santa Clara the next day and halted at El Capiro Hill. The commander of the unit, Colonel Florentino Rosell Leyva, chief of the Engineer Corps, deserted to Miami on December 26. The train was derailed on December 30, after Che Guevara's men removed 30 feet of rails. When the officers asked for a truce, the soldiers began consorting with the rebels. At 7 PM, the train and its soldiers surrendered to the rebels.

---

[75] $4,000,000.00 is equivalent to 40 million dollars in value in year 2020.

Those are the cold facts. The story behind the events is that Colonel Florentino Rosell Leyva, who seems to have been an incredibly talented manipulator, started to conspire when he concluded that the United States Government was doing its best to put an end to the Batista Government. He invented a conspiratorial theory of a military uprising to take place on Christmas day in Santa Clara, the most important city of the Province of Las Villas. In his conspiracy, the Colonel falsely included the names of distinguished military officers, like General Eulogio Cantillo, as participants. He also mentioned General Alberto del Rio Chaviano, who was conspiring with him. Audaciously he made contact with the July 26 Movement underground leadership in Havana, inviting the rebels to join the hypothetical military uprising and proposed the unification of forces, rebels, and soldiers, to topple the Government jointly. As the chief of the Engineer Corps and, therefore, commanding officer of the armored train, he proposed its surrender in exchange for specific considerations. He was able to negotiate the terms and conditions of his proposal directly with "Comandante" Ernesto "Che" Guevara.

There was no military uprising in Santa Clara on Christmas Day, which was a figment of the Colonel's imagination and a part of his pitch. Still, he was able to deliver the armored train to Guevara. As agreed, and, according to substantial evidence, was handsomely rewarded for it. Guevara ordered that the soldiers and the officers on the train be allowed to leave and go home. No one suffered detention, likely also a part of the agreement.

Rosell narrowly escaped to Miami in his yacht, *Barlovento II*, on December 26, 1958[76]. Anticipating his persecution, he had already sent his family abroad. A day before, General Alberto Rio Chaviano deserted and asked for asylum in the Dominican Republic. Both were very fortunate not to have fallen in the

____

[76] Winds of December pages 281-283.

hands of Cuba's Secret Military Intelligence (S.I.M.), which was already aware of their conspiratorial initiative and had orders to arrest them. Lieutenant Colonel Irenaldo Garcia Baez, head of the S.I.M., had been closely following both officers for some time and by Christmas of 1958 had sufficient proof of their treason to order their immediate arrest.

There is no doubt that many of the highly publicized battles[77] that were won by the rebel forces during the insurrectional process were not the result of fierce confrontations but, manipulated purchases, or bribes, effectively realized by the leaders of the revolt. Fidel Castro had a multimillion dollar war chest at his disposal, courtesy of Cuban donors[78]: mostly wealthy businessmen and landowners, as well as rich ex-political figures opposed to Batista. After reaching power, in a unique way of showing his gratitude to these generous donors, he systematically stripped them of all their money by confiscating their businesses and their estate. Most, if not all, fled Cuba with their family and asked for asylum in other countries. Some were accused of counterrevolutionary activities and sent to prison.

The demoralization of the Cuban Armed Forces, mostly as a result of the U.S. Embargo, led some high ranking officers to sell their arms and their strategic positions to their enemy. Francisco Rodriguez Tamayo, AKA "El Mexicano," who was a captain in the Rebel Army and Humberto Olivera Perez, who was a captain in Cuba's Regular Army, declared[79] in the United States, while in exile, that "Colonel Ernesto Rosell sold the armored train in

---

[77] Grandiose battles narrated by the Communist Propaganda Machine; deformed historical versions of what really happened. Systematic deceit and outright lies are part of the Communist propaganda machine.

[78] Fidel Castro also collected tributes (taxes) rom established businesses (mostly sugar mills and landowners) in the areas that he controlled. A form of extorsion.

[79] New York Times, June 25th 1959.

Santa Clara to "Che" Guevara. He sold not only the whole train but also the arms and troops aboard it." Some sources say that Rosell received $350,000, and others say it was $1,000,000. The amount of money is not the issue; only the fact that he sold the train to Guevara is significant. His was an intentional act of treason[80]. Colonel Rosell went on to establish himself in Miami as a wealthy, successful businessman directing his building firm until he died in 2007.

It was not the first time that a large sum of money was paid by Che Guevara to army officials for safe passage through otherwise hostile territory. Crossing the vast planes of Camaguey without opposition or the need to fire a shot, Camilo Cienfuegos and Ernesto Che Guevara, leading their rebel columns, entered the city of Santa Clara. A safe journey across the Province of Camaguey, before the Santa Clara offensive, was the result of a bribe. The officer who sold the safe passage to the rebels was, Colonel Victor Dueñas, the military head of the Province of Camagüey, who betrayed his Army for a payoff of fifty thousand dollars.

The almost mythological glorification of Ernesto "Che" Guevara, Comandante of the Cuban Revolution, and one of the three top-ranking military leaders of the revolt is merely a myth. It is the result of multi-millions of dollars invested by the communist in an intense and constant barrage of propaganda to rewrite history following their interests and goals. The distortion of history is one of the outstanding traits of communist propaganda. They invest heavily in what is now popularly called "fake news."

Cuban communist historians refer to the Battle for Santa Clara, as one of the most significant examples demonstrating the military genius of "Che "Guevara and his incredible talent in military strategy. Che himself in his diary talks of the battle as

---

[80] Fulgencio Batista's Santa Clara Armored Train Story - **by** Henry Louis Gomez.

a ferocious struggle crowned by Molotov cocktails setting the armored train on fire under a machine gun barrage of bullets and wounded soldiers. Is this true, or is it false?

Eloy Gutiérrez Menoyo (December 8, 1934; Madrid, Spain—October 26, 2012; Havana, Cuba) led the guerilla force Second National Front of the Escambray Mountains during the Cuban Revolution against Fulgencio Batista and later opposed the Government of Fidel Castro over its pro-Soviet leanings. In 1990 he started to put together documents to write his memoirs. Among these documents, there is a letter that tells the story of the surrender of the armed train. You must remember that he was there and that he took part in the military battle as one of the revolutionary leaders. In this letter[81], signed by him, he unequivocally recounts that the surrender of the armed train was not a military victory, but an acquisition made by Guevara. Colonel Ernesto Rosell Leyva sold the train, including the arms and the soldiers on the train, to Comandante Guevara for a specific sum of money. Not one of the soldiers or officers of the armed train was wounded or hurt in any way. After the surrender, they peacefully returned home, mostly to Havana. None arrested. "Che" Guevara supervised their release.

There seems to be sufficient evidence to demonstrate that the Battle of Santa Clara was won principally with United States Dollars rather than with blood and bullets. It puts into question the validity of the historical event according to the communist narrative and the war diary written by "Che" Guevara himself. Insisting on the truth is a moral obligation of all historians, the facts put into question Che Guevara's "genius" as a guerrilla strategist[82]. If the battle of Santa Clara was his most significant

---

[81] Letter written by Eloy Gutierrez Menoyo forming part of his memoirs. Archives of Memoires in the hands of Menoyo's daughter, Patricia.
[82] Fulgencio Batista's Santa Clara Armored Train Story - by Henry Louis Gomez.

military achievement, we are left with little substance to uphold his legendary talent as a guerrilla strategist. Later in his career, he failed miserably, militarily speaking, in the Congo, and after that, his guerrilla initiative in Bolivia also collapsed; he was caught and executed after his arrest. His legendary reputation as a genial guerrilla commander is eloquent, a sham.

Batista says Adios.

It was a great goodbye to Cuba. In the end, the same man that overthrew the representative Government of Cuba on March 10, 1952, with a coup, now, at the very end, ironically aimed to correct his legacy. Throughout his Presidential years since the overthrow of President Carlos Prio Socarras, Batista made an effort to revalidate the Cuban Constitution of 1940. However, the political upheavals caused by the Revolution sustained by his opponents, principally, but not only, by Fidel Castro, made it impossible for him to govern with the steady democratic and liberating guidelines of the Cuban Constitution. It was merely and reasonably untenable.

His last-minute aspirations were realistically futile, but he forcefully applied his will to the task and proceeded to realize what he felt was the right thing to do. He decided to give his departure an apparent Constitutional ending. Perhaps he imagined that this would be his last and most significant gift to the Cuban people without understanding that by that historical moment, the people had, generally speaking, no love for him and just wanted him to leave. He failed to realize that his initiative went from the sublime to the ridiculous because whatever he could achieve by then did not have a chance to stand for long.

General Eulogio Cantillo understood that morally speaking, his duty was to aid his President to end his Presidency peacefully, quietly, and in a safe and orderly manner. The General had no personal aspirations, but he did want to end the civil war immediately and then retire from the Army to live peacefully and lovingly with his family.

Before his exit, Batista organized his departure executing the transition by following the laws, rules, and regulations of the 1940 Constitution. It was merely a performance, a circus.

In the absence of the Vice President, not located[83], and the planned departure of the President of the Senate[84], the Constitutional Solution called for the most senior justice of the Supreme Court to be named President. Not the oldest but the one that had been in the court the longest. That was the regulatory order to follow. The next President of Cuba[85] would be, for a brief moment, an old judge by the name of Carlos Piedra.

On the early hours of January 1, 1959, shortly before his departure, Batista read a handwritten letter of resignation to his most intimate supporters gathered before him at the Presidential Residence of the Columbia Military Camp. He read it, he signed it, and he passed it around those present at this official gathering. Frankly, the letter of resignation was a rationalization of why he was departing. I say rationalization with a purpose because it means attempting to explain or justify behavior or an attitude with logical reasons, even if these are not appropriate or truthful. In his letter, he said that the highest military commands were "advising him of the impossibility of establishing order in the republic, considering that the situation was grave...saying that he should resign his office." It was not true. General Cantillo or any other top-ranking officer never gave him a desperate military assessment of the situation, and no one in the military had ever

---

[83] The Vice President, Guas Inclan, had gone on a hunting trip and could not be located.
[84] The President of the Senate, Anselmo Aliiegro, was also going into exile.
[85] According to Article 149 of the 1940 Cuban Constitution.

asked him to resign. Top loyal officers in the Armed Forces and the Police still believed that the war was far from being lost. But it is clear that Batista had premeditated his departure and had set his mind to leave the country days before. He had lost his will to fight on. He caved in to the pressures and setbacks suffered in the last weeks and months; the U.S. Embargo, the military treasons, the formal notifications of the U.S. Government suggesting that he should leave, and his marked and growing lack of popularity with the Cuban people. Understandably these are vital human considerations, but facts are facts. Batista was ready to go and was prepared to wash his hands off the Cuban conflict. The frustration felt by those present was immense. Frustration and anger were manifest. Isabel Collado, President-Elect Andres Rivero Aguero's wife, angrily confronted Batista and deeply frustrated stated:

"So now you decided to leave, just like that!"

Minutes after the resignation, the stampede commenced.

Crammed into three DC4 planes, most of Batista's closest collaborators, accompanied by their families, departed. At exactly 2:40 AM on Thursday, January 1, 1959, the aircraft carrying Batista and his wife, President-elect, Andres Rivero Aguero, his wife, and other intimate associates, took off from the Columbia Military airfield in Havana. Little did they realize at that moment that this would be the last time that they would ever set foot on Cuban soil again, that they would remain in exile for the rest of their lives. In time they would all die and be interred in a foreign country.

Left holding the bag was General Eulogio Cantillo Porras, an excellent soldier, but a man ill equipped to assume such a responsibility. He was not a statesman, he was politically unknown, and he lacked the charisma and the ambition of a caudillo. Yet we must not forget that his real aspiration was to retire and go home. His genuine interest was to end the military conflict and civil strife. The last thing in his mind was to gain power.

Cantillo's empathy and deep concern for the safe departure of those abandoning the reins of power put him in a critically delicate position. For sure, Batista must have known, must have realized, that the General that had saved his life, whom he had officially named, moments before his departure, chief of the Cuban Armed Forces, could not possibly retain power. If you are left holding the bag, you assume a situation where you are responsible for something, often unfairly because other people fail or refuse to take responsibility for it. This is precisely what happened to General Cantillo.

Hours after the safe departure of Batista and his closest allies was behind him, an exhausted and perplexed General ordered the release of Colonel Ramon Barquin[86] from the Isle of Pines prison. The Batista government jailed Barquín and a few other military officers for leading a failed coup attempt in 1956. The conspiracy was called the "Puros" scheme, which in Spanish means the pure ones. They had been in jail for close to two years with other political prisoners, including some crucial leaders of the July 26 Movement. There was hope that Barquin, having been a distinguished military officer who fervently opposed Batista, could perhaps keep intact the integrity of the Cuban Army from the revolutionary takeover. As soon as Colonel Barquin arrived at the Columbia Military Base in Havana, he met with General Eulogio Cantillo, who immediately and voluntarily resigned his command and named Barquin Commander in Chief of the Cuban Army.

---

[86] Ramón M. Barquín (May 12, 1914 – March 3, 2008) was a Cuban military Colonel and opponent of former President Fulgencio Batista. Barquín was jailed by the Batista government for leading a failed coup attempt in 1956. He later fled Cuba in 1960 following the 1959 takeover by Fidel Castro.

By this time, General Cantillo had been informed by Colonel Jose Rego Rubido, who was his second in command in Oriente, that Fidel Castro accused him of treason for having betrayed their agreement of December 28, 1958, at the Central Oriente when they met. Aware of this information, Colonel Barquin supposedly offered General Cantillo a plane to leave the country, which the General turned down. Perhaps the General had no idea of Fidel Castro's level of vindictiveness. He would soon find out.

General Eulogio Cantillo, was arrested within a few hours of surrendering his command by Jose Ramon "El Gallego" Fernandez, an army lieutenant imprisoned with Colonel Barquin and just released, was soon condemned by a Revolutionary Court in La Cabana Fortress in Cases numbers 184/59H and30/59H, to 30 years in prison and forced labor. Fidel Castro came close to shooting him without a trial but settled for the long sentence resulting from trumped charges. Major General Eulogio Cantillo only lasted 15 hours as the nominal official head of the Cuban Government when Batista abandoned Cuba until he surrendered his command to Colonel Barquin. Of the 30-year sentence that he received, he served just over eight years under extremely adverse conditions[87]. Eventually, he was allowed to leave Cuba and died in Miami in 1978.

Ramon Barquin rapidly tried to optimize and leverage his command to save the Cuban Army, the institution, from its disintegration to the rebel initiative. Still, his manipulations met with Fidel Castro's firm resistance to sharing power with any other

---

[87] General Eulogio Cantillo served most f his sentence in the Isle of Pines Prison known as *Reclusorio Nacional* also know as *Prison Modelo*. It is interesting to note that he met Fernando Pruna, who was also serving a sentence at this same prison and they became good friends. Cantillo and Pruna studied Italian together while in the Isle of Pines and their teacher was First lieutenant Ricardo Rodriguez de Castro, an ex military pilot that had been sentenced to 30 years in prison by the communist.

movement or organization. Fidel was not going to allow anything or anyone to usurp his Revolution. He had sacrificed and risked his life for two years in the Sierra Maestra, and he was not going to allow anything or anyone to snatch his accomplishments. Therefore, Fidel ignored Barquin's communications and ordered Comandante Camilo Cienfuegos to take the Columbia Military Garrison. Barquin felt outplayed and realized that there was nothing that he could do, so he prepared conditions to allow Camilo Cienfuegos to assume the command of the Columbia Military Garrison. On the early afternoon of Januray 2nd , 1959, Camilo Cienfuegos took control of the military complex from Colonel Barquin. He came with all his rebel force of his Column 2 with approximately five hundred men. Inside the Colombia Military stronghold, there were five thousand well-armed soldiers and officers, including tanks and heavy weaponry who surrendered without firing a shot.

Batista's departure opened up the flood gates of pent-up energy and enthusiasm of a people that clamored for change. No one could have gauged precisely before this moment the absence of popularity that the Batista's Government enjoyed. The country was profoundly divided, but those that favored Batista were a small minority that suddenly became smaller when faced with the outburst of support for Fidel Castro and the Revolution.

The Surrender

Fulgencio Batista did not, in any way, lose, in the strict meaning of the word, the war. For whatever reasons he may have had at the last moment, what he did was deliver the power of Government to the Revolution. It was not a defeat; it was a surrender. Batista succumbed. With a standing army of forty thousand well-armed soldiers and a well-organized police department that numbered in the thousands, with the most crucial military strongholds still under his control and command, Batista chose to run away on critical short notice. He informed the closest and most loyal members of his Government of his departure only minutes before departing. It meant that he was only thinking of himself and his family. His fear guided his selfishness. It was a surprise to all. For sure, none of his top officers or closest associates expected him to leave. His decision's last-minute notification did not give any of his close associates time to prepare for it. Most were caught totally off guard and had to depart abruptly, leaving behind their personal and family patrimony and arriving in another country penniless. On the other hand, Batista took his time to get ready, and when he put his affairs in order, he left.

The human stampede caused by his departure motivated deep anger and entrenched hostile resentment that persists even today. Many top officers and renowned politicians that had faithfully backed Batista throughout the years felt deeply betrayed. Those close to him who had the opportunity and luck to leave the country on time could save their lives. Those who did not have the chance to evade the vindictive "Revolutionary Justice" faced many years of prison or the firing squads of the Communist Revolution. Those that left were a measly minority. Yet, those that had no other option but to stay and face the consequences of his policies, numbered in the thousands.

The avalanche of popularity that the people of Cuba regaled on Fidel Castro was, doubtlessly, unprecedented in the history of the island. Close to the entire country, the whole population, men women and children, embraced Fidel Castro and his fellow rebels, as their flesh and blood. It was a fantastic experience to witness such a phenomenon. Fidel had won the love and trust of his people entirely, and this was his real victory.

Although most of Fidel Castro's most renowned revolutionary initiatives were catastrophic failures, to the point of his extreme personal exacerbation in which he attempted to kill himself for his malfunctions, not once but twice, he still had the tenacity to persist. Fidel tried to kill himself after the failed attack on the Moncada Garrison, and he wanted to kill himself again after the failed Granma landing. But his closest associates managed to keep him from harming himself, and Fidel persisted.

Fidel produced and directed two major military initiatives of historic proportions. First, he organized an attack on the most crucial military bastion in the Province of Oriente in Cuba. For this action, Fidel went to prison and did time. He then left Cuba, went to Mexico, only to organize and prepare an invasion. Fidel carried out the aggression and landed in Cuba with a group of armed men. The point that both military initiatives were failures is irrelevant to the fact that he created a pattern of actions that won him legitimacy, which awarded him revolutionary credentials. Despite these two failures, Castro goes into the mountains and organizes a military rebel force that the Cuban armed forces are not able to eradicate. For two long years, he persists and exists and grows in strength. His epic struggle has the connotations of a David and Goliath symbol of the underdog fighting against impossible odds. Then an influential newspaperman comes along from America, picks up the story, and turns the revolutionary leader into the legend of the Robin Hood of the Sierra Maestra. Herbert Mathews and the New York Times turn Fidel Castro into a superstar, an international revolutionary icon.

When Batista decided to succumb, to flee, no one was more surprised than Fidel Castro himself. The rebels could not believe what was happening; they did not expect it. It was a revolutionary miracle. Batista just took off, left. And the walls came tumbling down. When Batista went, the Cuban Armed Forces folded like a house of cards. It was a revolutionary tsunami.

When the Batista Government toppled, and the Constitutional Army surrendered, Fidel Castro Ruz instantly became a living legend; his overwhelming popularity was such that none of the other revolutionary organizations could stand up to him. Fidel and his July 26 Movement swallowed in one gulp the Revolutionary Directory and the Segundo Frente del Escambray and the multiple leaders of the Autentico Party and those that returned from exile after their significant opposition to Batista. His physical appearance and his fiery oratory helped him immensely. He looked and spoke like a real caudillo, and Cuba fell head over heels in love with him. Blind to his deceitful traits, Cuba embraced him with unconditional love.

Never before had the people of Cuba bestowed such absolute power to a single man. It was shocking to the objective eye. He could have done so much good for his country. And yet few imagined that he had other plans. His fanciful dreams of turning Cuba into a "Communist Paradise" soon condemned the country into a permanent food rationing regime. Hunger and misery, intellectual and social stagnation, thousands of executions, tortures and murders, countless political imprisonments, the exile of millions of Cubans and the reign of a repressive and totalitarian tyrannical system that gave no truce to dignity and human rights, that denied the individual freedom of man and enslaved a people.

Fidel Castro had pledged to make the 1940 Cuban Constitution and its Bill of Rights the Cuban Republic's law. He never kept his promise. Instead, within days of taking over the Government, he modified the Constitution to legalize the death sentence.

After January first, 1959, the 1940 Constitution never again became the law of the land. Instead, it was superseded by a variation of Socialist Constitutions, which led to converting a fundamentally democratic society into a totalitarian communist state.

Figure 38 On the left, the Someillan Building, overlooking the Gulf of Mexico. On the right, the decapitated SS Maine Monument. The American Eagle statue that crowned it, considered an Imperialist symbol, was removed by the Communist Government.

17

DARKNESS DESCENDS

Out of the night that covers me,
Black as the pit from pole to pole,
I thank whatever gods may be
For my unconquerable soul.
- Invictus – William Ernest Henley

In 1957, one of Cuba's tallest buildings, the Someillan, was built two blocks away from the mammoth Nacional Hotel and the massive FOCSA apartment complex. The apartments started to sell immediately. It was, by far, the most exclusive building of the Vedado district, not to say the most elegant in all of Cuba and probably the most expensive. Its thirty-story gleaming and spacious apartments, soaring paradigm and modernity, seemed to challenge the scenic Malecon Boulevard that bordered the open sea. From the flats, one relished the most spectacular panoramic view of the city of Havana and the Gulf of Mexico. Each apartment occupied an entire floor, so in fact, there were only thirty apartments. However, the builder, Guillermo Someillán González, a colorful retired air force officer, lived in the penthouse, which occupied the top two floors, and included a swimming pool. They say that Santos Trafficante Jr., a capo of the mafia operating in Cuba, provided the necessary funds to construct the building but this was probably not true. One of the apartments in the building was purchased by Charlie White, who was a good friend of the actor George Raft, a front man for the mafia. White, whose real name was Charles Tourine, was a member of the Genovese family from the New York mafia, and he owned a piece of the Capri Hotel Casino a block away from the Nacional Hotel.

The Pruna family had acquired the spacious apartment that occupied the entire 17th floor. Now, Fernando made use of it to celebrate the arrival of the New Year with close friends, beautiful ladies, and good wine. The windows were left open to allow full access to the tropical breeze coming in from the sea. The commanding view from inside was breathtaking.

"It's a bit strange, isn't it? "A friend suddenly said.

"You hear laughter. Music. Party rumors. The distant sounds. And then. An overwhelming silence. As if"

He didn't complete the phrase. The rebels had recently obtained a succession of victories. Three days earlier, Castro had launched an offensive attack over Santa Clara City, in the center of the island, with two separate groups. One headed by Ernesto "Che" Guevara and the other by Camilo Cienfuegos, respectively. The rebels counted on the support of frustrated people. They also relied on the permissiveness of a corrupt Army officer that allowed the rebel columns safe passage of the province of Camaguey in exchange for a hefty payoff.

Crossing the vast planes of Camaguey without opposition or the need to fire a shot, the two rebel columns entered the city of Santa Clara. It was a success and a crucial moment for Guevara. The revolutionaries had acquired a significant number of weapons and commanded critical strategic points of the city. At the same time, Fidel appeared to threaten Santiago de Cuba, while his brother Raúl Castro, according to rumors, was ready to move against the city of Guantánamo. The rebel chief vigorously announced his successive wins over Batista's troops.

"Nevertheless, it all seems eerily quiet now."

And yet, Havana appeared undisturbed. There had only been a few isolated episodes of agitation, like the two American professors who were in Havana on vacation and were held at the airport for some hours, after shouting "Long live the revolution!"

At the Riviera Hotel, the saloons overcrowded with guests. The roulettes rotated at a vertiginous speed at the Deauville Hotel in Malecon Drive. In the Hotel Saint-John's, cards ceaselessly shuffled. The slot machines sizzled with their shining coins at the Nacional Hotel. Rivers of champagne ran at the Capri Hotel. The showgirls swayed their hour glass shaped bodies at Tropicana. The glasses clinked with acute crystalline notes at the Monseigneur. The men stood, impeccably dressed, around the gambling tables and the women, covered in jewels, were courted on the dancing floors, while others stayed outside, laying under the porches.

"Do you want me to wish you a happy New Year, darling?"

They tapped on the streets with their heeled shoes, swaying their purses, or they launched their looks at you, from their open windows, ready to make revolutions with their bodies, putting generous commissions inside their bags.

During this time, some had raised their eyes to the sky of a Havana assailed by shadows.

When the agitation reached its peak, the confetti spread on the streets among laughter and made it appear that everything was well. The tempo of popular songs masked the distant gunfire that was mistaken for the sound of fireworks. It was midnight. The twelve chimes marked the time for kissing and eating the traditional twelve grapes. It was proof of happiness and prosperity and deeply felt wishes for a most prosperous new year.

It was finally at the Capri Hotel Casino, about 3 a.m., that Fernando and his friends chose to end their New Year's celebration. They did not stay long because, by that time, very few people remained.

Leaving the nightclub, they noticed that it was eerily quiet in the neighborhood.

Fernando drove Nidia Ríos and Norma Martínez to their residence. Andy, his brother, accompanied them. He left the ladies at the door of a discrete guesthouse located in the corner of the Victor Hugo Park, on I and 19 streets in Vedado. They were all exhausted and decided to go to sleep in their respective homes.

Years before, Fernando had met Nidia Rios[88] by chance at a 4th of September celebration hosted by the president of Cuba, Fulgencio Batista. It was a substantially lavish party at the Officer's Club of the Columbia Military Compound, the most critical military complex in Cuba. At the time, Nidia was only 16 or 17 years old. She had recently graduated from a strict catholic school, and she was there accompanying her parents and enjoying her newfound freedom.

Fernando also came with his parents and did not have a date. He was probably bored to death when he unexpectedly encounters this very slim, vivacious teenager with an unusually beautiful face. Nidia was very friendly and struck a conversation very naturally with Fernando. They danced and chatted a good part of the night. Fernando remembers that Nidia was very funny and always bubbling with laughter and fun. The party came to an end, and they parted that night without imagining that they would meet again.

I fail to remember how or specifically when I met Nidia Rios again after that party. Most definitely, it was years later, probably in the

---

[88] NIDIA RÍOS was, before and after the Communist Revolution, one of Cuba's most famous fashion models. The celebrated Cuban photographer, Korda, contributed to her fame. His photos were published in multiple magazines and were part of the many exhibits realized by the photographer. In 1959, Korda became Fidel Castro's personal photographer and was also the author of the icon photograph of Commander Ernesto "Che" Guevara that became famous around the world.

NIDIA RIOS

last months of 1957. Of course, I continued to see her in 1958, and we dated. In 1957 she was 19 years old, and the slim teenager that I met at the party years before was now an amazingly beautiful woman with a fabulous figure. Despite her youth, by far, she was a well known high fashion model doing commercials for some of the most prestigious firms in Cuba. I particularly remember her modeling for Jantzen bathing suits, Visant cigarettes, and a modeling agency displayed every weekend a full page of advertising starring Nidia in the Diario de La Marina newspaper, probably the most prestigious publication in the country. She advertised everything from real estate to wedding dresses. Simultaneously, Alberto Korda, the photographer who later took the well-known photo of Ernesto Che Guevara, discovered Nidia and photographed her. Nidia's photos by Korda became famous and are, to this day, exhibited in many world recognized exhibitions.

I vividly remember one afternoon I invited Nidia to an elegant Sunday lunch at the Habana Yacht Club and she informed me that she was wearing a fabulous black and white dress designed by the famous couturier Felíto Mojena. The dress FIT her body like a glove with exquisite taste and caused a sensation. The Governor's son, who was there, invited us to his table, but I preferred to dedicate the occasion exclusively to my companion and kindly declined the invitation. I can assure you that all eyes were focused on Nidia, who later told me that the couturier, Mojena, had received a barrage of calls from the ladies of the club interested in hIs creations.

Sometime in December 1958, I invited Nidia to come to our apartment to spend the last day of the year together. I told her that I was not planning a party, but just a nice get together with very intimate participants. She asked me if she could invite her friend Norma Martinez and I said of course. It was not the first time that Nidia and Norma came over to our apartment to visit us. They used to hang together often. I much enjoyed their company and their conversation. Nidia, who was very natural and informal in her manners, sometimes would join my younger brother Andy to paint. They would sit on the floor to paint together, which Nidia seemed to enjoy much. At the time, Norma Martinez, also an incredibly beautiful young lady, was beginning to do some modeling. A very humble and modest girl from Santiago de Cuba, she had come to Havana penniless to restart her life after a torrid divorce in which she left behind two young daughters that needed care. Norma left her kids with her mother and father and decided to move to Havana to try to get a job. The first person that she met in Havana was Nidia, who was living at this pension in the Vedado section, where Norma also came to live. She was fortunate to have met Nidia, who immediately did her best to help her adapt to her new surroundings and introduced her to modeling. It seems that she made the most of the introduction.

Later, I learned that Norma had a dizzying career with the Revolution. She soon became an actress, and eventually an assistant director and film producer. She joined the ICAIC (Cuban Institute of Cinematographic Art and Industry) in 1959, and, as an actress, she made the first color short film of Cuban cinema, "Carnaval," under the direction of Fausto Canel in 1960. From that moment, she represented Cuba in the first Weeks of Cuban Cinema and in different international festivals. She participated in the films "A little more than blue", and in the story "The end", by Fausto Canel, in 1961.

Norma developed a short but pleasant friendship with Fernando's brother, Andy, in the closing months of 1958. Her humble origins and beauty provided her with the perfect credentials to join the communist revolution, which she did immediately, with great success, as soon as the Revolution took power. Her career ended when she became the lover of the communist ideologue, Armando Hart, one of the main leaders of the Cuban Revolution who held the position of Minister of Education and Culture for many years.

Nidia Rios and Norma Martinez spent the last night of the year 1958 and the first hours of the year 1959 with the Pruna brothers at the 17th-floor apartment of the Someillan Building. They came to spend the year's end with their friends and arrived at the Pruna apartment at around nine in the evening.

Before leaving for Bellavista Farm, Mrs. Pruna set the table with some delicious dishes and, of course, Spanish nougats, nuts, hazelnuts, and the grapes *de rigueur*, to say goodbye to the ending year and to welcome the new one. Unexpectedly, two other beautiful girls showed up. One of them declared having been invited by Fernando. But they did not stay long since they felt displaced by the models, and the one who had allegedly been invited by Fernando said goodbye visibly upset.

Besides this unfortunate incident, the gathering was delightful. Everyone enjoyed the food. The night ended with a champagne toast to welcome the new year. Nevertheless, the intense joy of such a big night was absent. Maybe, it was the presage of the disastrous cataclysm that was about to occur with the coming of the new year.

The engine of an airplane buzzed, it took off at the Columbia Military Compound, and immediately flew over the Vedado district a few hours after Havana welcomed the New Year. Onboard were General Batista, his family, and his acolytes. The twelve chimes of Batista's era had sounded for the last time.

Long before daybreak, people spread the news on the streets of Havana: "Batista has left! Batista escaped!". Later, radio and television echoed the story. "Long live Fidel! Down with Batista!" screamed the mobs in different parts of the city.

Fernando woke up, startled by the noise coming from the street. It was six in the morning! What was the cause of such a scandal? The sound of broken glass cut the early hours of the day.

Theyoungmanwenttothebalconythatsurroundedtheapartment and took a look at the streets seventeen floors below. Some people were destroying the recently installed parking meters that were not immensely popular at the time. They hit the parking meters with bats or metal objects to destroy them and also to pocket the coins that they possibly held. Fernando contemplated the ferocity of the aggressors. The mob took to the streets to destroy whatever they could. The noise, the music at the casinos, had given way to the clamors of the crowd, which grew more intense after the heavy silence of the first hours of the new year.

"Let's take revenge and attack the Government's wallet! Let's destroy the parking meters!"

With the first lights of that January 1st, the parking meters became the slot machines of the mob and the disturbers. The telephone cabins pillaged as well. The crowd, entranced by delirium, just wanted to destroy whatever they could. Their anger was overwhelming. The Vedado district was invaded, and the shops gave in to the assault of the multitude. The Capri and the Saint John's hotels were almost swept away under the astonished eyes of the tourists. The casinos where ransacked. The furniture tossed out to the street. The Plaza Hotel overflowed by the mob and men carrying machine guns, identifying themselves as agents of the revolution. At the Deauville, tourists rubbed shoulders with underground agents of the revolution. At the Tropicana, the owner, Martin Fox, prepared himself for the assault of the mob. The tourists were bewildered.

"What if we don't find a plane to fly back to America?" asked an American lady.

"Will we have to stay here, blocked? The rebels are everywhere! They have taken the Hilton too. And also, the Deauville and the Plaza." Commented another.

"Do not panic. The agents are here to protect us. So that the mob can pillage at ease." Commented another disconcerted visitor.

When it was not on the streets or the parking meters, it was at the casinos where the crazy mob launched themselves over the real slot machines, symbols of the manumission of the huge incomes collected by the government. They were thrown to the outside, torn apart, burnt.

"Come on, boys, we have to put everything upside down at the casinos," they shouted.

From time to time, some shots heard along with the honking of cars speeding down the boulevard. Through the vehicle's windows, some men showed their weapons and shouted slogans. As soon as Fernando turned the radio on, the informative bulletin gave him the news.

Fernando received a call from his father, who was in the countryside, near his Bellavista Farm. "Father, I'm very worried. This is a disaster."

"So am I. Everybody is. But you must keep calm."

"Is it true that Batista has left the Island?"

"Yes, just last night, after midnight. He left without telling almost anyone."

"What should we do?"

"Get to safety. As the saying goes, keep calm, cool, and collected. How is Havana?"

"It's in the middle of chaos. Everybody has a gun! Thousands of men have popped up, saying that they are members of the revolution. I presume opportunists. People have gone mad. They pillaged the casinos when they were not smashing the parking meters with bats! They are also ram sacking homes and apartments belonging to important Batista collaborators."

"What about our apartment?"

"No, we are fine. No one has bothered us yet. However, some apartments in our building were pillaged."

"It's too dangerous. Just in case, don't stay at the Someillan."

"It's the…"

"Yes, exactly, it is the Revolution."

"They are arresting anyone who they think had anything to do at all with Batista."

"Don't stay there! Go to a quiet place. Let us wait until things calm down. Castro won't last too long. You know what happens in situations like this. They come, and others immediately replace them. I suggest that you ask Mickey's[89] mother if it is alright for you to hide at her apartment."

"I will call her as soon as I hang up with you."

"I think it will be the wisest and the most practical thing to do now. I don't think it would be smart for you to go to the countryside either. I do not think you should join me at Bellavista. Above all, don't go to Nazareno. Everyone knows you there."

Fernando had considered a more attractive idea, but now his father had blocked it. Just a few months before, he had met an unusually beautiful girl who had visited, together with others, his mother in Bellavista. He was motivated to see the young beauty again, but he decided to follow his father's advice. The girl lived in the town of Nazareno.

____

[89] Referring to his cousin Zoraida Bertot whom everyone called "Mickey".

***Figure 39** First Communion – Nazareno, Cuba: Under the guidance of Carolina Bertot Ortiz, (Carolina Pruna) center.*

It was common to see a significant number of young people at Bellavista. They came to see Fernando's mother, who always opened her doors to them. Carolina Bertot[90] loved young people, and she did everything in her power to help them and prepare them for the future. In the town close to the farm, Nazareno, Carolina, was an idol. All the families of the village loved her and considered her to be a part of their own family. A devoted Catholic, for years, she prepared hundreds of boys and girls for their First Holy Communion at the village's small, modest church. She purchased, with her own money, clothes to dress them adequately for the special occasion. She also dedicated her time to spread literacy, teaching children how to read and write for

---

[90] In Cuba, when a woman is married, she does not lose her maiden name. In the case of Fernando's mother her official married name in Cuba was, Carolina Bertot de Pruna.

miles around. She did everything within her powers to promote health, to the point of even taking doctors to the most remote areas, as well as free medicine.

My mother, Carolina Bertot Ortiz, was an extraordinary woman and a wonderful mother. She dedicated her life to helping the needy, mainly the children of that village she loved so much: Nazareno. In my memories, I see her surrounded by hundreds of young boys and girls about to attend their first communion. But, despite her constant beneficiary activities, she always had time for us, her children, Andy and me, and she filled us with infinite love. She defended her own, her family, unconditionally, like a wild tigress. For her, her people were perfect. I am sure that the people of Nazareno still remember her, with love and gratefulness. In time she has become a legend, which my brother and I have been able to confirm. We are blessed to have had a mother like her.

The young beauty, named Nora Ramos, dazzled Fernando when he met her. Tall, slender, with delicate features, she looked like a model from one of the most prestigious international fashion houses. And yet, she was a humble young girl from the small town of Nazareno in Cuba. She was only 15 years old when she met Fernando, and there were rumors that she had fallen deeply in love with the young man. With the unstoppable force of a first love, when in Bellavista, they always tried to be together but pretended not to be so close avoiding gossip. There appeared to be a bond between them that promised to be long lasting. They kissed, secretly, with the reciprocal intention to continue without restrictions, the burning force of love. But fate had other designs, and they saw each other for the last time just before Christmas. There were no farewells or reencounters. Destiny chose to separate their paths. In the first months of 1959, the revolutionary government confiscated the Bellavista estate, and Fernando and Nora never saw each other again. In his mind, permanently, the unforgettable memory of the beautiful girl, lying next to him.

She was illuminated by the moonlight, deliciously emanating the subtle fragrance of green grass exuded by the dew, and the sweet and promising lips that touched his, unaware, that it would be for the last time.

Father and son feared retaliation. One had taken part, as a candidate, in the elections that Fidel Castro had condemned, the other one was a lawyer in some of Batista's matters. The situation was possibly not so difficult for them, given that they had not taken an active part in the government. Still, in these moments of terror and confusion, the most sensible thing to do was nothing at all, just to remain quiet and discrete. Fernando walked for some minutes among the noisy Cuban mob and the tourists who rushed to lock themselves in the hotels or decided to leave the Island. The crowd was enflamed, and their behavior was threatening.

Fernando remembered that Fidel Castro had decreed political ineligibility, for the next thirty years, for all those who had participated as candidates in the elections of November of 1958. The triumph of the Castroist revolution meant for the young man that he would never be able to get involved in Cuban politics for almost the rest of his life. This thought cast a shadow on his existence when meditating about it. Later, he calmed down by believing that a communist revolution could not possibly be supported for a long time by a people that loved freedom as much as he did. He passionately believed that the Cuban people loved freedom and would never allow themselves to live indefinitely under the boots of a totalitarian tyranny. In addition, he also figured that Cuba was only 90 miles from the United States. The Americans would never allow a communist country at their doorsteps.

In time he would understand that he was completely wrong in all his predictions.

Military vehicles were everywhere. Women screamed hysterically in the middle of the street and threw themselves on the bearded rebels to hug them and kiss them, January 1st, heroes. Some were so young that they couldn't even grow a rebel beard. Many opportunists started to grow a beard as of the moment, and they needed to show a beard to take advantage and be a part of the new regime. To be an authentic rebel, you had to have a beard!

On the streets, thousands of people shouted the same leitmotiv: "Down with Batista! Long live Fidel". The use of his last name evoked the one, and the other one was called by his first name. The people were sold on Fidel. They referred to him with affection and familiarity. True, Batista was on the edge of an abyss, as E.M. had suggested. The Americans had not understood the storm before it formed. They chose the rebel over the general, political blindness. They knew that Raul Castro and Che Guevara were communists, but they thought that Fidel Castro was only a "fellow traveler." At most, a socialist democrat. Little did they imagine that Fidel already had a master plan to slowly, but surely, convert the island of Cuba into a Communist State adhered to the Soviet Block. He executed his plan by following, step by step, the guidelines of the Manifesto of the Communist Party, published in the year 1848 by Marx and Engels.

At daybreak, Andy Pruna decided to take a look around. The revolution resounded strongly inside his head. He wandered among the mob, whose arms ended up in firearms or baseball bats. He saw young rebels with faces framed by long hair that fell on their shoulders. They looked at each other. They were the same age.

There was a curious mix of festivity and danger on the boulevard. The young man took the invaded Malecón Drive and then decided to come back and enter the Someillan. On the 17th floor, the apartment was silent. Everything was in perfect order. He took the elevator down. Some neighbors were at the garage in the basement, talking. Some apartments owned by relevant Batista officials were abandoned. Their luxurious apartments plundered.

"Haven't you seen my brother?"

"No."

"Well, I'm leaving. I don't know where Fernando can be. Shit! "If you see him, please tell him I will be back in an hour."

As soon as he left the building, Andy ran into a group of armed men coming in his direction. One of them raised his weapon arrogantly. He looked pretty nervous. He pointed his machinegun at Andy.

"Are you running away or what?"

"Shit, man, leave me alone! I live here, and I am just going out."

A neighbor interrupted. "Listen, I can guarantee that he lives here."

Calmly, the neighbor intervened, seeing the predicament. The young rebel put his gun down. At sixteen, Andy was easily upset and was often fired up by his rebellious temper. He never bit his tongue. He was not interested in politics, and he never cared too much until these last months, when tensions shook the Island. He looked at the rebel in the eye and said:

"You know, you are a real piece of shit! You cannot just go around pointing your gun at people. You probably don't even know how to use it!"

"Shut up, you, asshole! You better stay out of my way!"

"Oh, fuck you."

Those men left as fast as they had come, quickly merging into the tide of passersby.

The twilight was quickly coming to an end. Darkness had arrived.

18

THE LIZARD

Chameleons are reptiles that are part of the iguana suborder. These colorful lizards are known as one of the few animals that can change skin color. However, it is a misconception that chameleons change colors to match their surroundings.

"I think Castro has lizard blood."
Errol Flynn – Havana January 1959.

Hotel Nacional Gardens, Vedado, Havana, Cuba, the first week of January 1959

"I caught one!"

The persecution had started on a beautiful, sunny day—impatient, aggressive oppression. The hand clenched around the prey that continued fighting in vain. As soon as some suspicious movement was detected, the process of hunting of other game began.

"I see another one trying to escape over there!"

The second fugitive crawled cautiously on the grass, attempting to go unnoticed—a chameleonic tactic with the perfect camouflage when the olive-green colors merged. The hunter didn't ask for explanations. It was happening so fast! It knew the strategy it should use in case of an attack. To escape, it only needed to climb a palm tree rapidly. Which it did, hastily. There was only one thing the hunter could do: wait for the fugitive to come down. The pursuer was not willing to desist. It was essential to catch this one at any cost!

When she rose her eyes to the top of the palm tree to locate the inaccessible prey, the noise of an engine disturbed the peace. The noise caused the palm-tree branches to vibrate. The apparatus approached and ended up finding a spot to land. Not scared at all, the young and fragile hunter waited for the helicopter's helixes to stop to meet the two soldiers that descended from it. Each one was carrying a weapon, and their olive-green uniforms crossed by cartridge belts full of copper bullets shining under the sunrays. They looked too young. One could speculate that one of them was still a teenager.

"Good morning! Hola. Buenos Dias. What's your name?"

Claudia liked to use those holiday mornings to give herself to one of her favorite activities in the peaceful green manicured gardens of the Nacional Hotel in the Vedado neighborhood of Havana: lizard hunting. She wondered which one she would choose to take back to New York with her, hoping her parents would approve her plans. The young girl had managed to catch one. The second one she could manage to get would make an excellent travel mate. She would now look at the tree trunk in desperation, fearing she wouldn't be able to evict the fugitive that mocked her some meters up, under the palm tree leaves—appearing completely safe.

"You can play outside if you want to, but don't leave the hotel premises or venture into the surroundings of the hotel either," Solange told her that morning.

Rumors had been circulating about people getting shot since early that morning, followed by some distant gunshots later. From time to time, there was uncommon shouting, mixed with the whistling of bullets flying around. Agitated conversations in the Nacional Hotel lobby reflected uncertainty and speculation, and most tourists had already packed their suitcases.

However, children splashing in the pool went on barely undisturbed by the whirls agitating Havana, except, of course, for the helicopter that had just landed. Claudia had heard about the President who escaped. He must have been scared. She knew some people wanted to get rid of him. That's why, when she saw the shadow of the helicopter turn around over the hotel, the palms, and the helixes whirling, she smiled confidently.

The aircraft landed near the swimming pool, and she approached with all naturality and unafraid of the presence of the two-warrior looking, smiling young men.

"Hola, my name is Claudia.... I want to ..... catch...," she wanted to explain in rudimentary Spanish, accompanied by gestures.

If these two strong men were there to help people, they could also help her accomplish her mission.

"I want to ..... catch..... big..... lizard..."

"What? Yes, I see. You want to catch a lizard?"

They looked up to the top of the palm tree and smiled. To Claudia's delight, one of the rebel soldiers climbed up the trunk of the tree, skillfully, and almost as fast as the lizard. He came down with the reptile in his hands. In the absence of any of Batista's men, he could at least praise himself before his superiors for having caught a lizard! Claudia rewarded him in her way.

"Thank you. Thank you very much! Come to my room! I have something to eat. And we can also draw!"

In her hotel room, the child drew a big city, with such tall towers that the Nacional Hotel itself looked small next to it, even the Statue of Liberty looked small. The soldiers looked at the drawing with interest.

"This is what it looks like where I live," she said, looking at them earnestly.

While the girl's pencil built beautiful buildings, the young rebels drew airplanes, rebel soldiers, gunshots, and explosions, warriors in a battle.

So began the first days of January 1959. Hunting down soldiers and police officers of the Batista Government by revolutionary rebels in Havana, and the hunting of lizards in the garden of the Nacional Hotel by a seven-year-old girl. Young men whose fragile lives had been crossed by some ideals and a girl's universe in the golden palace of her fantasies.

"I will name my Lizard Fidel," the child stated convincingly.

"I think that it is a perfect name, said one of the young rebel soldiers."

"Yes, I agree," said the other." "Claudia, you have found the perfect name for your lizard."

Claudia beamed proudly.

"I think Castro has lizard blood." These were the terms in which Errol Flynn described Fidel Castro, impressed by the rebel's energy. The actor had landed on Havana some weeks earlier. During Batista's government, Errol Flynn, was often seen gambling at the Capri Hotel, arm in arm with beautiful ladies.

Both Claudia Podell and Errol Flynn had pegged Castro correctly. They had subconsciously asserted in both name and description. In time the people of Cuba would also come to realize that Fidel was the perfect lizard, with the capacity to turn the colors of his ideals, from green, the color of the Cuban Royal Palm, to red, the official color of a totalitarian communist regime.

A new actor had made his appearance before the cameras of the international scene: Castro. Flynn was fascinated by the character. While some groups happily dealt with the slot machines and reduced them to dust, waves of students left the University to mix with the growing crowd.

American tourists tried to ease themselves and enjoy their last days in Cuba. Others preferred to leave their hotels and go to the American Embassy escorted by American jeeps. The Nacional Hotel suddenly looked like a cinema plateau. Tourists in their swimming suits discussing politics with rebel soldiers and taking souvenir photos. Actresses hastily packed their suitcases, and singers voices hoarse from screaming instead of talking to be overheard in the noisy crowd.

During the late hours of the evening, the Segundo Frente rebel troops, commanded by Commandante Eloy Gutiérrez Menoyo, a Spaniard who had emigrated to Cuba with his family after the Spanish Civil War, entered Havana. At the same time, Fidel Castro made his victorious entry into Santiago de Cuba, which would become the capital city of the country provisionally. He appointed Manuel Urrutia president of the nation. When Fidel appeared in the balcony of a hotel in Santiago with the new President, his voice drowned by the crowd was unheard. He called for a general strike from the new capital city.

Fidel trusted that his troops in Havana, led by Commanders Camilo Cienfuegos and Ernesto Guevara, would take the command of the Columbia Military Garrison and La Cabaña Fortress. Amazingly, in forty-eight hours, the Constitutional Army toppled and surrendered. Morally broken by the absence of their unquestionable leader who had chosen to flee the country hours earlier, thousands of armed and trained soldiers surrendered to dozens of rebels, instead of fighting. No inch of Cuba's strategic military territory seemed to have escaped the olive-green Revolution.

Parapets were placed even in the gambling paradises. At the Capri Hotel, George Raft, manager of the place, moved among the cars dodging some non-existing gunfight.

Then, someone screamed at him:

"Hey, Georgie, do you think you are playing some part in a movie?"

Standing at the door of his club, he shot back,

"I am an American actor. I have nothing to do with Cuban political affairs".

There were hundreds of young rebel soldiers and hotheaded young people in the middle of the urban mob. Raft tried to calm the spirits, and he even offered food to the troops that had taken the Capri Hotel by assault. Like he was playing the best and most crucial part of his life, he overwhelmed the rebels with revolutionary slogans, and so he managed to save some of the hotel furniture. The Capri barely survived from total pillage.

The morning editions had no time to print the fantastic revolutionary slogans. In the afternoon, during the sunset in a Havana burning with rebellion, the paperboys restlessly repeated the front page news: "Batista is gone."

Leaving Havana seemed to be the wisest thing to do. Hide in the countryside and wait for the spirits to calm down.

"Pruna is gone, Pruna is gone...," some friends must undoubtedly have announced.

But Fernando had not gone anywhere. The whole debacle caught him by surprise. He could not have imagined that Batista would leave without even packing his bags. He was perfectly aware of the existing political complications, but he never imagined that it would come to this. For him, it became a shocking, traumatic experience that froze in his mind forever after. His first reaction was an incredible surprise, but soon anger and frustration replaced those feelings. He failed to justify the decision taken by Batista to flee. Because he had the privileged of being briefed by Captain Labrada about who the leaders of the Revolution were, he understood that communism would be the result of the Revolution.

Havana, January 1959 – First Month

Fernando preferred to distance himself from the turmoil of a convulsed city. He prudently decided to stay out of sight for the next few days, accepting the gracious hospitality of his beautiful young cousin, Mickey[91], very dear to him, and her mother, Zoraida, in the peace and safety of their small but comfortable apartment. From his hideout, still in the Vedado neighborhood, he could discreetly monitor the current events of the incipient Revolution. It was not the right moment for reckless actions.

Amazed by what was happening, he kept his eyes glued to the TV set. From the very beginning of the revolutionary takeover, the news incessantly covered the persecution of those that had served the Batista government. Within days, the new government modified the Cuban Constitution of 1940, legalizing the death sentence. The thirst for vengeance was overpowering, and accusations became the order of the day. Revolutionary courts sprung throughout the entire Island, and bearded rebel officers without any legal formation presided over the courts and sentenced to death anyone suspected of a crime. Firing squads executed the sentences automatically and immediately. Blood flowed like never before in Cuba.

Trials entirely covered by TV allowed all viewers to witness the implementation of revolutionary justice without due process or any legal procedure. Defendants were defenseless and sentences pre-dictated. The trials were a circus, but Fernando soon understood that these demonstrations of aggressive and

---

[91] Mickey was the nickname given to Zoraida Bertot by her father. She was Fernando's cousin.

severe punishments had a political purpose. The purpose was fear. It was the process of creating Revolutionary Terror—a way to instill profound fear of the power of government. It was clear, terror as the institution of revolutionary threat.

The press, void temporarily of censorship, allowed the publication of graphic photographs of prisoners before, during, and after being shot before a firing squad. Newspapers and magazines carried atrocious pictures of mutilated bodies riddled with bullets. Still, mobs hollered in unison the word "PAREDON"[92] repeatedly in favor of the executions by firing squad. Again, intense fear was generated to subdue the general population. It meant that the Revolution was serious about its purpose and that it could put an end to your existence openly without the need to do it covertly.

Fidel Castro began to give interminable speeches that lasted for hours. Divisions amongst the different revolutionary organizations immediately became evident. It was the result of sectorial ambitions to gain some sort of power. The various anti-Batista groups were unsuccessfully clamoring for a piece of the pie. Fidel, with exceptional political maneuverability and inflammatory oratory, manipulated the masses and managed to usurp total power for himself and the July 26 Movement.

Comandante Ernesto "Che" Guevara immediately showed his sanguinary predilection staging daily executions in la Cabana Fortress and inviting crowds to see and enjoy the show. It became a source of thrilling entertainment for radical spirits that were turned on by such bloody events. Dozens of condemned prisoners were shot every day by firing squads in the early hours of the morning or late in the night. There were rumors that "Che" Guevara, the charismatic Argentinian rebel comandante, had

---

[92] PAREDON in Spanish means the wall. It refers to the wall in fron of which prisoners stand before being shot.

personally assassinated some high-ranking Batista officers in his office with a bullet to the head from his 45-caliber pistol.

The most extreme case happened less than two weeks after the Revolutionary takeover. On Monday, January 11, 195[93], in the early evening, while the population of the city of Santiago de Cuba, like the rest of the country, was still celebrating the triumph of the Revolution, several cars and trucks moved at moderate speed through the streets of the city. Their destination was the military firing range at San Juan Valley.

The caravan had just departed from a revolutionary trial that was abruptly cut short by Fidel's youngest brother, Comandante Raul Castro, who cried out: "If one is guilty, all of them are guilty."

Arriving at the firing range, about 200 bearded rebel soldiers dressed in olive green uniforms stepped out of the vehicles. They were all carrying weapons of different types and calibers. Once there, they unloaded a group of prisoners, with hands tied, from the trucks. Other trucks arrive in the next hour, bringing more prisoners. Later, a caravan of cars and jeeps arrived, and Comandante Raul Castro exited one of the jeeps. With his long hair tied in a knot behind his head, the beardless Comandante, wearing a black beret with a single gold star, ordered the prisoners to move and stand before a deep, wide trench previously dug with a bulldozer. Father Chabebe was the priest present who tried to give some spiritual assistance to the terrified prisoners.

At approximately four o'clock in the morning on Monday, January 12, 1959, 73[94] ex-police and ex-military officers fell into

---

[93] A headline on the official July 26 Movement newspaper "Revolución", published on its front page on January 14, 1959: "EXCLUSIVE! SEE THE LIST OF THOSE SHOT IN SANTIAGO! "The list of all seventy-three men that were shot that day was published with their full name.

[94] "Carteles" Magazine, a well known Cubsan magazine published the trench executution on one of its publications on January 1959.

Figure 40 CUBAN NEWSPAPER DATED JANUARY 15, 1959 REPORTING HUNDREDS OF EXECUTIONS ORDERED BY COMANDANTE RAUL CASTRO, FIDEL CASTRO'S BROTHER. THE HEADLINE SAYS: "RAUL PROMISES MORE EXECUTIONS."

the vast open trench massacred by a barrage of gun fire. The bulldozer quickly covered them with the same dirt drawn from the excavation. The next day a newspaperman, **Antonio Llano Montes**[95], visited the tomb area and saw a hand clutching an object protruding from the ground. It appeared that some of the prisoners, only wounded, had been buried alive. It was a summary mass execution ordered, directed, and supervised by Raul Castro personally[96].

David and Solange Podell, accompanied by their daughter Claudia and a Lizard named Fidel, were finally able to book a direct flight from Cuba's Rancho Boyeros International Airport to La Guardia airport in New York. Solange was incredibly nervous and fearful of what might happen to Fernando. Since meeting him at the 23 Street entrance of the Nacional Hotel, she could not keep him out of her mind. They had only been able to see each other for a few hours, but enough to unbalance her peace of mind. All her feelings for the young man had come rushing back to haunt her, and she could not stand the idea of not seeing him again. Although he had met Andy for lunch and enjoyed a couple of daiquiris with him, David was unaware that Solange had also seen Fernando. David was quite fond of Andy. Claudia tucked Fidel in her handbag and passed customs without any difficulty.

On the plane that took her from Cuba, Solange was leaving her memories behind, as well as the Island. She wondered how

---

[95] The journalist Antonio Llano Montes, witness and connoisseur of what happened, recounted in a program broadcast on the WAQI Radio Mambí station (Miami), on Monday, January 28, 2002 at 9 am what happened in Loma de San Juan.

[96] In 1966, Raúl Castro took the precaution of making the bodies that remained in the mass grave at the Santiago de Cuba shooting range disappear. He had large concrete coffins built, which were carried on ships to be thrown out to sea, as far as possible from the southern coast of the East, into very deep waters. The traces of the crime would never resurface.

Fernando would survive in the middle of the revolutionary storm. She had asked him to please leave Cuba and meet her in New York, but he had not answered. It seemed to her that perhaps he had other plans, and this filled her with apprehension. The mere thought that something terrible could happen to Fernando disturbed her acutely.

David and Solange had Errol Flynn as a fellow traveler, some seats from theirs. The actor was returning to New York. He wore a black kerchief around his neck, a revolutionary scarf made by some rebel ladies, and given to him by Fidel Castro himself. He, who had played the Robin Hood of the Woods on the screen twenty years before, felt proud to have met his double in real life.

George Raft, who was also leaving Cuba, was on board the same aircraft. The pillage to the casinos and, at the same time, the persecution to the Mafiosi happened in just one week. The safes of the Capri Hotel, as well as any money found, had been stolen before Raft's restless and powerless eyes. Meyer Lansky had left, not without having first toured his clubs to pocket the dollars. He, however, counted on the possibility of negotiating with the new government. Supposedly, however, Castro hated casinos. Would the Mafiosi try to obtain any advantage from the rebel chief? Once Batista fled, the gangsters were fairly sure that their empire would immediately fall. Castro had just occupied the renowned Hilton Hotel to make it his General Headquarters, and he had no plans to present the underworld kings with gifts. He immediately outlawed any form of gambling. Meyer Lansky's brother, Jake, could verify it some weeks later when they arrested him at the Havana Airport with fifteen thousand dollars in his suitcases, which the Revolution confiscated.

"My Christmas Holiday."

In Cuba, I played to catch lizards in the park. A lizard climbed a palm tree. I couldn't see it. Then, a helicopter appeared.

Two soldiers came down from it. They had rifles and wore cartridge belts full of bullets around their chests. But I wasn't afraid, because they were friendly soldiers who helped me. One of them climbed the palm tree and caught the lizard to give it to me. Then we painted together in my hotel room, and I gave them something to eat to thank them for their help. They were good soldiers. Then I named my lizard Fidel, and they were pleased.".

Claudia was delighted with the written composition the teacher had requested. The title was "My Christmas Holiday." Sure. A seven-year-old child makes up stories or beautifies them in their way. Everybody knows that when a child cannot catch a lizard, a helicopter lands next to her, as if by magic, and two armed-to-the-teeth soldiers come down from it to help her get the lizard! The teacher gave her an outstanding grade and wrote a very gratifying note for her: "An excellent imagination."

The popularity frenzy of the Revolution continued unabated. The mobs grouped and shouted: "Long live Fidel" holding posters in which they had written "Thank you, Fidel" or other revolutionary slogans: "Long live the July-26 Movement". Catchphrases appeared written wherever, on a dress, on a helmet, and even on foreheads. The guerilla rebels hoisted berets on their rifle muzzles and cheered "Long live Fidel!" while they posed smiling for the photographers. The crowd, bursting with joy, huddled together in the square, dotted with flags showing the colors of the Revolution and posters with their revel slogans: "We support the revolutionary government," "Welcome, Fidel," "Fidel, this is your home!". Some jeeps arrived full of soldiers holding flags and screaming, "Long live our revolution." Castro and his guerillas had just entered Havana with great fanfare and were lovingly acclaimed with arms waving by everyone standing in every balcony overlooking the parade. Screams of joy filled the streets in welcome to the passing bearded leader and his closest collaborators. They saluted the people from army war tanks and jeeps courtesy of the Constitutional Army. Aroused by Fidel's presence, the delirious mass, blinded by the triumph of the Revolution, even compared Fidel Castro to Jesus Christ himself, in both spirit and appearance. The next day, almost a million people gathered before the presidential palace, dazzled by Fidel, who hastened to pronounce a speech to his troops of bearded men who were sitting, while he stood in the balcony and raised his arm to salute the crowd. The overwhelming popularity of the new leader and his troop was an extraordinary experience to witness. Fernando, glued to the TV set, was amazed and wondered how long this popularity would last. How long would it take for the people of Cuba to understand that the joy that they were expressing was the result of masterful deceit studiously realized by an expert manipulator who represented what he was not?

Already a few days had passed since the triumph of the Revolution. Fernando decided to risk momentarily, leaving his hideout. He felt that he needed it, wanting to see if Andy and his mother, Mrs. Pruna, had everything they needed. Casually walking by the FOCSA building, a brand-new red Mercedes Benz convertible had just come to a stop on the sidewalk right in front of him... He almost ran into the uniformed rebel who had jumped out of it with an arrogant and energetic air. He assumed that the revolutionary officer had just confiscated the brand-new car from a dealership. Probably he stole the vehicle from Ramon Santé[97], Fernando mused. The rebel officer dressed in an olive-green uniform was wearing a black beret with a gold star pinned on it. Only a few feet away from him, the beardless officer with long hair and a ponytail walked briskly passed Fernando towards the entrance of the FOCSA building. Fernando just kept walking, a little bit faster now, towards the Someillan Building.

---

[97] Ramon Santé, Fernando's acquaintance, was the owner of the Mercedes Benz dealership in Havana.

Fernando and Andy had not seen each other since the first day of the year. They had a remarkably close relationship, and they embraced when they met at the family apartment.

"Bro, I have been thinking a lot these past few days, and I believe that you should leave the country as soon as possible. Cuba has become too dangerous for you to remain here. You will never guess who I have just seen. I almost ran into him: Raúl Castro entering the FOCSA! Can you believe it? He was exactly right there in front of me. Although I think that he is about twenty-eight years old, he looks nineteen. He was driving a gorgeous Mercedes convertible, one of those with wing doors. I think it is a 300 SL Gullwing."

"Coño! What a coincidence."

"Yes, I know, this guy just had a bunch of people shot in Santiago de Cuba. Batista officers. He is an extremely dangerous man."

"Why do you want me to leave Cuba, brother? My studies at San Alejandro are coming along great. It is a great school. Probably the best art school in the world."

"I know, but Andy, Cuba, will be transformed into a communist dictatorship. It will be a totalitarian state. It is only a matter of time. We would never fit in that type of government; it is a foreign thing to us. You are exceptionally talented; you have a wonderful future ahead of you. America is the place for you. Besides, you speak perfect English, and you will be at home there, thanks to our father, who had the foresight and was able to afford our education in the United States."

"What about you. Will you be coming with me?"

"Andy, I have been giving it a lot of thought. I am seriously considering staying. Perhaps I am crazy. I would have no problems in the States. I have so many good friends there. But I don't know, I feel an obligation to Cuba. I feel that we cannot just let our country fall into the hands of communism without a good fight. It is crazy, but that is how I feel."

"Are you planning to get into politics again?"

"No brother, I will not be able to get back into politics in Cuba again for the next thirty years. Castro passed a law while still in the Sierra Maestra, banning anyone from politics for the next thirty years, that participated in last year's general elections as a candidate."

"But that is fucking crazy!"

"You can say that again, but now he is running the show. Things are pretty bleak for us here; there is no doubt about that. These guys are shooting people every day in La Cabana. We have never seen anything like this in Cuba. For sure, this is not a regular revolution, its more than that, much more."

"But the people love him and don't seem to care who he is shooting."

"Yes, I know, and that is precisely why you have to leave the country."

"And what about you, brother, what do you have in mind? If you stay, I will also stay."

"I think that we cannot all go. I believe that some have to stay and see how we can confront this problem. Andy, this is about freedom. I think that this guy wants to change the system of government. We are not talking here about a change of power, no, not at all. He wants to change everything. Somehow he must be stopped."

"Fernando, I think that you are playing with fire. The guy is immensely popular; it will take years. I believe that you are crazy to get involved, at least for now. If you fuck up, it might cost you your life. These people are not playing games. We both have to leave."

"I know, I know, I'll think about it. I will start preparing the paperwork for both of us. You now need a signed permit to leave the country. Other than that, we are in good shape; we both have visas."

Fernando had not made up his mind regarding leaving Cuba or staying. But Andy had convinced him that perhaps the right thing to do was to go. So, he discussed it with his father and started to work on all the legal formalities with the thought in mind that they should both leave the country, convinced that if Andy felt that he was not going to go as well, he would refuse to leave. They were that close."

Dr. Pruna cleared the idea of departing and agreed that both brothers should leave the country. However, in the last weeks, he had met several times with his close friend, Jose Luis Pujol, at their home in Vedado, and they had discussed the feasibility and possibility of conspiring against the revolutionary government. Mr. Pujol had a close association with the past Batista government. He ran or managed the enormous Central Washington Sugar Mill near the city of Santo Domingo in Las Villas province, which, everyone knew, was owned by the departed President. Mr. Pujol's son had been elected to congress for the second time in the last election and was a man of influence in the past government. Dr. Pruna had become enthusiastic with the thought of conspiring against the Revolution and talked to Fernando about it. The conversation sparked an interest in Fernando, who was already pondering what to do to oppose the new political reality.

In the beginning, It was just talking about it. Interchanging thoughts and ideas and discussing and analyzing the latest news from the States. In New York City, Rafael Diaz Balart, Fidel Castro's ex-brother in law, an elected senator in the last suffrage, had just founded the first counterrevolutionary organization, **La Rosa Blanca**, after a well-recognized poem authored by the venerated Cuban apostle, Jose Marti.

Fernando was able to clear Andy's documentation before completing his own. He did not think that it would take long to resolve his paperwork, maybe a couple of weeks, and then he would catch up with his brother. At the airport, the departure was always tense and sometimes chaotic. Customs officers searched the passengers, as well as the bags, meticulously. Only one handbag allowed, no jewelry, and not more than one hundred dollars.

On January 24, 1959, Andy took a flight from the Rancho Boyeros International Airport to New York City with a very brief stop in Miami. It was a cold but sunny Saturday morning. After a quick embrace and some encouraging words, Fernando ran up the stairs and saw him off from the top portal of the airport building. He pulled out his white handkerchief and waved it in the air so Andy could identify him in the gathering crowd. Andy responded with his own, waving his arms high in the air. Although they felt confident of meeting again, in days, it was still an emotional parting, a sad and agonizing separation. The uncertainty of the future that lay ahead and the predicament of the present inspired tears in the brothers' eyes. Fernando had given his brother a long list of trusted friends and acquaintances that his brother could call in the big city. "You are going to be OK, Bro," Fernando repeated. "In a few days, I will be with you."

But things did not turn out that way. Sometimes fate, like the wind, has unpredictable twists and turns. Little did the brothers imagine in that last embrace, that it would take twenty long years for them to meet and embrace again.

Figure 41 Andres "Andy" Pruna. Copy of Passport photo when he left Cuba. January 24, 1959.

Note: "BEFORE THE AFTER," THE FIRST BOOK OF THE "HAVANA 505" TRILOGY, ENDS HERE. THE SECOND BOOK IS IN THE WORKS.